Action Research in Classrooms and Schools

Action Research in Classrooms and Schools

EDITED BY

D. Hustler
School of Education, Manchester Polytechnic

A. Cassidy
Teacher in a comprehensive school in Stockport

E. C. Cuff
School of Education,
Manchester Polytechnic

London
ALLEN & UNWIN
Boston   Sydney

Allen & Unwin (Publishers) Ltd,
40 Museum Street, London WC1A 1LU, UK

Allen & Unwin (Publishers) Ltd,
Park Lane, Hemel Hempstead, Herts HP2 4TE, UK

Allen & Unwin, Inc.,
8 Winchester Place, Winchester, Mass. 01890, USA

Allen & Unwin (Australia) Ltd,
Napier Street, North Sydney, NSW 2060, Australia

First published in 1986

British Library Cataloguing in Publication Data

Action research in classrooms and schools.
1. Education – Research 2. Action research
I. Hustler, D. II. Cassidy, A. III. Cuff, E. C.
371.1′02′072   LB1028
ISBN 0-04-370164-7
ISBN 0-04-370165-5 Pbk

Library of Congress Cataloging in Publication Data

Main entry under title:
Action research in classrooms and schools.
  Bibliography: p.
  Includes index.
    1. Action research in education – Great Britain
Case studies. I. Hustler, D. (David) II. Cassidy,
Anthony. III. Cuff, E. C.
LB1028.24.A28 1986   370′.7′8041   85-28589
ISBN 0-04-370164-7 (alk. paper)
ISBN 0-04-370165-5 (pbk. : alk. paper)

Set in 10 on 12 point Bembo by Columns, Reading
and printed and bound in Great Britain by
Biddles Ltd, Guildford and King's Lynn

Contents

Acknowledgements   xi

Notes on Contributors   xiii

General Introduction: Teachers in Action   1

SECTION A   *Issues in Action Research*   7

1 Does Action Research Require Sophisticated
Research Methods?
MICHAEL BASSEY   18

2 Classroom Enquiry: an Approach to Understanding
Children
STEPHEN ROWLAND   25

3 Teachers' Professional Knowledge
CAROL CUMMINGS AND DAVID HUSTLER   36

4 Action Research: an LEA Adviser's View
HARRY PICKLES   48

5 *Curriculum in Action* in Action
ANGELA ANNING   56

6 Teachers' Perspectives on Matching: Implications
for Action Research
CHARLES DESFORGES, ANNE COCKBURN AND
NEVILLE BENNETT   67

SECTION B   *Case Studies: Starting with Teachers'
Concerns*   73

7 Towards a More Open Classroom
JOHN GROARKE, PETER OVENS AND
MARGARET HARGREAVES   79

8   An Enquiry into Pupil-Responses to Non-Literal
    Art Objects: a CRISES Case Study
    JIM NIND   87

9   Making Sense of Literacy
    EILEEN BOOTH AND NIGEL HALL   95

10 Changing Schools
    DIANE TRANTER   105

11 Mathematics, Teachers and an Action Research
    Course
    LILIAN STREET   123

12 Initiating and Encouraging Action Research in
    Comprehensive Schools
    TONY CASSIDY   133

SECTION C   *Two Large-Scale Projects: Externally
             Initiated Concerns*   143

13 Some Unseen Effects of GIST
    JOHN THOMPSON   148

14 Curriculum Innovation and Evaluation
    SIDNEY SLATER   156

15 Single Sex Science Teaching: a Route to Bias-Free
    Choices in Science for Third Year Pupils
    DAVID BOWES   160

16 Observing with GIST
    GLYNIS WARD   166

17 Teachers' Perceptions of the GIST Project: an
    Independent Evaluation
    DAVID HUSTLER AND TED CUFF   172

18 The Alternative Curriculum Strategies Project
    MIKE COCKETT   183

19 The Alternative Curriculum Strategies Project at
   Arden
   ROD HILL   187

20 Parents, Teachers and the Alternative Curriculum
   at Arden
   LORNA HODGSON   190

21 Two Bites of the Cherry at Arden
   BRIAN ROLLINS   197

22 Emerging Strategies at Newall Green
   ROY DAVIES   201

Concluding Comments   207
Bibliography   212
Index   217

Acknowledgements

First and foremost we must record our continuing sense of loss upon the death of George Payne, who died on 23 December 1983. He was heavily involved in much of the work with teachers represented in this book and the editorial work here is greatly diminished through his absence – as we are, as colleagues and friends.

Many teachers, particularly in the Manchester area, have worked with us, talked with us, and helped us generally in the compilation of this book. To them all we owe our appreciation, as we also do to Jean Davies for her patience, good humour and unstinting effort in deciphering our hieroglyphics and producing a beautiful typescript.

Notes on Contributors

ANGELA ANNING was head of a Salford infant school, and is now at the College of Ripon and York St John.

MICHAEL BASSEY is at the Centre for Educational Research, Trent Polytechnic.

NEVILLE BENNETT is at the University of Lancaster.

EILEEN BOOTH teaches at a school for the hearing-impaired in the Manchester area.

DAVE BOWES teaches in a comprehensive school in the Manchester area.

TONY CASSIDY teaches in a comprehensive school in Stockport.

ANNE COCKBURN now works at the School of Education at the University of East Anglia.

MIKE COCKETT is project leader of Manchester's Alternative Curriculum Strategies project.

TED CUFF is in the School of Education, Manchester Polytechnic.

CAROL CUMMINGS is deputy head at a Trafford primary school.

ROY DAVIES teaches at Newall Green High School, Manchester.

CHARLES DESFORGES now works at the School of Education, University of East Anglia.

JOHN GROARKE is a primary school teacher in Stockport.

NIGEL HALL is in the School of Education, Manchester Polytechnic.

ROD HILL is now at Manchester's South Manchester College.

LORNA HODGSON works at Arden Sixth Form College, Manchester.

DAVID HUSTLER is in the School of Education, Manchester Polytechnic.

JIM NIND is a Leicestershire primary school teacher.

PETER OVENS is in the School of Education, Manchester Polytechnic.

HARRY PICKLES is senior adviser, Salford LEA.

BRIAN ROLLINGS is at Arden Sixth Form College, Manchester.

STEPHEN ROWLAND is co-ordinator of the Leicestershire Insights into Learning Project.

SID SLATER is head of a secondary school near Solihull.

LILIAN STREET is in the School of Education, Manchester Polytechnic.

JOHN THOMPSON teaches at a comprehensive school near Stockport.

DIANE TRANTER teaches at a comprehensive school in Manchester.

GLYNIS WARD teaches in a comprehensive school in the Manchester area.

Action Research in Classrooms
and Schools

General Introduction:
Teachers in Action

This book has a variety of purposes to it and a variety of audiences in mind. As such, it will inevitably annoy some people and disappoint others. It seems wisest, at the outset, to dispose of some purposes we do not have.

We are not attempting in this book to produce a theoretical treatise on the nature of action research. Instead, we are interested in what various parties, primarily practising teachers, are actually doing to examine, explicate and improve their own practices.

We hope that the materials presented here will help some others to involve themselves in practical issues of action research. The materials will help shape up the notions of what action research is, from an involved rather than a purely theoretical standpoint. The studies will illustrate some prospects and some problems, will stand for some readers as examples of good practice, and for others will capture worries about both action research and those who write about it. Last – but far from least – these materials provide ideas for practice. They point in places to possible procedures, methods, techniques, and, as such, may open up ideas about implementation. In all these senses the materials in this book provide *resources*.

In our view they provide particularly powerful resources for one vital reason. All the contributions in this book are grounded in examples of research; all are in a sense close to being case-studies. We have deliberately not entertained contributions which involve extensive discussion of action research abstracted from practice. All the contributions are tied clearly to some research exercise or possible framework for a particular research exercise. This point does represent one of our clear commitments, and through it we would argue that our first central purpose is established, i.e. to provide resources for those interested in action research to make up their own minds as to what it is, and what the possibilities are for them in connecting with it.

To provide these resources we have included large-scale and small-scale research enterprises, we have examples of both primary and secondary practice, and we have attempted to include reference to a wide range of curricular concerns and topics. What the selection also displays is a variety of differing starting points and contexts for the research, from LEA, SSRC funded, or DES initiatives covering a number of schools to one teacher's work in one classroom.

Our second central purpose for providing these particular resources is to point to the variety of possibilities and problems involved in collaboration between professionals working in differing sectors of the educational system. Here we are talking of professionals who see action research as a route forward, although they vary considerably in their conceptualization of that route. The case-study nature of the contributions once again, in our view, raises issues to do with collaboration in their sharpest possible form. They point to the problems and the possibilities in context. Many of the studies will raise for the reader questions whether they represent collaboration or imposition and also whose problem counts. Worries will surface about LEA involvements, school hierarchy and local politics, the 'arrogance' of traditional researchers and outsiders with a mission. Once again our choice here to include a range of professionals was deliberate: teachers with differing areas of concern and degrees of responsibility within the school, including headteachers; researchers and/or research facilitators working in institutions of Higher Education; teacher educators; LEA and LEA project representatives. These choices in this book are informed in part by the planning of an action research conference at Manchester Polytechnic in 1983. The major rationale for this conference was to bring together and establish a dialogue between, people working in differing educational sectors who had an interest in action research, were involved in action research, or who wished to speak to action research. For us, the conference was part of our attempt to clarify our own thinking and views on the possibilities of action research. One clear outcome, if an obvious one, was that different jobs in different educational arenas have built into them distinctive practical concerns. They carry with them particular frameworks for thinking about education, particular pressing day-to-day matters, particular issues of relevance, and particular notions of what is or what is not a legitimate research enterprise. Attempting to make these differing relevancies explicit is still, in our view, a necessary step towards any constructive collaboration in terms of action research. This book still reflects the concern which informed the planning for that conference.

One set of practical concerns is however the dominant one for us, and it brings us to the final and most important purpose behind this book. It is the set of practical concerns associated with being a teacher in the current context of low morale, the possibility of an imposed system of teacher appraisal, intervention from the Manpower Services Commission, and crude demands for accountability. Most of the contributors to this book are teachers: all of them work hard, think a lot about the business of teaching and about how to improve their effectiveness, and all of them are concerned for children and the educational development of children. In fact, almost all the teachers we know share these characteristics, remarkable though this might seem given some current characterizations of teachers and teaching. All the contributors to this book also attempt in a variety of ways to move their teaching forward, to improve their work as teachers of children, and they do so through what we are happy to call research. What follows is as close as we would wish to come to a definition of action research where teachers are the practitioners. They subject themselves and their practice to critical scrutiny; they attempt to relate ideas to empirical observations; they attempt to make this process explicit to themselves and others through the written word. Their prime concern is to improve their own practice in a particular situation from the standpoint of their own concern or worry. For them action research seems to be a practical way forward given their concern in that situation. They use and/or design aspects of their action as teachers to find out more about effective teaching and, in our view, they do so rigorously. It seems essential to continue pointing to the fact that teachers *can* do so and to display this fact to a range of audiences. We thereby establish not only the legitimacy of Stenhouse's (1975) notion of 'the teacher as researcher' for that range of audiences, but also we draw on the major resource available within the teaching profession for improving teaching, i.e. the teachers themselves.

This reference to the 'range of audiences' perhaps clarifies one aspect of the overall style to this book. We have attempted in our editorial introductions to make the materials as accessible as possible for a wide variety of readers. We do not therefore intend to engage in any lengthy characterizations of the development of action research, and, as we have noted, we are not suited best to this task anyway. Reference to Lawrence Stenhouse does however point to the need to at least briefly point to some aspects of the action research movement, with references which readers can pursue if they wish.

DEVELOPMENT IN ACTION RESEARCH

A Teacher's Guide to Action Research edited by Nixon (1981) did indeed 'represent another landmark in the history of the teachers as researchers movement' as John Elliott commented in his foreword in the book. The book not only consisted of contributions mainly from teachers, it also provided a strong sense of the roots of the action research movement, through the useful foreword by Elliott and collation of key references and associations. In particular we would point to the role of the Class-room Action Research Network (CARN) and the bulletins it produces.

In terms of that movement, it is clear that Lawrence Stenhouse's contribution was central, through his direction of projects such as the Humanities Curriculum Project (HCP), starting in 1967 and based at the Centre for Applied Research in Education, University of East Anglia. Essential reading must still be his *An Introduction to Curriculum Research and Development* (1975) where he develops the notion of 'the teacher as researcher', first expressed strongly in the HCP, and interpreted in distinctive ways in the Ford Teaching Project. This latter project, directed by John Elliott, with Clem Adelman as research officer, generated some very influential collaborative action research strategies, especially one form of 'triangulation' (Adelman, 1981).

It was with Schools Council Programme Two – Helping Individual Teachers to Become More Effective – that the action research movement began to really spread out beyond those who had had direct contact with either the Centre for Applied Research in Education or the Cambridge Institute. Our own involvement, and the involvement of several other contributors to this book, was more specifically as members of 'outer network' groups attached to the Programme Two project Teacher–Pupil Interaction and the Quality of Learning (TIQL). The working papers stemming from this project are extremely useful though still unpublished. We would particularly recommend 'Action-research: A framework for self-evaluation in schools' (Elliott, 1981) and 'Teachers as researchers: how four teachers co-ordinate the process of research in their respective schools' (Ebbutt, 1982).

The central aims of the TIQL project displayed a shift of emphasis within action research away from thinking about my classroom to thinking, with others, about my classroom within the institutional context of the school (Elliott, 1983). Other projects within Programme Two had similar emphases, one particularly interesting example being *Teachers in Partnership: Four Studies of In-service Collaboration* (Rudduck, 1982). For those who wish to pursue arguments relating to whether the focus of attention should be the individual teacher or the school, see Holly (1984). The materials in this book provide further resources for considering this question, although in our view the either/or formulation is misplaced. As we see it, action research necessarily embraces a central connection with perceived problems or worries: perceived that is by the practitioners, and perceived as related to their concerns, in their situation. Collaboration and facilitation within the school, and between outsiders and school personnel may lead to the discovery of shared relevancies, but it must connect with these relevancies. One clear-cut message, for us at least in working with teachers, is that the ideas of Lawrence Stenhouse and John Elliott in particular speak to these relevancies.

We have deliberately selected out a very narrow range of sources in the above. They do serve, in our view, as useful starting points. One consequence of the selection is that action research might be seen to be intrinsically linked to education, which it is not (see Cohen and Manion, 1980). Another consequence is to see it as peculiarly English, which it is not. On this, we would point to a particularly useful body of work linked to Deakin University, Australia, and especially Kemmis *et al.*'s *Action Research Planner* (1981) together with the more complex *Becoming Critical: Knowing through Action Research* (Carr and Kemmis, 1983). Some further readings, particularly concerned with the distinctive nature of action research, are referred to in the concluding comments to this book.

ORGANIZATION OF BOOK

The book is divided into three sections, each of which has an editorial introduction. Section A consists of materials which, in our view, raise most sharply some general recurring issues associated with action research. The latter part of the introduction to Section A provides a general overview of these issues. We find these issues surfacing, sometimes more explicitly, sometimes less so, in the other two sections. Section B has as its focus relatively small-scale action research studies of different sorts. This section also includes contributions which raise some questions about facilitating action research within the school, and building an action research dimension into a lengthy award-bearing course. Section C centres around materials from two large-scale projects. One of them, the Girls into Science and Technology Project (GIST) raises questions about externally initiated collaborative ventures: this project explicitly claimed an action research thrust and rationale. The other is Manchester's Alternative Curriculum Strategies project, a local version of the 14–16 Lower Attaining Pupils Project (LAP). The project was not explicitly built on an action research model, yet the work done by many of the teachers involved captures for us some of the most fundamental features of what action research is. The material from the Alternative Curriculum Strategies project here displays some aspects of the work done by a few of the involved teachers. They are not intended to convey a picture of the project.

SECTION A

ISSUES IN
ACTION RESEARCH

There is no doubt that nearly everyone with a direct interest in classroom teaching is disenchanted with traditional educational research. Whether they be teachers or teacher educators, HMIs or LEA advisers, heads of school or heads of departments, they regard such research as lacking in relevance and practicability for what they all regard as *the* prime task: helping teachers to improve the learning experience of the children in their classes. This is not to say that these parties see no need for research. They do, and plenty of it, for the problems are many and pressing. But it must be research which is positive, leading to action in the classroom and can help with these problems. In short, there is a huge demand for 'action research'.

Although there is this broad agreement on the irrelevance of traditional educational research and on the need for a more direct, pointed approach, loosely dubbed 'action research', there is less certainty on what is involved in such an approach. Is it more a question of 'action' rather than 'research'? Can 'action' and 'research' be combined? How can teachers be involved? What methods are available? Are they valid? What about the LEAs? Has traditional research nothing to offer? Can any use be made of extant published materials?

The five contributions in this section are all committed to the notion of direct involvement in classrooms and between them they give some answers, in the light of their own practical experience, to these key questions concerning how we can obtain studies of what goes on in classrooms which can lead to effective and practical action.

In his chapter, Michael Bassey points at two major faults of traditional research: it is verbose and it is general. If we are truly interested in action in the classroom, doing something about something, then the brevity of a report is at a premium. Given brevity, busy teachers can be realistically encouraged to examine and report on what they are doing; and their colleagues can involve themselves in the report without having to labour through a weighty tome. As such reports are particular to a specific setting or situation, unlike most traditional research documents which are general and abstract, the chances of interesting and involving other colleagues are greatly enhanced. Here Bassey stresses the essential difference between the academic researcher and the teacher-researcher as being that of watcher and actor respectively. As he shows, both can have access to and can gather the same kinds of data which are available in the classroom, but this difference in relevance – acting rather than observing – is crucial.

He illustrates these points with two seemingly mundane – even trivial – examples of teachers' short reports, each written on only one side of A4 paper: one on classroom queueing, the other on storytelling. In the realities of the classroom, however, they are not trivial and can form the basis of the sort of discussion between colleagues which can go on to reshape school policy on basic questions of classroom management. Indeed, such discussion could lead to the formulation of a paper for dissemination to teachers elsewhere, possibly via a teachers' journal. For Bassey, an essential feature of his approach to action research is the explicit involvement of the children in the problem being investigated. Rowland develops this feature even further. In his view, 'classroom enquiry' presupposes an approach to teaching which depends on learning *from* children rather than transmitting knowledge *to* them. A primary aim of classroom enquiry is to try to grasp the children's viewpoints: what is their perspective on the subject matter in the classroom? As teachers, we can then use this vantage point to review our own understanding of the subject matter.

It is not enough, however, to try to see how children understand the world. We also have to realize that knowledge is not the same as experience. It is foolish for us, as adults, to attempt to 'transmit' knowledge. Such knowledge has meaning only in terms of our own experiences as adults. Instead, we have to create learning situations in which adults and children can go about exploring one another's meanings and making mutual sense of what is going on. Children have to make knowledge part of their experience and adults have to find out what it then looks like. The outcome is that Rowland's model of classroom learning is very much a conversation among equals. This approach will help children to restructure knowledge in terms of their own experiences, thereby giving it meaning and significance for them. It will also help to avoid regarding knowledge in a piecemeal, mechanistic way as attention will be focused on incorporating it into the children's whole experience. Currently, there is far too much emphasis on the subject itself, its internal logic and sequential development, rather than on what it means to children.

Rowland advocates the need for 'classroom enquiry' because he feels that the term 'action research' does not necessarily incorporate this approach to children which he regards as indispensable. Also 'classroom enquiry' is focused on an aspect of children's learning and might not be directed to a specific problem, unlike some versions of 'action research'. Like Bassey, he draws a distinction between academic research and teacher enquiry and reiterates the importance of such enquiry *not* pursuing generalizations. In fact, for him it is a virtue to have a 'subjective' approach, i.e. an approach which stresses the importance of interpreting what is going on in classrooms. 'Objectivity' comes from teachers sharing and discussing their interpretations and here there are problems in developing a suitable language and conceptual framework. In this respect, traditional academic research is of no help as its jargon is a barrier to teachers sharing understandings.

He goes on to show how the Leicestershire Insights into Learning project has served to turn many of these ideas into a practical reality for serving teachers. This project has facilitated the growth of classroom enquiries over a wide range of topics and schools, involving a considerable number of teachers. There are three levels of overlapping and interlocking involvement: (1) teachers on full-time secondment, (2) teachers released for two or three days a term, to form discussion groups, (3) teachers within schools developing school-wide schemes of enquiry for staff. He points out that the first two levels are needed to create the 'intellectual space' for teachers to embark on careful reflection and a genuine sharing of ideas. Ultimately, however, it is vital to locate classroom enquiry in the schools themselves so that it becomes a standard activity in the taken-for-granted routine of school life. In Section B, the chapter by Jim Nind illustrates some of the work produced in the Leicestershire project.

Carol Cummings and David Hustler illustrate how in a different context they helped to generate 'intellectual space' for reflection and the sharing of ideas. A special feature of their approach is its team nature, i.e. the close collaboration of a practising teacher and an 'outsider' researcher, albeit one with a particular interest in teacher education. They also draw attention to the need for some explicit methods for examining what goes on in classrooms.

A key methodological problem in 'action research' is how to achieve apparently contradictory aims, viz. how to *research* a situation and how to *act* on it. The problem here is one of relevancies. What is important to some researchers (e.g. development objectivity, acceptance of findings by fellow researchers) is unlikely to be as relevant to practising teachers who have their own priorities (speed, improvement, practicability, acceptability in school). What collaboration between two parties with these different relevancies might do is to generate research which is acceptable academically *and* is relevant and practicable in the school situation. It might be, however, that such a collaboration hinges on gaining access to each other's relevancies.

To secure these aims, however, some sort of methodology is required. How exactly did Cummings and Hustler go about the task? Can other potential collaborators do the same?

Part of their answer is the methodic production and analysis of tape-recordings of classroom talk. It is cheap, easy and convenient to produce tape-recordings. The recordings provide a basis of data which checks and circumscribes the imaginative and idealistic leaps to which retrospective memories and discussions are so prone. Further, by transcribing some of the tapes much can be learned, and data which can be analysed in finer, more penetrating detail is produced.

In fact, these transcriptions – supplemented by the tapes on occasion – can provide a fertile basis for the sorts of insightful discussions advocated by Rowland. In allowing much of the detail of classroom events to be recaptured, discussions of transcriptions do much to reconcile the relevancies of researcher and teacher, allowing for analysis which can be both practical and relevant. Cummings and Hustler argue that it is through these discussions, closely tied to everyday life in the classroom, that teachers' professional knowledge becomes more accessible.

A further advantage is that teachers can collect data, and begin analysis on their own without undue interference with the class or undue expense and bothersome technical preparation. By making available and circulating the transcriptions, analyses and suggestions for action, teachers can plug into a network or group of teachers. Cummings and Hustler report on one such group and network, the Schools Council Outer Network group on Teacher–Pupil Interaction and the Quality of Learning (TIQL), based at Manchester Polytechnic. In fact, historically the initiative for doing transcript-based analyses was generated by this group and individual members developed the approach in their respective schools.

From his distinctive standpoint as a senior LEA adviser, Harry Pickles has high expectations of action research in assisting him in his task of stimulating changes and improvements in school practices. In his chapter, he shows in fine detail the great attention LEAs have to pay to the frequent government (DES) and other educational publications that are produced each year. It requires considerable powers of judgement to determine which issues are genuine 'straws in the wind', which will eventually acquire DES approval and government backing as official policy, and which recommendations can safely be ignored. He shows how successive reports time and time again focus on the key point made so lucidly by Rowland: what do classroom experiences mean for the children? Whether the focus is on mixed ability teaching, or on teaching mathematics, whether the focus is on the curriculum or on the way children spend time in middle schools, the same point emerges: what is it like to be a child in the class, what is it like to be on the 'receiving end'?

A fundamental conclusion of these reports, argues Pickles, is that many teachers do not ask themselves this question, do not see it as important. Consequently, they see what they want to see, make assumptions about what the children in their charge 'must be like'. In short, they do not examine and reflect upon what is actually happening in their classrooms.

Even in the age of the computer, the basic resource for teaching children rests in the skills of the teachers. So the problem facing Pickles and his colleagues is in refining and developing these skills in directions indicated by all these straws in the wind. They all show the strength of the pressures for empathizing with and developing from the needs and experience of the children in the classroom, i.e. what the children are really like, not what they are *assumed* to be like. His own LEA, Salford, has usefully produced a broad framework for the necessary self evaluation by teachers in the form of two schemes, one for primary and one for secondary. These schemes focus on the need to improve the curriculum for the children by providing guidelines and a framework for development. Of course, these are not sufficient in themselves; teachers and schools have to take action and to operate in autonomous ways. Hence action research can be invaluable in helping teachers to diagnose honestly what is happening in their classrooms, to identify and to evaluate their own skills in relation to what they find, and to seek to develop their skills on a co-operative basis.

What this argument looks like in the reality of schools is illustrated by Angela Anning in her chapter. She was, at the time of writing, a headteacher in the Salford LEA and she graphically sketches her own teaching biography from a beginning primary teacher to a fully fledged teacher, to teacher with responsibility for language, to deputy head including responsibility for curriculum development, to being, finally, headteacher with also a major involvement in the LEA-wide scheme described by Pickles.

Angela Anning, as a practising and involved teacher, expresses dissatisfaction with the inservice education she has encountered and which she fears is typical. Such education tends to purvey traditional academic research which practising teachers find jargon-ridden and off-putting. Besides it is at most weakly relevant to everyday teaching and is usually lacking in practical details. Such education, whether at undergraduate or postgraduate inservice level, also tends to be of the knowledge-transmission kind, negating or ignoring the students' own experiences as practising teachers.

Yet there are alternative paths to teacher self-improvement and development. She herself has had the task of trying to involve teachers in *radical* changes and approaches to their classroom teaching. Here there are published materials which are of great assistance and, like Pickles, she praises highly the Schools Council *Curriculum in Action* as being inspirational. Its pivotal six key questions all stress action: what can the teacher actually *do*? Such materials are invaluable within the general thrust given by the drive towards action research in a school.

She is involved in action research both in her own school and across a number of other schools in the LEA and sketches some of the difficulties of involving teachers. Even when they agree to examine practices, they tend to select 'safe' ones – at first anyway. Thus she brings out the great importance of securing the right atmosphere and relations between colleagues if a group of teachers is to achieve the necessary free-ranging discussion, detailed analysis and genuine self evaluation of what goes on in the classroom. As her chapter shows, such outcomes are possible and were achieved from using video-recordings which are clearly an extension of the methodology suggested by Cummings and Hustler, though the nature of any practical problems caused by the use of equipment more elaborate than a tape-recorder is not discussed. In the teacher discussions she also brought out a problem referred to by other contributors: the absence of a suitable language. She feels that we can move out from particular to more general themes once a suitable vocabulary has been developed. Perhaps a suitable language might enable practising teachers to talk to traditional academic researchers, rather than being put down by them.

The final contribution in this section argues that a suitable vocabulary can only develop along with a general commitment to research. Action research needs to be built into every teacher's job description, rather than resemble a suit of clothes to be put on for local trouble shooting.

The piece by Charles Desforges, Anne Cockburn and Neville Bennett takes its inspiration from a strictly traditional piece of academic research in which researchers from outside schools examined the matching of tasks with pupil ability in sixteen top infant classes. Desforges *et al*. then go on to discuss what they consider to be the implications of this work for teacher-based action research and the conclusions are generally critical. Teachers' interpretations of classroom problems are likely to be inadequate, because they lack a 'clear and explicit framework of judgement'. Without it teachers' conceptions are 'deficient in a way which is fundamental to the whole notion of research and development'. The primary function of action research should, therefore, be to articulate an interpretative framework, and this can only be done in a situation where alternative interpretations are advanced in an adversarial fashion. The use of a collaborator from outside school, a practice which is common to many projects, is felt by Desforges *et al.* to be inadequate for this task as their role is habitually supportive rather than critical. The apparently startling demand for 'a respected and credible enemy' to play devil's advocate to the teacher–researcher turns out, however, to be no more than a call for the teacher himself to be self-critical, questioning and patient, and most contributors to this section would probably agree with this prescription. Yet when Desforges *et al.* equate research with 'the development of a body of objective professional knowledge, and a commitment to 'the adversary model of research traditional to British scholarship', then some might feel that they are drifting from the central concerns of action research back into the waters of academic respectability. Their point, however, would seem to be that the research mentality is not a framework which can be tacked on to the job of teaching. To endure, it must be a central aspect of that job.

At this point, the reader may well wish to move directly to the studies in this section. The rest of this introduction attempts to provide a brief outline of some central issues about action research, which these studies raise, if at times somewhat implicitly.

Desforges *et al.*, Anning, and Rowland all stress the crucial role of 'writing' in action research and we would agree with them. Through writing, the records of observations, the analysis of observations and the attempt to generate ideas and materials become accessible to ourselves and others. They become, if one wishes, part of the public domain and, as such, teachers' work becomes open to a wider community of practitioners for scrutiny and debate.

Yet there are larger questions about research traditions which many of the contributors explore. Rowland, for example, is clearly unhappy about characterizing his work as 'research', and understandably so. 'Research' for many teachers has connotations of something which others do 'to' or 'on' teachers and teaching, and these others dwell in places such as universities, distant from any real understanding of, or concern to understand, teachers' practical concerns. Anning speaks for many when she complains of 'jargon'. At times there seems to be a two-way resistance, with traditional researchers jealously guarding their preserve and teachers happy to leave them to it. Other teachers feel uneasy about viewing their own research as legitimate, as 'real' research. In our view it is not only legitimate to view most of the studies in this book as research, it is necessary to label them so. The label may be challenged, but at least it may play some part in bringing different communities of practitioners into some dialogue with one another.

There are other connotations of 'research' as well. 'Research', for many people, relates to the large-scale, relates to surveys and measurement, relates to extreme detachment and objectivity, as well as the testing of hypotheses derived from prior theory. How it can relate to 'me' and 'my classroom' is a natural question and one which Bassey raises on behalf of teachers. Interestingly enough, there are well-established traditions within the social sciences which stress the small-scale, the need for involvement in the situation one is studying, the importance of gaining access to people's perceptions, the virtues of qualitative data as opposed to quantitative data, the need to génerate theory (see for example Shipman, 1981, ch. 9; Cuff and Payne, 1984, ch. 6; Hammersley and Atkinson, 1983; Woods, 1983). These traditions are somewhat loosely labelled 'interpretative' or 'phenomenological' (see Tranter, Section B). It is hardly surprising that many action researchers have found these traditions more amenable (Elliott, 1978). There are four points we wish to make drawing on the above.

First, there is some legitimacy already there, within the academic market place, for those who need this particular sense of security. Second, these 'interpretative' traditions have generated many teacher-usable, data-gathering techniques and have influenced the construction of data-gathering strategies involving teachers, pupils and outside researchers. One of the best known examples of the latter is the development of a particular kind of 'triangulation' within the Ford Teaching Project, where the attempt was made to elicit honest accounts from teachers and from pupils (Adelman, 1981, ch. 5). Third, the 'interpretative' traditions are perhaps particularly appropriate for coming to terms with children, their perceptions and understandings. This is explicitly crucial to Rowland, for example, and to Pickles and Anning and Bassey, although in very different ways. At times action research, in its focus on teachers' problems and concerns, does seem to neglect the central audience for all of us: the children. Fourth, action researchers do tend to emphasize the virtues of qualitative data, almost at times to the extent that any use of quantitative measures seems 'wrong'. In our view this emphasis is usually appropriate, but at times quantitative data can be extremely useful. In particular, we would draw on another sense of the term 'triangulation' to point up this view. The use of differing data-gathering techniques can complement one another, feed off one another; they can cross-validate at times and raise legitimate questions (see Hammersley and Atkinson, 1983).

Whether it should be the business of 'outside' collaborators to raise legitimate and even awkward questions opens up debates on action research collaboration which have operated at a variety of levels, including for example discussions as to the relevance of Habermas's treatment of 'discourse' (Tripp, 1980). In the introduction to Sections B and C we do discuss forms of collaboration, if only briefly. What we note here is the argument that some form of dialogue with an 'outsider' is not only desirable for action research, but almost one of its defining characteristics. It so happens that almost all the studies in this book do involve some form of collaboration between those inside schools and those outside, and Cummings and Hustler make explicit one sort of argument for one form of collaboration.

Meetings between collaborators, whether 'outsiders' and 'insiders' or collaborators within one school, require time. As Bassey notes, action research may not require as much time as some imagine, but as Rowland and Hill (Section C) sharply point out, 'quality time' is a rare but essential commodity in schools. To suggest building into actual job descriptions the role of teacher-as-researcher as Desforges *et al.* suggest, would be a solution, albeit an unlikely one.

If it were to come off, an ensuing problem would be how senior management in schools and LEA administrators regard the time allocated for the research project. Whose time would it be, and whose problems would figure in the agenda? Obvious, but very worrying, issues are raised here to do with what relationship, if any, could or should obtain between LEA guidelines for self evaluation or school-based evaluation and particular notions of action research (Elliott, 1981, pp. 3(i) and (ii)). Harry Pickles's contribution, as well as Angela Anning's, will disturb some readers though, given our knowledge of their work, not us. One source of discontent might be the view that the very use of standardized evaluation frameworks and structured materials such as 'curriculum in action' cuts right across and denies the particular features of specific teaching contexts and teachers' perceived concerns. At the same time, it is our strong view that to stand up and be counted for a notion of action research which must not be contaminated with the involvement of the LEA or senior management in schools is misplaced and self-defeating. In addition it is based on a somewhat narrow notion of whose problems are suitable candidates for action research. We are brought back to the need for a dialogue, albeit between different partners in this case. Whilst we recognize the differential power positions which the partners may have, we would argue that many of the studies in this book display a resource in schools, amongst teachers, which any authority should be reluctant to alienate through imposition. The first task must be to recognize that there are different relevancies involved, to make them as explicit as possible and to attempt to see and understand and build on the relevancies with which teachers, in particular, are operating. Agendas must be mutually constructed. This point is pursued again in the introduction to Section C.

One item which would have to be high on the agenda in the above context particularly, but which demands attention in any action research study, concerns the areas of confidentiality, control of materials gathered and negotiation of access to these materials. This set of issues about ethical considerations is only touched on in this book. They are however vital issues and we would recommend the discussions raised in the evaluation context by MacDonald (1976) and Simons (1982). Experienced action researchers have paid a considerable amount of attention to these issues (for example, see Classroom Action Research Network Bulletin no. 4, 1980).

Finally, there is one issue which for many readers must seem long overdue for attention. Just what *is* action research? In our general introduction we have indicated major resources for pursuing this question and here we do not intend to involve ourselves directly in what can become a purely theoretical and fruitless discussion. We note, however, that many of the studies in the book provide definitions or criteria or build on well-known frameworks for pursuing action research (see for example Bassey, Street, Groarke *et al.*), and we have argued, much earlier, that the studies presented here are one central resource for considering that question. The very compilation of this book has changed our own notions of action research, has left us unclear in places where we thought we were clear before, and vice versa. This experience suggests several final points. First, the action research movements are developing and dynamic movements and cannot be tightly defined. Secondly, there is clearly tension apparent in the combination of 'action' and 'research' (for one discussion of this, see Cohen and Manion, 1980, ch. 8). This tension, this seeming contradiction between acting in a situation and researching into it, can spoil the comfortable nature of having a sharp clear-cut professional identity. The educational world becomes not so easily compartmentalized into some places where people teach and other places where people do research. One possible consequence for some teachers can be a sense of unease and isolation within the school; unease with other colleagues, with themselves as they once were. It can breed dependency on action research 'facilitators' in Higher Education, facilitators who themselves may regret at times the loss of firm identities they once held as sociologists perhaps or psychologists! If such unease suggests that action research can be an uncomfortable enterprise, then we would agree. We also suggest that Stenhouse's notion of the teacher-as-researcher is still for many a bizarre, unconventional formulation. The emergence of 'fuzzy' identities however is an inevitable consequence of the weakening of boundaries between what were once different communities, between those who teach children, those who teach teachers, those who administrate and those who research. It is one indicator of the development of a real partnership between individuals working in differing sectors of education. The action research movement is growing and, if the contributions in this book are anything to go by, the children in our schools seem to be benefiting from that growth.

1

Does Action Research Require Sophisticated Research Methods

MICHAEL BASSEY

I am tempted to write the shortest chapter in this book by responding to my title with one word: NO. This would also illustrate one of my strongest contentions about classroom research – that reports should be brief and to the point! But the editors, and perhaps the reader, require more of me.

One of the characteristics of action research is that it is research which people get on with and do quickly. As such it can be contrasted with academic research. The academic world enjoys the intellectual delights of rigorous thinking about minutiae and is able to devote long periods of time to it. Thus an M.Phil. student will spend usually about two years of full-time study to gain the research degree, and a PhD. student longer. But a school teacher with a classroom problem which might be illuminated by research methods is likely to have only a few hours to devote to the search for a solution.

One of the handouts used on our Primary Generalist B.Ed. at Trent Polytechnic is adapted from the writing of W. G. Perry and entitled 'Discoveries of the Obvious'. It includes this paragraph:

> My fifth discovery was that I am not a watcher of the world, but an actor in it. I have to make decisions and some of them have to be made now. I cannot say 'Stop the world and let me get off for a bit, I want to think some more before I decide.' Given so many differences of opinion among reasonable people, I realise that I can never be sure that I am making the 'right' decisions. Yet because I am an actor in the world, I must decide. I must choose what I believe in and own the consequences and never know what lay down the roads I did not take.

Academics are watchers of the world: teachers are actors in it. Teachers make decisions and search for 'right' decisions. Sometimes research enquiries may help in the search for 'right' decisions. Sometimes the research evidence is in a published report which teachers can relate to their own classrooms, but other times they need to obtain the evidence themselves for every classroom is unique and one teacher's solution may not be appropriate for others.

The actions of classroom teaching can be expressed in this way. Classroom teaching entails assessing the educational needs of children, identifying intentions for what you hope they will achieve, locating suitable resources and working out appropriate strategies whereby the intentions may be achieved. The acts of defining needs, intentions, resources and strategies all entail decisions which, although involving value-judgements, can be illuminated by empirical data. And the collection of empirical data implies research.

The following preliminary list of some of the kinds of data which can be collected in and about classrooms illustrates the scope for classroom research.

DATA FROM PUPILS

(1) Observation of activity

This includes descriptions of what a single child, or a group of children, or a whole class, do over a period of time. Notes may be written in a book, or whispered into a tape-recorder, by an observer during the activity, or written after the activity and based on his memory or on audio- or videotape-recordings of the activity. Tape-recordings may be used to produce detailed transcripts of what was said. The notes may be a freewheeling account phrased according to the immediate perception of the observer, or a structured account based on pre-determined questions. Or the record may be simply a tally of the number of times that certain activities on a checklist occur.

(2) Reports of experience

The two major methods for obtaining reports of experience are (a) by asking questions about experience either in an interview or through a questionnaire, and (b) by reading a diary which gives accounts of the experience under study. An interview is, of course, an activity and so the methods described in (1) above are applicable.

(3) Tests

There are many tests of basic skills published by the National Foundation for Educational Research and others which can provide sources of data. These include measures of competence in curriculum subjects such as music, mathematics and reading at different levels of achievement, as well as tests which purport to measure a variety of cognitive attributes such as intelligence, creativity, divergent thinking and memory. Many of these tests have been standardized against large populations and so results obtained from children of a particular age can be compared to norms.

Other tests which purport to measure characteristics such as curiosity, moral maturity and achievement motivation can be found in the literature of education.

Tests of knowledge can be added to this list – which are often *ad hoc* tests devised by a teacher for a particular sequence of lessons.

(4) Expressions of opinion

Children's opinions and attitudes can provide data if elicited by interview or questionnaire.

(5) Classroom artefacts

This includes anything which is made or produced in the classroom by children and so includes their exercise books, writings and creative work.

DATA FROM PARENTS

(6) Reports of experience

As with children this kind of data can be collected by diary, interview or questionnaire.

(7) Expressions of opinion

These can be collected by interview or questionnaire.

DATA FROM TEACHERS

(8) Observation and activity

(9) Reports of experience

(10) Expressions of opinion

Similar procedures to those listed under 'data from children' apply.

(11) Classroom artefacts

These include teaching aids, displays and records.

DATA FROM SELF

(12) Observation of activity

This can be done by the playback of audio- or video-recordings.

(13) **Reports of experience**

Here the diary is a particularly successful method of collecting data.

(14) **Expressions of opinion**

These are of particular interest when recorded over a period of time and reveal a shift in opinion which can be explained introspectively.

(15) **Classroom artefacts**

These are as listed under 'data from teachers'.

I consider that there are two kinds of pedagogic research, i.e. meaning research that attempts to improve the quality of teaching and learning. One kind attempts to produce general statements about teaching and learning. Thus Neville Bennett in *Teaching Styles and Pupil Progress* and Maurice Galton, Brian Simon and Paul Croll in the ORACLE reports, base their conclusions on surveys of relatively large numbers of teachers and pupils and try to draw general conclusions. I describe this kind of research as 'search for generality' and although there is much of interest to teachers in these studies, I find little that gives guidance to the individual teacher in the day-to-day work of the classroom. The other kind of pedagogic research I describe as 'study of singularities', which means accounts of the happenings in single classrooms. It may be the description of a particular piece of teaching, with an explanation of why the teacher works in this particular way; it may be an account of an experiment in which pupils learn in some way which the teacher has not tried before; it may be the results of interviews with the parents of one class on what the children tell them about life in school. In each case there is no attempt to generalize the findings beyond the classroom, but there is recognition that there may be aspects of the results which stimulate other teachers to try something similar. The York Street School examples on the following pages are of this latter kind: they are studies of singularities. I have invented them to illustrate a number of points about classroom action research.

The York Street School Action Research Reports could only be produced in a school where the staffroom is supportive of this kind of professional enquiry. The snide comments that 'Martha's obviously after the deputy head's job' or 'Penny ought to get on with it instead of fretting about' would kill this sort of initiative. Years ago these responses might have been common, but today many teachers are prepared to share their experiences with colleagues and to learn through staffroom discussion.

The reports illustrate a number of points about classroom research by teachers.

York Street School

ACTION RESEARCH REPORT 23   12 February 1983

Classroom Queue

I was concerned about the length of the queue at my desk of children wanting their assignments marked or seeking assistance with their work. I discussed it with the class (3rd years), the children agreed that too much time was being wasted in the queue, and we decided on two kinds of monitoring. During individual work periods one of the children would keep a record every four minutes of the people at my desk (we used an egg timer) and I would keep a record of why each child came to me at the desk. Each morning first thing I would announce the average queue length for the previous day.

After the first week it became clear that of the 30 people in the class 8 were spending much more time than the rest in the queue and so I discussed with them the importance of their learning to be independent and self-sufficient. Also I changed the routine for handing work in (two wire trays at the other end of the room instead of piling it on my desk).

By the end of the second week the queue had shrunk from an average of six people to an average of two. We agreed that the study had been worthwhile and decided that if the queue grew long again we would repeat the monitoring.

I don't think that either my pep talk to the persistent queuers, or the wire trays, explain the change. My guess is that it was due to class interest in shortening the queue. But the experiment achieved what I wanted it to do, and the children obviously enjoyed being on the 'inside'.

Martha

The issues under study were classroom issues identified by the teacher as worthy of investigation – queues and fidgeting. This should be an essential feature of any classroom action research – that the issue is one of concern to the teacher. But they have another essential feature – in both cases there was a reasonable expectation that investigation would lead to some improvement in classroom practice.

Both reports are written on one side of a sheet of A4 paper and would have been run off on the school duplicator. Both reports convey part of their message through a line drawing. Also the reports are written in the first person vernacular without any pompous academic forms such as 'in the opinion of the present writer'. They are chatty, but brief and to the point.

In both cases it is clear that the children have been 'on the inside' of the research. Martha's children knew she was trying to shorten the

York Street School

ACTION RESEARCH REPORT 24   3 MAY 1983

Story Telling

Elaine Moss's article in *Education 3–13* (edited by Colin Richards, 1978) on 'story telling' inspired me to carry out an experiment on my first year junior class.

For story time over the last fortnight I had chosen *Charlotte's Web* by E. B. White. Instead of reading aloud every chapter, I read alternate chapters but told the in-between ones. This meant quite a bit of work each evening in preparing the chapters which were to be 'told'. I put a few notes on a postcard so as to get the sequence of events right.

In order to monitor the effect on the children I asked Marian (the nursery assistant) to join us and count the number of 'fidgets'. She used a hand counter for this and sat with it hidden in her lap. We had a few trial runs beforehand at recording the level of fidgeting. Obviously there is an arbitrary element in deciding what constitutes a 'fidget', but we found that Marian's counts over several days accorded with my subjective impression of the children's fidgeting. On the first trial run I told the children that Marian was joining us to listen to the stories and that she was also going to see how much they fidgeted – but we made no further reference to this. (I hope this was ethical!) I also told the children that I was going to experiment with reading and telling the story and that afterwards I would ask them which they preferred.

These are the results over ten days. The height of the histogram represents the number of fidgets; 'R' means that I read and 'T' that I told the story.

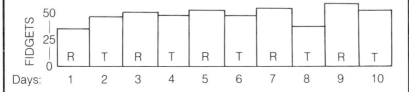

The difficulty is in measuring fidgets, but Marian and I both thought she was recording consistently. It would seem that, apart from the first day, my story telling held the children's attention more than my reading aloud.

In a show of hands on day 10, 18 of the children voted for 'telling' as better and 12 for 'reading' as better. Some of their comments were interesting: 'It sounds more like you were there' (pro-telling); 'I was worried that you might miss something out' (pro-reading).

Penny

queue and Penny's children knew that Marian was counting how much they fidgeted. The academic researcher may snort and say, 'No wonder that the children's behaviour changes since they knew what was expected of them.' But to the action researcher this is immaterial if the situation is improved. Democratic involvement of as many people as possible is an important feature of action research.

The only reference to the educational literature is to Penny's source of inspiration. There is no tedious reference to queueing theory or to physiological explanations of fidgeting. Action researchers use the literature only to the extent that there is something significant and germane to the issue under study; they do not genuflect to Pavlov and Piaget in order to impress their readers!

Most writers on action research see it as (1) seeking improvement in the action, (2) democratic in its involvement of the participants (not 'research subjects'), and (3) reflective. The latter point is not brought out clearly in these reports so let us expect that after three months, these two teachers would be writing further reports on the basis of careful reflection and discussion with colleagues of the issues involved.

Suppose that other members of staff in the school also started to study the problems of classroom queueing. It could become a school issue, with a staff working party meeting regularly to consider progress. This could eventually lead to a more extensive paper which might be submitted to a teacher's journal for publication. I add this comment simply to establish the view that action research reports are not necessarily limited in scope!

2

Classroom Enquiry: an Approach to Understanding Children

STEPHEN ROWLAND

In this paper I want to explore the concept of 'Classroom Enquiry' as an approach to the relationship between learning, teaching and understanding children. While the ideas I shall present are to a large extent personal they do, I believe, form the basis of much of the work that has been done in the Leicestershire Insights into Learning project.

The argument I want to develop rests upon two fundamental viewpoints, one concerning children and childhood, the other concerning the nature of knowledge. It is difficult to see how either viewpoint could be proved, although I think they can be clarified and demonstrated by a close study of what children do.

CHILDREN AND KNOWLEDGE

Children's work is worth taking seriously, not merely as reflecting the fits and starts towards some ultimate goal of adulthood, but as a contribution in its own right. The limitations in children's experience of the world, and in the knowledge and skills that derive from that experience, are obvious. However, within the limitations of that experience, we can see children as thinkers, with ideas they want to explore and express and as having purposes and intentions which underly their activity. In these respects they are no different from adults. Their activity and expression can thus be interpreted not only as evidence that they have reached a certain 'stage of development' or 'level of understanding', nor simply as evidence that they have more or less understood an idea that we have intended to put across to them. Their activity can also be interpreted as representing or expressing an understanding of the world which can be significant to us. It takes a considerable effort of the imagination to empathize with young children sufficiently to begin to understand their perspective on the world as expressed by their activity in the classroom. But it is an effort which can reward us by stimulating and often challenging us to reconsider our own understanding. I am reminded here of how my understanding of the concept (is it a concept?) of subtraction was radically developed by considering how, from a group of seven year olds, seven different strategies emerged for finding the difference between pairs of numbers all less than ten. 'Subtraction' was a more diverse and complex notion that I had initially thought. My claim here is not that these children's understanding of subtraction was greater than mine, but that their insight and their activity was sufficient to provoke me into reconsidering what I understood subtraction to be.

Children, then, present us with a twofold challenge: to understand how they understand the subject matter, and to review our own understanding of it. Unless we are prepared to learn from children and with children, I think it unlikely that we will learn much of significance about them.

My second fundamental viewpoint concerns the nature of knowledge. As a teacher of young children, I can claim to have, or to have access to, more knowledge in most fields (though by no means in all) than the children I teach. It therefore might seem reasonable to suppose that my duty is to pass on my knowledge to the children. Surely, that is what teaching is all about? But there is a danger here of misunderstanding the relationship between knowledge and experience. Knowledge is rooted in experience. Therefore to 'pass on' knowledge requires me to 'pass on' experience. Clearly, there is a sense in which we can 'pass on' experience: we can represent our experience in language or art, we can reflect with others on their experience drawing parallels from our own, and we can construct learning situations which we believe might produce appropriate experience. But our experience itself cannot be passed on. It has to be interpreted by us, reinterpreted by others, and related to their experience before they can make use of it. For this reason, any knowledge which children gain from our experience must be a reconstruction of the knowledge which we gained from that experience. How different the children's reconstructed knowledge will be from our own knowledge will depend upon the differences in our personal histories and the differences in our cultural and linguistic backgrounds. To underestimate or ignore these differences may result in complete failure of children to reconstruct anything of value from our experience, or may lead to an unjustified imposition of our culture upon them.

There is a further problem with the notion that knowledge can be passed on. This concerns the structure of knowledge. The prevailing view in modern industrial and technological society has been that true knowledge – scientific knowledge – is analysable into component 'bits' which can be taken apart and assembled rather like the component parts of a clock. This mechanistic view of knowledge, whose origins we can trace back to the influence of Newton and Descartes, has led to the fragmentation of academic disciplines and to the supremacy of so-called scientific knowledge over aesthetic knowledge and other forms of knowledge. Capra (1982), traces in some depth the influence of this Newtonian paradigm, and the limitations it has imposed on a range of human thought and activity. In the classroom, this view of knowledge has reached its apotheosis with the dominance of programmed learning packages, limited behavioural objectives and rigidly structured syllabi.

However, since early in this century, physicists have seriously begun to question mechanical models as appropriate tools for understanding the world. It has become increasingly apparent that aspects of many complex phenomena cannot best be understood by simply reducing them to their constituent parts. An important trend amongst much of the scientific community – though perhaps not yet amongst educationalists – is towards a more holistic view of knowledge, that is, an understanding of reality in terms of integrated wholes whose properties cannot be reduced to those of smaller units. The implication of such a change in approach for the classroom is that we cannot best understand children's learning as following a linear sequence as more 'bits' of knowledge are added, but must instead view the growth of their knowledge in relation to their wider experience, from which it gains its meaning.

This more holistic approach to knowledge clearly should lead us to view the 'learning package' with some scepticism, to be less certain of our ability to predict what learning will result from which experience, and so places a greater obligation upon as, as teachers, to try to understand the understanding of children as it develops in the classroom.

To summarize, then, the position I have sketched out with regard to children and knowledge. Children's learning activity is worth taking seriously as an active and purposeful expression of significant ideas, rather than as a passive response to a situation. The knowledge they gain from that activity is a construction from their experience of it, or a reconstruction from the experience of others. It is not merely a replication of knowledge that exists outside them. Such knowledge is best viewed as being integrated into their wider understanding, from which its meaning derives. It is not separable into all its constituent elements which can be learnt and viewed independently, only to be assembled and thereby given meaning at some later stage.

TEACHING – AN INTERPRETATIVE APPROACH

The implications of these ideas for us as teachers are apparent. We cannot accurately predict what knowledge will be gained from a particular experience, nor can we assume that it will be gained according to a prespecified sequence. Therefore we must be concerned in our interactions with the children and their work continually to interpret how they understand the subject matter. Of course, any thoughtful teacher attempts to do this anyway. But what I am suggesting here is a shift in emphasis. As we talk and work with children, the central question in our minds should not be 'has the child understood what I'm getting at?' but 'have I understood what the child means?' It is our answer to that question which guides our contribution to the learning that is taking place between us and the child.

It might be said that the art of good conversation rests largely in each party's ability to empathize with the other, that is, their willingness to attempt to see a question from the other's viewpoint, if only to challenge this viewpoint more effectively. Good conversation provides an appropriate model upon which to base our interactions with children. Its success demands and promotes an expanded awareness on both sides of the teacher–learner relationship, a relationship from which both parties learn and to which both contribute their significant experience. It also assumes a sense of quality: the meaning and purpose of any learning interaction is not defined solely by the teacher, but emerges from the attempts of both parties as they seek to understand each other, and to understand the subject matter which lies beyond them both.

Such an approach to teaching does not rule out the role that direct instruction might play in the classroom. On the contrary, it provides a context in which we are more readily able to judge the appropriate content and methods of instruction that the child can use. Many instructional packages and programmes fail not because they are instructional, but because they are designed with little regard to the concerns and wider knowledge of the learner. Their use then produces, at best, a kind of knowledge which is alienated from life outside the schoolroom, possibly leading to success in the narrowest of examinations in the short term, but to a general disillusionment with the educational process in the longer term.

Nor does this approach envisage the rejection of educational objectives. They are vital if we are to provide for and stimulate the children across a wide range of experience. However, when it comes to evaluating what learning has taken place, it is important that our interpretation of the children's activity is not restricted by the objectives we have in mind. Our objectives comprise our prior hopes and expectations about where the children's activity might take them and thus inform our plans. Without them, we would not have a starting point for understanding their activity. But too narrow a focus on our objectives can prevent us from seeing what it is that concerns the child. In such cases, our further contribution to their activity will be misinformed. Thus our objectives, while providing a frame for planning and interpreting what takes place in the classroom, should always be viewed as provisional, as providing a perspective from which we are always ready to take a sideways step in order to engage with the child.

CLASSROOM ENQUIRY AS A WAY OF UNDERSTANDING LEARNING

Throughout these comments I have referred to the need to be continually interpreting children's activity – their actions, their language, their writing and so forth. However, given the real classroom situation, with thirty or more children often engaged in a wide variety of activities and only one teacher, much of our interpretation is done very rapidly and on the spur of the moment. The speed with which we have to make decisions on our feet often allows little time for cool reflection. For this reason, the interpretations we make in the classroom are likely to be based upon rules of thumb and everyday assumptions about the children and the subject matter which we use uncritically. A more careful investigation of what children's activity really means requires not only time but a certain 'intellectual space': an opportunity to reflect, preferably with others, and to develop and share insights into the children's concerns, skills and understandings. Certainly, we cannot reflect with this degree of intensity upon all the children's work, nor even upon a major proportion of it. Nevertheless, the in-depth study of selected samples of activity from our classrooms can lead us to challenge, modify and at times radically alter those assumptions from which we work when we interact with children in the classroom. It can help us build an understanding of the learning process and of the concerns of children which are expressed and developed through that process. We must develop such understanding if we are to realize our role as educators rather than merely as purveyors of knowledge.

It is this attempt to study in depth, or analyse, selected samples of children's activity and work from the classroom that I call Classroom Enquiry. I use the term 'Enquiry', rather than 'Research', because what we are doing differs from normal academic research in several fundamental respects. Our enquiry starts with our experience of the children and their activity. This experience is necessarily subjective. It is quite obvious that any two observers – and especially any two teachers – presented with the same classroom event will perceive different things. For example, a piece of writing that strikes one teacher as showing a poor grasp of grammatical conventions, for another may be evidence of ingenuity in self expression.

This essentially subjective way in which we interpret children's activity has been considered by many educational researchers to be something to be avoided at all costs. 'Unreliable' accounts by teachers are dismissed in favour of such devices as observation schedules which list categories of behaviour to be noted and ticked off at regular intervals, and questionnaires and tests whose results can be readily subjected to statistical analysis. Such attempts to gain understanding again reflect a view that knowledge about the world – our knowledge about the children as well as their knowledge – can be mechanically broken down, or reduced, into 'bits' without regard to the subjective experience of the observer or the observed.

On the contrary, explanations of the learning process itself must be concerned with the children's intentions, their intepretations and the thinking they bring to bear upon their activities. It is these non-behavioural aspects of classroom life to which we must gain access. Such access cannot be achieved by an observer who is separated from the children both physically and psychologically by the research tools used to measure behaviour. As teachers, however, with our close involvement with children and our professional skills which are intended to enhance our understanding of them, we are in a privileged position. The inner thoughts and intentions of children will never be quite open to us and we shall always have to speculate. But we are, nevertheless, in a position to relate closely to children, to prompt their thinking and thereby to begin to reveal it.

Our own writing plays an important part in this process of revealing the children's understanding, of sorting out our ideas about it. One can only get so far by thinking alone. With children's writing in mind, Bruner (1966, p. 105) described writing as 'a calculus of thought for ill-informed problems – problems, that is, without unique solutions'. For the enquiring teacher, writing is not so much a means of recording data – although it certainly has that function – or even of communicating ideas, as much as it is an important part of the process of reaching closer understandings; understandings which are always provisional and are the subject of further reflection.

However, once we accept that it is our subjective experience and reflections upon that experience that provide the richest material for our enquiry, there are serious difficulties we have to meet. How sure can we be that our interpretations of the children's activity will not merely reflect our prejudices, our personal framework of values? Will not the understanding we thereby gain serve to confirm our position rather than challenge it?

In order to meet these difficulties we have to think carefully about how we can share our descriptions and interpretations of classroom activity with each other. Whereas conventional research seeks to minimize the subjectivity of the observer and make generalizations from as wide a sample as possible, classroom enquiry capitalizes upon the different viewpoints of teachers in order to evolve deeper understandings of the particular. We therefore have to construct opportunities for exploring these different perspectives. Our classroom enquiry, then, is not only an individual's reflective analysis of what has taken place, but it also must invite the reflections of others. It goes without saying that this sharing of ideas must be critical, that is we must welcome the expression of contrary viewpoints in an atmosphere that is secure enough for individuals to reason with and reject each other's ideas. The results of such open sharing of our understandings of children's activity will not result in generalized and objective truths about how children learn. To search for these would be a hopeless enterprise. Rather, it aims to produce intersubjective understanding of the complexities of the learning mind and a more articulate language with which to share such understanding. The difficulties we have in understanding how children's minds, and indeed our own minds, grow are arguably not so much the result of a failure to establish the 'true facts' about learning, but more the result of a failure to develop a language and a conceptual framework for interpreting and communicating our experience of learning.

It is our task, through classroom enquiry, rather than the task of the professional researcher, to develop this framework. Traditionally, the functions of production and consumption in educational research have been separated by the institutions of research and schooling. Academic research has produced 'findings'. Teachers have been encouraged to make use of those findings. That we have largely failed to do so reflects not only the difficulties we have in finding the time to interpret research that is often written in a language that is inaccessible to many of us. Nor does it simply reflect an inevitable opposition to the conclusions which such research has reached. Rather, it is based upon our conviction that it is the teachers' and children's experience of the classroom which is authentic, their reflections upon it which are most significant, and that it is in these that our understanding of children in the classroom will be rooted. But that understanding will not develop by itself. It requires our concerted effort to make opportunities of sharing our experience, reflecting upon it and thereby making it more articulate.

AN ENQUIRY PROJECT

It has been the aim of the Leicestershire Insights into Learning project to provide this opportunity for teachers to investigate some of the work from their classrooms in depth. The project was previously called The Leicestershire Classroom Research Inservice Education Scheme, but the title was changed largely because it was felt that the term 'research' was misleading in the context of our investigations into children learning. Originating in the experience of two intensive classroom enquiries that were conducted in primary school classrooms during 1976–7 and 1978–9, and reported in Armstrong (1980) and Rowland (1984), the project now involves teachers in Leicestershire from across the age and subject ranges. It has the support of the Leicestershire Education Department for a trial period of three years from 1982–5 during which time I act as its co-ordinator while on secondment to the department's advisory team.

The project operates at three levels. At the most involved level are a few teachers – usually two or three each year – who spend a year on a secondment from their schools. Most of this year is spent doing fieldwork, teaching alongside a colleague, usually from another school, who has agreed to 'host' the enquiry. During this period, the seconded teacher is largely free from the normal managerial responsibilities of school life and can concentrate instead upon working closely with the children, collecting and recording samples of activity from the classroom, and writing detailed descriptive and interpretative fieldnotes of some of the work with which they have become involved. These analytic notes are discussed with other seconded teachers at regular seminars. Eventually, they are used to compile a report, usually in the form of a research thesis to be submitted for a higher degree.

The support for these enquiries comes almost entirely from the group of teachers. Some of the teachers, seconded in earlier years and now returned to the classroom, meet at the seminars for seconded teachers, thus enabling experience to be passed on from one year to the next. While the focus of these seminars is the interpretation of children's classroom activity, they also provide an opportunity for sharing the problems which inevitably arise from a concentrated period of work in a new context, and for developing a methodology whose discipline is appropriate to our aims.

The subject matter of these enquiries has varied widely from a study of the development of scientific ideas amongst a group of fourteen year olds to a study of influences that affect children's artwork in a multicultural primary school classroom. While such diversity of themes might appear to present problems in fact throughout these studies runs a strong and developing current of thought rooted in the ideas about learning and knowledge discussed in the earlier part of this paper. In particular, we have been concerned to follow the implications of teaching and learning situations in which the relative autonomy of the child is given a high priority. This theme reflects the view that an emphasis upon the children's freedom to choose and interpret their activity is not only a precondition for effective learning, but also enables the teacher, as enquirer, to gain greater access to the thoughts, intentions and plans of the children as they learn.

The second level at which enquiry takes place is amongst a group of about twenty teachers from a wide range of schools. This group is called the Research Consultative Group (RCG). Teachers in the RCG have their normal commitments at school, but meet for two or three days each term to share material and notes they have made about children's activity in the classroom. Much of their work is done in subgroups of about five or six teachers. Each subgroup chooses a theme which draws together the individual teacher's investigations. Periodically, they make presentations of their work to the full RCG, write papers, and contribute to the journal of the project 'Teachers Studying Children's Thinking'.

The RCG provides an initial experience from which some teachers can focus their ideas prior to taking up a more intensive enquiry on secondment. For those who are seconded, it provides a wider audience with whom they can share their ideas as they develop.

The title themes of the subgroups of the RCG have tended to be very broad and interdisciplinary, for example, 'Children's Concerns', 'Talking and Learning' and 'The Social Implications of Literacy'. Perhaps one of the main achievements of these groups has been the realization that teachers of infant children and of teenagers, of mathematics and of the arts, share the same concerns in the classroom and can develop a language which transcends the barriers of curriculum and age group. Such barriers, it would seem, reflect more the institutions of schooling than the needs which they supposedly serve.

The extent of the problem of sharing insights gained during classroom enquiry with other staff has been suggested by the reports of seconded teachers who have returned to their normal teaching role. They have, at times, appeared to feel a sense of frustration, isolation and perhaps alienation, even though the school has given sympathetic support to their secondment. Their appetite and faculty of critical reflection about children's learning has been sharpened, but, on return to the school, with its constant pressures, they received little opportunity for further expression with other teachers. Staff have to meet regularly in order to discuss timetabling, examinations, parent evenings and all the other managerial issues that demand immediate decisions. The discussion of children's learning through sharing classroom enquiry rarely produces immediate and tangible results. Therefore, even though the desire to understand children may be the prime motive of many teachers, it tends to be the 'soft centre' of educational practice, the part which yields most to the increasing pressures of school life.

The work of the Insights into Learning project points to further reasons for tackling this problem by institutionalizing classroom enquiry within schools. Although it would be facile to view the activities of the teacher and those of the children as though they were unrelated aspects of classroom life, the prime focus of classroom enquiry, as understood here, is the activity and understanding of children rather than the performance of a teacher. We have found that directing our attention in this way allows for a less threatening situation when we come to share our analyses with colleagues. For it is not directly our performance which is open to challenge, but our understanding of children. Nevertheless, any attempt to interpret children's work leads us to make more explicit and articulate the educational values which inform that interpretation. In this way, a group of teachers can explore those values upon which their teaching strategy is based, without necessarily feeling under pressure to defend the way they perform. Within the context of a school staff, this means that the values and aims upon which the curriculum is constructed can be made more explicit and open for critical review. All enquiring teachers would contribute to this review from the basis of their observations of children. Such a development raises the classroom anecdote to the level of more deliberate case study, thereby transforming it into a powerful tool for curriculum change.

It is with this aim that the project is now being extended to a third level, with groups of teachers within schools setting up their own classroom enquiries. Opportunities are available for these school-based groups to share their experience with the RCG which, together with the seconded teachers, continues to develop strategies and frameworks for observing and understanding children. In this way it should be possible to complete a continuing cycle of development which extends from the classroom, through the more intensive discipline of sustained enquiry and returns to influence the school.

IS THIS ACTION RESEARCH?

In a book which addresses the general theme of educational action research, I have not used the term 'action research' in relation to our work. I would leave it to the reader to decide, in the light of this paper and of the case study by Jim Nind in Section B, whether classroom enquiry can be subsumed under the general heading of action research. Whether or not it is seen as an approach within the same field, or as an essentially different form of enquiry, would seem to depend upon such questions as these:

- Classroom Enquiry presupposes a certain approach to teaching. Does action research make any such presuppositions?
- The focus of a classroom enquiry is not necessarily a particular problem. Need it be for action research?
- The subject of a classroom enquiry is an aspect of children's learning. Does action research, on the other hand, necessarily concern itself directly with teaching?

3

Teachers' Professional Knowledge

CAROL CUMMINGS and DAVID HUSTLER

INTRODUCTION

Our starting point in this article is teachers' professional knowledge, and how to make that knowledge more explicit, or at least available to ourselves and others. For both of the authors, in our differing professional settings, this concern for clearer access to professional knowledge has gradually come to dominate our work together and with others. The core of the article consists of accounts of two differing forms of collaboration between tutors in teacher training institutions and teachers in schools. One ambition was to get some grip on what teachers know as teachers. More specifically, then, what follows is about collaboration, or at least our experience of collaboration as it relates to teachers' professional knowledge.

The notion of professional knowledge with which we are working is in brief nothing more than the knowledge which reasonably competent teachers use to do what they do as teachers. One way of addressing it is to take note of a problem which many student teachers face. Students can often recognize competent teaching, they can see it or even hear that it seems to be getting done in a tape-recording. To their regret, however, students often find that the experienced teacher cannot provide much help as to how it is being done. The routine manner in which an experienced teacher handles a class may perhaps be so taken for granted that she cannot easily explain the trick to others. This very way of pointing to the general sense of what we mean by teachers' professional knowledge also raises a central issue to do with collaboration. For the tutor in a teacher training institution, one key professional concern is precisely how best to enable students to get access to professional knowledge which works. For the teacher in the classroom the concern with professional knowledge may be very different and may stem from a concern to make more available to herself what she is doing and how she is doing it, as this relates to a particular classroom worry or problem. We also feel that it is important to recognize the different professional practical concerns which people have, practical concerns which are associated with differing sections of the educational system. These of course lead to distinctive ways of seeing, to distinctive 'relevancies'.

We return to these issues in the concluding discussion, but they also have implications for how materials are presented to an audience in written form. In the following section we provide two accounts of collaboration. The first involved the attempt to take on board some of the ideas associated with action research with reference to working in one infant classroom in 1981. At the time these ideas were relatively new to us and we present a small part of a report which we produced at the time to communicate our experience to other teachers. The second account, written by Carol Cummings, is a more recent description of her interest in the use of tape-recordings. A full account of what emerged for her from the focus on news-time in an infant classroom is reported in Payne and Cuff *Doing Teaching*, together with the transcript. In the concluding discussion we draw on these two accounts in relation to how to make teachers' professional knowledge more accessible.

TWO ACCOUNTS

Action Research in an Infant Classroom: a Collaborative Attempt

Action research seems to be well on the way to being accepted as not only a feasible enterprise within schools, but also a legitimate enterprise. The appearance of books such as Jon Nixon's *A Teacher's Guide to Action Research* mark, by their very publication, some recognition that teachers can and do generate worthwhile research in their own classrooms. In addition, many inservice courses for teachers are taking up the notion of 'teachers as researchers' and building more on the existing experience and skills of teachers themselves. Until recently, teachers were largely viewed as having two sorts of roles as far as educational research is concerned; the first was teachers as the objects of researchers, the second involved teachers in the role of applying the research findings of others. Both roles are remarkably passive. In the former, teachers have been subject to the scrutiny of various 'outsiders', whether these be sociologists, psychologists, curriculum experts or whatever. In the latter role, the products of such 'outsiders' are returned to teachers in the form of findings, prescriptions, suggestions, curriculum projects, evaluation programmes, etc., to be taken account of. We realize that this is a somewhat exaggerated characterization which neglects the possible benefits of traditional research on education, but it does help us to make a little bit more explicit, by contrast, just what appealed to us both about the ideas associated with action research. In what follows, we intend to take this up first, after a few words about how we came to be able to attempt some action research. Next, we will give a brief report on some aspects of the experience itself.

To begin with, a few words about the background to the project. One of us, Carol Cummings, is a teacher at Flixton Infant School. She is the teacher of a vertically grouped class of children aged 4½ to 6 years. David Hustler is a lecturer at Didsbury School of Education, Manchester Polytechnic. Thanks to the staff and headteacher of Flixton Infants School, and the support of the Senior Primary Adviser for Trafford, David Hustler was able to spend most of one term in Carol Cummings's classroom.

What then was appealing to us about action research? There are two attractive features in the literature which we would like to emphasize. In discussing these, we will attempt to take up a few of the implications of these features as we tried to take account of them in our preparations. First, action research in the classroom starts with attempts to uncover 'problems' or 'matters of concern' as perceived by teachers, rather than problems as perceived and conceptualized by those not directly involved in the day-to-day business of classroom life. Starting points for much research on education stem from concerns linked with particular educational disciplines, where the problem is first and foremost a problem within some aspect of that discipline, whether it be to do with learning theory, language development or whatever. Research also stems from national considerations and worries, which must be taken on board, but which the teacher in the classroom may find difficult to translate into a 'problem for me'.

Our view certainly is not that action research is 'better' or should replace such research, only that it is different and one central aspect of that difference lies in this focus on 'problems' as perceived by the practising teacher. By 'problem' we could be talking about anything which emerges or forms a starting point: from a niggling worry about how much time some children are spending queuing up for the teacher, or a feeling that more could be done with story-time, to some strong concern as to how the present pattern of allocating children to tables may be affecting progress in particular areas, or a growing lack of conviction about aspects of the teaching style we generally adopt. One implication that we read into this was that David Hustler had to involve himself in the classroom, had to participate in some sense as a teacher, so that at least, up to a point, he could come to share, through experience, some of the concerns of being a teacher in this particular classroom. To operate as a detached observer was not a viable basis of collaborative action research as we viewed it here.

A second feature is that action research cannot be pre-planned or pre-structured in the same way, for example, that traditional experimental procedures demand. As the research develops, so do ideas develop which can lead to action of some sort, which leads to more information and analysis and more ideas and so forth. The goal is not to produce a study which meets, as a major target, the criteria for 'respectable' scientific work and which can stand as a contribution to learned journals. The goal is to illuminate and, if possible, attempt to resolve issues as the research develops. As the name implies, action research involves action, which feeds back into the situation and can lead in unforeseen directions, which are followed up because it seems to the teacher *at that stage of the research* that it is worth pursuing them. It can be seen then that action research is to do with discovering hypotheses and ideas as well as with attempting to test them out. One implication of this for our own work was certainly that we would need to spend a lot of time discussing the research and possible next moves as the research developed. Another implication, given our attempt at a collaborative project, was that we should attempt to monitor fairly closely our own collaboration – our own perceptions of the work as it developed.

So far, so theoretical! Now to some aspects of the experience itself. First, we attempt to provide some indication of our perception of the process of collaboration. Secondly, we will touch on some aspects of what the research came to focus on and some of the techniques used.

Given natural worries about being an 'outsider' in the classroom, we thought researchers would be more interested here in some account of the teacher's perceptions. We monitored our collaboration in a variety of ways, e.g. initial thoughts and anticipations written down separately, diary materials, tape-recordings of discussions, and a technique by which we interviewed each other and tape-recorded the interviews. What follows is a retrospective reworking of some of these materials from Carol Cummings' viewpoint.

Initially, my fears and worries were numerous, overcoming the enthusiasm which thoughts and plans for this research had engendered. They took four distinctive avenues. The first was personal. How would I react to another ever-present 'body' in the classroom; another adult, and one who, for much of the year evaluates student teachers! How would my 'performance' stand up to the test? And, as David Hustler had been a tutor on an inservice course on which I was a student we had exchanged views on teaching – did I, in fact, do what I said I did?

The second cluster of concerns was perhaps more of a problem, and one which was, in fact, easier to talk through and resolve. How would the presence of an outsider affect the children – would they react with difficult behaviour, with lack of application to the tasks set – would, in fact, the 'normal' life of the classroom be upset and, perhaps, be difficult to retrieve. We resolved this problem with the understanding that, should David's presence in the classroom lead to any major problems, we would abandon our attempt at research.

The third consideration and worry was purely practical. In an already busy life, where would we both find time to discuss what we felt was emerging, a part of our joint enterprise which we both felt was central to our concept of collaboration. In fact, we managed many lengthy discussions which began to clarify what we felt were issues that we might profitably look at and I, personally,, found those discussions helpful and illuminating, both as an opportunity to talk with someone 'outside' the infant world about my own concerns, and as an opportunity to hear a 'stranger's' reactions to my daily experience.

Finally, as a member of the staff of a school, I could not act in isolation. Although David's presence would not have any direct impact on other classrooms and other teachers and children in the school, his anticipated presence inevitably provoked questions and discussions, and his presence in the staffroom might be a 'burden' that the staff would be called upon to carry. Colleagues were bewildered by the open-endedness of what we planned, by the relative lack of quantitative techniques, by our inability to pre-specify the 'problems' we were hoping might emerge. Nevertheless, their support and encouragement were ever present. The anticipated problem of the staffroom was resolved in much the same way as the problem of the 'outsiders' in the classroom, and David's presence became no more noticeable than that of a frequent and familiar visitor, although I did not think he was ever party to the most relaxed and informal 'in-house' discussion that occasionally takes place. Unlike children, adults never quite seem to 'let go' in the presence of an outsider.

As time progressed, the feelings of my being evaluated largely disappeared. Indeed, David became almost a 'fly-on-the-wall' during class-time – although a useful fly!

At first, I felt that I should attempt to provide 'jobs' for him, but this initial disease soon vanished and the children provided an excess! They revelled in the luxury of two adults to whom they could go to talk, for information or approbation. And, as David became more an insider in the classroom, feelings of collaboration grew and our discussions began to move towards defining possible problems. From an initial feeling of being researched an atmosphere of us both teaching and researching developed, although, of course, the balance reflected our different areas of expertise; we both felt it important that my role as class teacher must be maintained.

The children, at first interested and questioning, soon accepted David as an integral part of our classroom, and, although the tape-recorder never really ceased to provoke comment, the presence of another 'teacher' was more an added resource than an intrusion.

We were both initially concerned about the unaccustomed presence of a man in the all-female world of the infant school (adults, that is!), but this was never mentioned by the children and David managed to disguise his towering height by adopting the semi-crouching (and, incidentally often back-breaking!) stance of most teachers of young children.

Now some words on the research. Gradually this focused on how children of different ages participated in the classroom, and how their activities were differentially structured (by Carol Cummings and other children). Tape-recordings of story-times and news-times, as well as the morning and afternoon setting up of activities, led to this interest and provided the initial data on it. At half-term a new group of 'youngies' joined and their integration into the group and classroom activities received particular attention. Qualitative and quantitative data-gathering techniques were used: the former, for example, providing details on how Carol Cummings oriented to the different ages, and how the children identified themselves as 'oldies' and 'middles'. Quantitative measures were built up of participation and class oral work, and a regular schematic profile displayed shifts in friendship allegiances.

It became increasingly clear to David Hustler that, at different stages in the term, there was increased or decreased emphasis placed by teacher and children on the age-groupings within this vertically grouped class. As half-term and the transition of some children to other classes approached, it was noticed and hotly disputed that not only was age-status a frequent referral point, but also that the teacher spent considerably more time with the oldest group of children although they did not form a classroom 'group'. This provoked considerable discussion mostly centred around Carol's belief that children were, in fact, being treated 'as individuals'. In fact it was through discussions of this issue that Carol's use of her knowledge about children and particular children, became really explicit for perhaps the first time.

Nevertheless, such differentiation can be seen to have served various purposes. It, perhaps, provided an entry into a new status for all three groups of children: the oldest as future members of a new class, the middles as future 'oldies' and the youngest as now-competent members of the class, ready to accept a new group of novitiates.

One matter for concern however was how, for one particular older child, his approaching transition time led to a structuring of activities for him which were probably inappropriate. Although the central focus of our research, in terms of appraisal and action of various kinds, remained on issues surrounding the age-groupings in the class, there were in our view a number of other useful outcomes. In general terms we both gained insights into a situation with which one of us was familiar and the other entered as a stranger. For both, this was an illuminating experience and engendered scrutiny of the routine practices of the classroom, with which, in our different ways, and for different reasons, we are both centrally concerned.

Secondly, it was an enjoyable experience, an opportunity to collaborate and, for the children, an additional adult with whom to interact.

And, thirdly, through our discussions, 'problems' emerged which were discussed and clarified, adding to our perceptions of how this particular classroom works and thus making more explicit much that was already known in an intuitive, misty sense. As stated earlier we do not see action research as providing prescriptions, generalizations or findings to be applied by others, but as illumination, as growing understanding of what we felt was happening both in terms of classroom practice and in terms of our joint commitment to notions of collaboration.

Tape-recording News-time

I intend to look at three questions: why do I and other teachers undertake research at all, why this particular method, and why pick news-time as a focus? Then I shall look at the uses to which a transcript might be put to illuminate various aspects of professional knowledge and, finally, I shall touch on the Schools Council Outer Network group and the ways in which talking through transcripts provided support and the opportunity to use the eyes of others.

A good question to start with is just why I and other teachers undertake research at all. First, it has become increasingly obvious to some teachers that we have relied on others to tell us what to do, why we act as we do and to what effect. This may be illuminating but it is only a partial picture and not necessarily the picture which is of more use to us with a particular class and its particular problems.

Secondly, my research stems from a desire to find out – memory plays tricks – we tend to gloss over a session and take from it selected 'bits' – so a more systematic way of monitoring classroom events is required. Thirdly, I am concerned about the 'hidden' curriculum aspects of my work, particularly with very young children. They are very trusting and unsceptical.

If the medium is the message, what can we discover of that medium? What messages are being transmitted? Finally, research might reveal some 'solutions' to the practical and ethical dilemmas of the practitioner – you can't move towards more systematic coping strategies without some fairly systematic appraisal of where you are to begin with. If as teachers we want to regain control of our professional status, we need to generate our own data to answer some of our own problems and not always look to the world of research on education as our salvation. The least we can do is to work more closely with researchers and with teacher trainers rather than passively accepting or more often rejecting out-of-hand what little of their work is disseminated as far as the staffroom.

Another general question area is why I have found tape-recordings useful. As a classroom teacher, what skill and expertise I have is not in the area of research methodology. Tape-recording is simple and within the control of the teacher who can use or reject recordings to suit her own purposes.

Although transcription and evaluation are very time-consuming, they can at least be done at any time. Any method of data collection which makes greater demands on the class teacher during class contact time is difficult, if not impossible, unless teaching/interaction time is to be forfeited. Tape-recordings seem to provide the most 'objective' data that the class teacher can hope to collect, although the picture presented is, of course, only partial. Nevertheless, much insight can be gained into life in a particular classroom at a particular time using this method. The data produced can be used to serve a variety of ends. For example, it could be used to evaluate question/answer techniques, pupil participation, starting and ending a session and teacher control. The nature of the data provides the opportunity and opens the door to collaboration with as many others and in as many contexts as may be desired. It could be of interest to other teachers, in or out of the narrow world of infant education, to teacher trainers and student teachers. Each will bring to and take from a transcript different concerns, different ways of looking at and evaluating the material.

A final question is concerned with the choice of session or part of the day. First, news-time was chosen for practical reasons. It is easy in terms of having the whole class together, in terms of very little extraneous noise and because the children are orienting to this session as a particular type of occasion: one in which there is a sort of dialogue between the children, almost as between one child and the teacher. Secondly, its very nature as an occasion makes it interesting in many ways. In most infant days the class is rarely treated as a cohort. The ideal is usually individualization. News-time as a complete chunk of the day, with beginning, middle and end, is an opportunity to look at the accomplishment of that totality as contrasted with data which abstract particular strategies from many sessions on certain recurring features. The data can demonstrate how the children and the teacher orient to this session as a particular type of occasion with its own format and rules.

A transcript can of course be evaluated in many ways. One possible area of concern may be teacher ideology and the extent to which mismatch between that and actual practice is demonstrated. Interest might centre around the ways in which pupils and teacher accomplish the business of the session which in the case of morning news-time seems to be partly formal – registration, dealing with parents and administration – and partly a time for children to link home interests with those of school and orient from one to the other which will then occupy them until home time.

It could be looked at in terms of ownership. Whose session is it? Is it really the child-centred occasion it purports to be? How many children are involved, in what ways and to what ends? What techniques are used by the teacher and by pupils to accomplish the occasion? For me, this question of ownership became increasingly the issue. It challenged my philosophical standpoint and my notions of a child-centred approach. As it became obvious that the degree of teacher-domination was much larger than I could easily accept, it forced me to look again at such sessions and change either the way I dealt with the children, or my view of my own teaching. Discussion of the transcript, talking about the talk, provided not only the support, but a way of uncovering the personal theories and practices, the 'knowledge' upon which my classroom action is based. In a very real way, the talk sessions challenged my taken for granted world and I shall look briefly at some aspects of it. We uncovered a pattern to the session, which starts with informal, mostly small group talk and ends with the administrative business of registration. Post-registration the session becomes more the formal and distinctive teaching of turn-taking, listening to others, paying attention and the transmission of knowledge and information became the central concern. Children seem, by their ways of entering the conversation, to be very aware of this pattern, and show remarkable ability to act appropriately. What I became clearer about was the ways in which the items children brought to my attention before registration were used in a very structured way during the post-registration work. I knew this happened, but seeing how it happened raised questions for me as a teacher. It also became clear, through looking at my transcripts, that the teacher seems in group discussions to act as the central pivot of conversation and that talk often follows a spoke-like pattern. As a group we challenged the necessity or desirability of this phenomenon which we found to be almost universal, we had the data which we could look at together, and in this way we were enabled to examine a frequently occurring but generally invisible aspect of life in the classroom.

Finally, the notion and practice of data-collection and discussion around that data seems to me to go some way towards bringing together the reality of the classroom and 'talk about classrooms'. We had available as central to our sessions actual classroom data and, therefore, were tied firmly into 'what really happens'. It was on this that our discussions were based, and the outcomes led back into the classrooms not just back into 'the' classroom, but into 'our' classrooms. It proved both illuminative and of practical value.

Discussion

The two accounts, 'Action Research in an Infant Classroom' and 'Tape-recording News-time' are relatively small-scale, and not particularly noteworthy in themselves. For both of us, however, and for many of the teachers and tutors in the Outer Network groups, they worked. Given our at times different concerns, our different relevancies, they seemed to be modes of collaboration which got us places as professionals. What does seem worth pursuing is why that may be so, although our focus here will be very much on the teachers rather than the tutors.

Perhaps the first dimension which both settings shared is a closeness to the practical business of classroom life. Our previous experience, whether it be in college or LEA sponsored inservice courses, or through the mainstream literature of research on education, has often been that the everyday pressing features of doing the job of teaching are somehow squeezed out. In both examples, the ad hocs, the sudden necessary changes of pace, the immediate as well as the long-term imperatives, the practical management issues, remain visible. They are part of the content and can be picked up on, or demand to be picked up on, whether this be through the fine detail of transcripts or through the business of talking over classroom incidents almost as and when they occurred. Discussions in both examples appeared to have the ring of reality to them and to be grounded in at least the teacher's sense of what it is to be a teacher with her children at this time.

Another feature in the examples we have takes us further than this. The classroom events and the transcribed readings are the materials which structured the discussion, but it was through the talk itself about these materials that teachers' professional knowledge emerges. Perhaps this is almost too obvious to be explicit about, yet it strikes us as extremely important. Usually, observational materials from schools are presented as the data – whether it be data for the researcher to work on, the student teacher to pick up the tricks of the trade from, or the teacher to note as 'what happens in my classroom or school'. For the teacher who wants to get more access to her teaching situation, and for student teachers, it is not only what teachers visibly do which is important. It is not, in our view, what we can capture on tape, audio or video, and observe which is so important: it is more important to retrieve the knowledge which teachers use to allow them to do what they do. What both settings encouraged was a form of talk in which that knowledge became more available to oneself and to others. Both settings also shared structured contexts involving collaboration, and some form of commitment, which could sustain this form of talk and move it beyond the normal features of, for example, some staffroom talk. In addition, both contexts were relatively free of the superordinate/subordinate relationships built into inservice courses, whether certificated or LEA promoted and neither seemed to be dominated by the question of whose agenda really counts *vis-à-vis* the hierarchical situation of schools.

The two central features we have concentrated on so far, have been, first, the recognizability of the talk that took place as being connected to the job of teaching and, second, that it was through the talk itself that teachers' working knowledge emerged, together with points about how some settings can make that form of talk more awkward. The third and final feature which we see as important to note is that in both examples, that talk actually moved us on. It gave pause for thought, it did lead to change in practice, and attempts to monitor these changes for their effectiveness. It might be particularly difficult to see why this was so in the Schools Council Outer Network group. After all, this was just a group of people talking about their own and each other's transcripts. We would suggest that one object of working with transcribed materials as a group is to bring into the open what you do intuitively so that you and others can look at it. On occasion, of course, there are surprises, there are the 'is this really me?' moments. More important, are the ways in which one's own professional knowledge as a teacher, including taken-for-granted knowledge, becomes part of the discussion. What we begin to look at then is what we know, but perhaps had never been particularly explicit about. Presumably the job of teaching, like any other job, just could not be done without a massive range of unquestioned assumptions, taken-for-granted bits and pieces of knowledge, which have gradually become part of us through the very process of doing the job in a particular context. This knowledge provides the bedrock for stability, for 'life as usual' in the classroom and the school. To have an interest in getting access to at least some of that knowledge does not bring with it by necessity any requirement that we should be criticizing it, or admiring it – the business of making such knowledge more explicit, if only describing it, does however tend to disturb at times. 'Life as usual' in certain respects may not seem quite so 'usual'. However, given that a teacher has a specific worry in the classroom, or a more general concern she wishes to address about her teaching, there is some motivation built in to risk being disturbed. Explicating professional knowledge can open up other possibilities. It can point to a greater scope for action where necessary. The point about taken-for-granted professional knowledge is precisely that it *is* taken-for-granted, and that as such it closes off certain aspects of how a teacher operates, or could operate. If self-appraisal means anything for a teacher, it must mean the capacity to find out more about how she ticks and whether, having done that in relation to a particular concern, she is more able to generate strategies for action.

4

Action Research: an LEA Adviser's View

HARRY PICKLES

The views contained in this chapter are mine; although reference is made to developments within the City of Salford, the views should not be construed to necessarily represent Authority policy.

I enjoy going to the theatre and am full of admiration for the top stars who can hold an audience in the palms of their hands. It is quite an art and although these stars suddenly appear upon the national stage or television screen, the suddenness hides what had, usually, been a long, hard, unnoticed apprenticeship. Theatre programmes outline the careers of the performers; some are famous, others on the way up and some has-beens; it's fun to predict who will become a well-known star and very satisfying if a few years later you are proved correct.

Elements of national reports are like that and one of the tasks in an LEA is to predict which issues will be big, which small and which will fade away into oblivion. I like to think of these trends as 'straws in the wind'; one such straw has been the emphasis on teaching methods that leads, inevitably, towards the need for school-based evaluation and classroom action research.

The major reports written over the past eight years contain references that point to the need for schools and teacher to increase their expertise in matching teaching activities to pupils' ability and interest, observing pupils' activities, assessing their value and effect, critically appraising their own performance and making decisions in the light of all this. Her Majesty's Inspectors, writing on mixed ability teaching, say:

> Many mixed ability classes observed, however, demonstrated that the practice of having small groups of pupils working together for particular aspects of a subject was rarer than the whole class working together or the pupils working as individuals. Providing appropriate content and task, matching these to pupils in the small group, and ensuring that discussion which genuinely promoted learning took place seemed to have proved very difficult for many

teachers. Where small groups were formed within the mixed ability class, their composition was usually self-determined by interest or friendship. Less commonly, the teacher selected group members, either to ensure a spread of ability or to form more homogeneous groups. However, regrouping of pupils when this would have been appropriate within the mixed ability pattern was not often practised even when timetable facilities and accommodation were suitable or specially designed for this possibility. Certainly there was some lack of awareness of such possibililties, or of expertise in creating them.

(HMSO, 1978, p. 36)

In the report resulting from the national secondary survey observations on mathematics and science included:

It might be advantageous for some science departments to review their methods and to adopt teaching approaches which are more successful in maintaining the interest and motivation of the pupils.

Oral work was often limited to brief responses from a few pupils, in answer to questions that provided no opportunity to exchange ideas or examine hypotheses. The work for the least able was sometimes designed to make the minimum linguistic demands. We quote some observations of this kind:

The lessons seen at all ability levels were traditionally presented with little demand being made on the pupils to use mathematical language other than in simple monosyllabic responses.

Very little opportunity was given for the pupils to express themselves orally in mathematics lessons and this resulted in some very confused statements in the exercise books when anything in the nature of an explanation was demanded.

The teachers used language only to instruct, explain and illustrate; rarely were questions asked of pupils requiring thought and alternative answers, 'But not in my classroom surely?'

(HMSO 1979, pp. 136, 200)

But HMIs are not the only ones to provide the straws. Schools Council in the best publication it ever produced, *The Practical Curriculum* (1981), observed:

For the children themselves the effective curriculum is what each child takes away. Schools and their teachers need ways of finding out what each child's experience is and how well they are learning what the school intends. This is a more difficult task in secondary than in primary schools. Class teachers in primary or secondary schools are well placed to take an overview of each pupil's experience and help the pupil to assess it. Specialist teaching and the typically fractured day of secondary schools make it a great deal harder for most secondary teachers to do this.

A form tutor may have a good overview of the experience his or her colleagues have planned; with sympathetic imagination a tutor may feel what the pupils experience. But there seems to be no substitute for sharing their experience, seeing the day as the pupils see it and listening to what they say about it.

One headteacher who checked what was happening in his own school found that one form was given workcards in one lesson after another throughout the day. We had to ask whether it was sensible either to use them to that extent or to exclude other methods of learning.

Similar checks on the experience of particular pupils may also be illuminating. One class of 10 year-olds studying their local community had an exciting series of lessons with visitors coming in to talk about their jobs. There were many opportunities for role play and much good work was done. Only afterwards did the teacher realise that one boy had first been asked to play the role of a heavily bandaged patient on a stretcher, then a member of a jury, all essentially non-speaking roles. By accident it seemed he had been denied access to rich areas of experience.

(*Schools Council, 1981, pp. 42-3*)

The findings of the survey on middle schools (HMSO, 1983a) provides yet another straw:

The survey indicates that much of children's time in school is spent in listening and writing. Not many opportunities are provided for extended discussion, for collaborative work in groups, or for the exercise of choice, responsibility and initiative within the curriculum. A greater diversity of teaching and learning approaches should be provided for children across the four years span, but especially for older pupils, as a means of enhancing motivation to learn and quality of work. In all schools the local environment provides an obvious though often ignored, starting point for children's enquiries; it is a rich focus for work which can involve children in observation, description, application of skills and ideas, and, increasingly as they grow older, explanation, reasoned argument and generalisation. An expansion in the range of learning approached, coupled with an increase in the demands made on children as they develop, will provide more opportunities for all pupils, from the least to the most able, to acquire and develop levels of skills and an understanding of ideas more clearly related to their capacities than is often the case at present.

(HMSO, 1983a, p. 124)

LEAs in partnership with the DES engaged in fundamental curriculum appraisal on the basis of their publication *Curriculum 11–16*. The outcomes are described in what is affectionately known as 'Red book Three', (HMSO 1983b) because of the colour of its cover. On pupil learning:

> Towards the end of the first phase of the enquiry, there was a growing recognition of a need to develop ways of examining the curriculum in terms of what children experienced and received, and of how they are motivated to enjoy learning. This led to the second phase of the enquiry to emphasise the clarification of curricular aims and objectives, their translation into classroom practice and the evaluation of pupils' learning. In this work, the development of new check lists of skills, attitudes, concepts and knowledge had a particular view. It encouraged schools to look practically at these aspects of pupils' learning across the boundaries of subject departments. It proved possible, for example, to consider certain skills to which many departments claimed to contribute and hence to coordinate approaches and minimise duplication. To evaluate what was happening, teachers, advisers and HMI cooperated to follow individual pupils through their course of daily lessons in 'pupil pursuit'. This process was found to be a valuable way of observing what pupils actually received from the learning experience planned by teachers.

(HMSO, 1983b, p. 10)

Bringing comments right up to date, on slow learning and less successful pupils HMI wrote:

> If demonstration was needed, the schools demonstrated that their most important resources are the skills of their teachers. However, such lessons were, for the most part, the result of an individual initiative or of an almost fortuitous partnership between two or three teachers – fortuitous in the sense that chance has brought into the school people of like mind. Very few schools planned a style of working on certain principles of classroom management which affected all teachers. Sometimes the school had enunciated principles, but they were not apparent in the classrooms because the schools had not proceeded to consider the necessary measures for putting them into effect. Thus, for example, the principle that each child should be enabled to work

at his own (i.e. appropriate) pace was seldom followed by steps to
see what the child's own pace was or whether it was somehow
'natural' to the child or the result of a specific malfunction. Nor
was it usual to find any method of checking that children were in
fact progressing at their 'own' pace not at some other. In many
cases it was assumed that what a child actually did represented his
'natural' level.

(HMSO, 1983, p. 46)

These straws are in the wind that gusts inexorably to the need for close
and detailed examination of what is going on in schools but more
particularly in classrooms. How to go about this is problematical for all
the straws are concerned with issues that are fundamental to the day-to-
day operation of teachers in schools and classrooms. If there is to be
progress, help and guidance are needed so that there is a match between
what schools and teachers intend and provide and what children
experience and gain. The well-established method of the school
inspection carried out by HMI or local authority advisers usually
highlights matters of use to the school; it is always hoped that some
good comes out of such exercises. Unfortunately when it does not, it
may be because the school was not ready for it, or that the purposes
had not been adequately explained or simply that the issues of concern
to those inspecting were not shared by the teachers in the school. Even
when the visit has been useful and successful, when the inspectors or
advisers depart, having delivered their findings, the school loses the
value of the experienced eye. But that need not be, for if the staff in the
school act as their own experienced eyes because they are there all the
time, school-based evaluation can take place as often as it is wished.
Armed with a framework to assist the exercise, the staff in a school can
do it for themselves.

In the City of Salford the framework has been provided by two self
evaluation schemes: the one for primary schools was introduced in 1982
(City of Salford, 1982) and the other, for high schools in 1983 (City of
Salford, 1983). This has been supplemented by *Curriculum in Action*,
described in detail elsewhere in this book.

Although the self evaluation schemes are very different in style and
operation they share a common basis of fundamental principles without
which successful evaluation is unlikely to occur. The most important of
these is that the staff are ready and willing to engage in the task, are
aware of one another's roles, trust each other personally and
professionally and have taken part in determining the aspects of school
life to be evaluated. This formidable list of pre-requisites should not be
viewed with too much dismay for it is found that such attributes as
trust, willingness, awareness, involvement and commitment grow as

staff become increasingly involved in the task and see its usefulness. For many teachers it has been professionally rewarding to discuss with colleagues such questions as:

- the arrangements made to ensure that pupils receive a balanced programme over a period of time
- identifying what is essential in the planning and forecasting of work and systems for monitoring it
- the time allocation to be given to the various curriculum areas
- the need to monitor carefully the work programme of pupils in more flexible learning situations
- the danger of imbalance caused by individual teachers' lack of curriculum knowledge
- the need for necessary support, in-service training and staff development work in the light of any curriculum weaknesses within the school
- the needs of the school in particular curriculum areas when appointments of staff are made

These questions come from the section 'Leadership in schools' (Salford, 1982) which is one of twelve sections that primary schools work through during a four year cycle; others include the learning environment, relationships, aims and philosophy as well as curriculum areas such as humanities, science and language development.

In the secondary framework schools have performance indicators that have to be expanded into the school's view of its ideal position. This can then be matched against the school's actual performance; prompts are provided to assist with interpretation. The clear links and inter-action between the individual, groups and the whole school are empha-sised as shown in the example on Staff Roles at the end of the chapter.

In both schemes the order and depth of consideration is determined by the staff. Local authority advisers, headteachers and teachers from other schools act as critical friends to moderate the school's view of its performance.

Evaluation by itself is interesting but of no consequence unless it leads to action. Careful study of curricular and management issues point to strengths and weaknesses which in turn lead to a definition of priorities for action, selection of support agencies, planned development of staff and eventually further evaluation. The weakness is that this kind of arrangement relies on the expertise of the staff who are operating it: if they do not possess the knowledge and skills to examine school performance in a systematic and educationally sound manner then the results will be suspect. It can reinforce mediocrity or make good, conscientious teachers paranoiac.

SECTION 1 STAFF ROLES

Key Issue 1.4 The Work of the Subject Teacher – this key issue is concerned with the teacher's responsibility to promote children's learning.

Indicators related to performance

	School	Sub-groups	Individuals
1.4-1	Matches teaching experience and knowledge to subject requirements.	Review and match teaching expertise and knowledge to particular requirements.	Are knowledgeable about the content of the subject they teach.
1.4-2	Establishes principles for the production of departmental guidelines and the subsequent monitoring of their application.	Provide departmental guidelines and encourage and monitor the development and use of appropriate teaching materials.	Evaluate, use and develop appropriate teaching materials and methods within departmental guidelines.
1.4-3	Fosters and provides resources for an orderly and stimulating environment.	Provide orderly and stimulating departmental environment.	Provide an orderly and stimulating working environment.
1.4-4	Expects professional approach to the management of learning experiences.	Identify factors related to the efficient and effective management of learning situations.	Manage learning experiences efficiently and effectively.
1.4-5	Defines the concept and requirements of good working habits in pupils.	Interpret the requirements of good working habits in pupils.	Foster good working habits in pupils.
1.4-6	Determines policy on assessment and record keeping.	Provide guidelines for assessment and record keeping.	Assess and record pupils' work, progress and attainment.
1.4-7	Establishes criteria for personal performance.	Contribute to and interpret criteria for evaluating personal performance.	Evaluate personal performance against agreed criteria and act accordingly.

This is where action research has such a large part to play in school development, particularly in classrooms, for it provides the skills and knowledge that are essential if school self evaluation is to succeed. In Salford it is exciting to witness schools engaging in evaluations of their very *raison d'être* but it is inspiring to see how *Curriculum in Action* (Open University, 1980) through its six questions and training in observation can provide the hard edge that is needed.

5

Curriculum in Action in Action

ANGELA ANNING

In this chapter I will be describing the process of professional development which lead me to use the Open University *Curriculum in Action* school-based packs; the impact this approach to inservice had on myself and colleagues; and developments of the approach into an action research project and a whole staff project. Finally I will deal with issues arising from this personal testimony.

THE WAY THERE

I came into teaching reluctantly at first, needing cash in the early stages of surviving as an arts graduate. I worked in a secondary modern school and later on vocational day release courses in Further Education. I was concerned at that stage with the day-to-day mechanics of learning how to teach. In the college of Further Education I had access to a changing population of working adults. I listened carefully to what the apprentices and craft instructors said about their own experiences of inner-city schooling – very different from my own academic training. I began to recognize the enormous gulf between pupils and their teachers in understanding what education was all about. I was married to an academic and I shared his healthy scepticism for the exclusivism and irrelevance to real life of the research projects which dominated the conversations of many of his colleagues. Two children later I had discovered a passionate interest in the development of the young child and as a mature student studied for a Postgraduate Certificate in Education so that I was qualified to be a 'proper teacher'. Against this background, my own concern for personal professional development began to extend outwards to a critical interest in inservice provision for teachers and the role of the professional educational researcher.

In the first few years of inner city primary school teaching – first in a junior school on a large council estate and then running a nursery in the heart of a Northern city – I dutifully attended inservice courses. I do not think I was naïvely expecting instant enlightenment, but I was looking for advice and support. I genuinely wanted to be a 'better' teacher. It required a supreme effort at the end of an exhausting day of teaching, juggling with already complicated domestic arrangements, to actually get myself to the course venue. More often than not I was disappointed that the course did not give me the kind of support I wanted. Sometimes the course handout was not specific enough about the content of the sessions so that theoretical models that were presented were far more accessible to me from personal reading. Sometimes the practical content offered seemed so remote from the realities of a hectic day in inner-city classrooms that I wondered whether it was me that was at fault; but it was apparently not expected that teachers should voice such doubts. Occasionally, I would return to school the next morning determined to try to implement some of the ideas I had gleaned from the previous evening session. My efforts were usually perfunctory. Very few of the teachers around me bothered with inservice (Bolam, Smith and Canter, 1978). It was easier to slip back into the safe undemanding rituals of teaching based on the 'pedagogic theory' that had evolved as the norm of that particular staffroom (Sharp and Green, 1975). The only productive thinking which made any difference to my classroom practice was done with groups of colleagues, either informally or through local pressure groups, who share my particular interests and convictions.

At about this time I became aware of the media hyperbole about the Lancaster research project on teaching styles and pupil progress (Bennett, 1976). My attitude to educational researchers was antagonistic. I was irritated by the negative tone of many of the research reports and suspicious of the methods used to collect data. The reports were often couched in jargon and statistics and were published in journals that rarely reached staffroom shelves (McCutcheon, 1981). Above all I felt frustrated that teachers lacked the language to argue coherently with the researchers. We seemed to live in separate worlds. A prestigious research industry seemed to be thriving at the expense of school practitioners rather than in support of them.

My role in schools, initially as a scale post holder for language development, then as a deputy headteacher, changed to one of responsibility for curriculum development throughout schools. The dilemma was now to persuade other teachers that it was possible to change their practice and encourage them to attend courses.

Any changes we made were strictly content based – a new language policy, a record-keeping system, an emphasis on a technique or resources that made teaching more efficient but not necessarily more effective – administratively impressive but basically cosmetic.

At the same time I was looking for personal intellectual challenge. I was still uneasy about the value of straight research. I rejected the idea of taking a higher degree which I saw as a course where I was simply going to regurgitate information second hand in order to gain a qualification. I opted instead to study for the Open University Diploma in Reading Development since I could at least see the relevance of this course to my own classroom practice and the benefits for the pupils I was teaching. During this period I read Lawrence Stenhouse's seminal book (1975). It seemed like a breath of fresh air.

> The improvement of teaching is a process of development. I mean by the first, that it is not to be achieved by a change of heart but the thoughtful refinement of professional skill; and second, that the refinement of professional skill is generally achieved by the gradual elimination of failings through the systematic study of one's own teaching.
>
> *(Stenhouse, 1975, p. 39)*

I responded to the idea of teachers researching their own classrooms and I began to follow with interest accounts of the Ford Teaching Project (Elliott, 1976) in East Anglia where teachers and researchers were working together using triangulation procedures. I also heard members of the Leicester team talking about the ORACLE project (Galton *et al.*, 1980) where attempts were being made to categorize pupil and teacher behaviours using systematic observation techniques. The team seemed supportive rather than critical of the teachers they had observed.

In my fourth year of study for the Diploma in Reading Development at the Open University Summer School we were asked to comment on some new materials the Open University was trialling for school-based inservice. They were packs aimed at groups of teachers working together in schools. There was evidence from the DES discussion paper (1978), *Making Inset Work* and from projects like the It/Inset (see Ashton *et al.*, 1983) that there was at last recognition of the fact that teachers working in isolation could not sustain curriculum change and that inservice was far more effective if the needs of a particular school were identified and inservice was geared to their expressed needs. My experience of leadership in curriculum development in schools had taught me that staff in school would tend to identify safe content-based areas for development resulting in superficial changes in practice. I saw the need for radical changes in the basic attitudes of the teachers which would modify the way in which the curriculum was taught. Amongst the papers we were handed by the Open University staff were extracts from the *Curriculum in Action* (1980) pack. I read them with mounting excitement. At last I had come across inservice materials that considered the pupil's experience of the curriculum as a critical starting point for evaluation and where the focus was firmly on an analysis of one's own classroom teaching. I had moved to a new authority, now as a headteacher, and when I returned from summer school, I contacted the LEA Senior Adviser with responsibility for inservice and asked if we could order some packs for use in our authority.

CURRICULUM IN ACTION

The following September I drew together a group of Salford primary teachers, through personal contacts, which included headteachers and their deputies as well as my own deputy. This small group had the qualities Stenhouse (1975, p.144) believed were essential to qualify teachers as researchers:

> The commitment to systematic questioning of one's own teaching as a basis for development. The commitment and the skills to study one's own teaching. The concern to question and test theory in practice by the use of those skills. To these may be added as highly desirable, though perhaps not essential, a readiness to allow other teachers to observe one's work – directly or through recordings – and discuss it with them on an open and honest basis.

The six core questions of the *Curriculum in Action* course pack appear deceptively simple. The questions are:

> What did the pupils actually do?
> What were they learning?
> How worthwhile was it?
> What did I do?
> What did I learn?
> What do I intend to do now?

We soon discovered that responding honestly to them requires rigorous self-discipline and the capacity to rethink many of the accepted beliefs about teaching and learning that seem to be at the basis of the collective consciousness of teachers.

Group members explored issues which they felt to be critical in improving their understanding of processes in their own classrooms. They talked with refreshing frankness about the problems they had identified through the careful and systematic analyses of classroom practice built into the format of the course. At the end of six months the issue they intended to pursue were identified as:

The function of groups in the classroom. How does the teacher allot time to groups within the class? How valuable is grouping to the pupils/teacher? How does grouping benefit learning?

Monitoring individual children on task. How can the quality of task be raised so that children's motivation to learn is improved? How can teachers organize effectively a curriculum based on the individual learning needs of pupils?

Criteria for grouping. What criteria do teachers use for grouping young children for learning? Is it their learning ability, social competence, emotional development? How does grouping perpetuate teacher expectations and thus pupil performance? What effect do different groupings have on children's ability to learn in the classroom.

Control. How important a factor is matching task to pupil in maintaining discipline with fourth year juniors?

Verbal interaction between pupils. What are the effects of (a) personality mix of a group, (b) the cognitive ability of members of a group and (c) the ethos of the classroom on the quality of verbal interaction within classroom groups? What organizing strategies would the teacher need to employ in order to maintain purposeful and thoughtful interaction between pupils?

The following year it was decided (1) that more *Curriculum in Action* packs should be bought for use in the LEA (2) that the next course should involve primary and secondary teachers and (3) that deputy headteachers would be in the best position to lead a 'bottom up' initiative for self evaluation in schools. The course was advertised in the LEA inservice brochure and was heavily over-subscribed.

In this larger group of primary and secondary headteachers members began to separate out into recognizable categories. A small group became totally involved in the process of looking critically at their own practice. As the weeks went on, it was clear that the process was having a profound influence on their attitude to teaching and learning and forcing them to modify their practice to accommodate some of the unpalatable truths they had discovered. One secondary deputy headteacher wrote:

> Initially I was fascinated to learn how much more I could derive from my classes by looking more closely at how my pupils react and perform. It was interesting to see how different pupils worked in their own ways to achieve a similar end result. Some needed discussion, some reassurance, some lacked confidence in practical others in written skills.
>
> The fact that surprised me and concerned me most, was how much the children needed me as a teacher and that their general

attitudes and performance depended on how our relationship progressed. I had always known that the teacher's influence was important but had not realized how great that influence is.

The whole ethos of a particular learning situation is moulded on our mutual agreement with our pupils regarding standards, behaviour, tone, etc. Each class is different and secretly establishes a different relationship with me as a person, with very little having actually been spoken on the system we will, or are prepared to accept.

Bearing this in mind, I now think more about what is happening and the reasons behind it. I do not always succeed in what I try to do in establishing the kind of atmosphere and relationship I require but I certainly think more and try more carefully to encourage an atmosphere in which we can derive mutual satisfaction and progress.

As I do more classroom observation and try to find out more about how I can improve the learning situations of my pupils, I realise even more that pupils are individuals and need to be approached according to their individual character, a very difficult task when I consider how many children I teach at a time and the fact that I see them for only a limited time each week.

I have also realised that the classroom situation is much more artificial than I had previously thought because of the very nature of control and trying to teach both a collection of individuals and a class of pupils all at the same time.

My plans for the future will try to take all this into account. I have always tried different things with my pupils to try to improve our mutual success but this will progress much more consciously now and in the future. 'There are no problems – just opportunities for success.'

Another category included, of course, members who simply went through the motions of attending sessions, fascinated by the data they had collected, but with little commitment to go back to the classroom and change their practice. Some dropped out altogether either because their priorities were elsewhere, or because they found it too threatening to face up to the realities of what was happening in their classrooms rather than what they wished to believe was happening, or because they could not see the point of what we were trying to do at all. Two-thirds of the original group of twenty-four completed the course. Committed participants focused on one particular aspect of their own practice and worried away at it, like a dog with a bone. These included:

Transfer of learning. How can we ensure that interesting class discussions are reflected in more thoughtful written work?

Independence in learning. How can organization in a classroom be structured so that children develop independent strategies for learning so freeing the teacher to teach groups without constant interruption?

Group work. How can group work be structured so that pupils gain the skills of co-operative learning? How can the teacher present group tasks that provide (1) a high level of motivation, (2) intellectual challenge and (3) a genuine sense of purpose.

Bright children. How can the teacher provide a rich diet of stimulating tasks for bright children in mixed ability classes?

Feedback. What qualities make for effective teacher feedback for learners?

Science lessons. How can the teacher motivate all levels of ability in science lessons within the constraints of an imposed school syllabus?

Exams. How can the demands of teaching for assessment be reconciled with the need to teach for understanding?

Below average children. How can one counteract the alienation from school of the below average child?

At fortnightly meetings the quality of discussion of the issues raised by the work carried out in the schools was always good and sometimes excellent. The regular meetings also provided a framework of mutual support which is an essential requirement for this kind of intense personal professional development. A small group of these deputy headteachers will continue to work either with colleagues in their own schools or with contacts in other schools who share their interest in a particular issue, again using the *Curriculum in Action* packs as a framework. Some of these teachers will include members of the original *Curriculum in Action* group. What is significant is that, unlike most inservice activities, the commitment to work within this framework has been maintained in some cases over three years; time enough for reflection and action.

THE WAY AHEAD

Research with Teachers

My own interest began to focus on the sections of the pack course members consistently found most difficult – what were the pupils learning? Somehow we could not find the language to express our understanding of how pupils were learning from the experiences we put their way. The hypotheses we made were loosely defined as a series of hunches and intuitions based on our knowledge of individual children's (apparent) capabilities. I had begun to use a video camera in school to record sequences for a course on problem solving which I was helping to run. As I ran and re-ran the tapes I began to identify patterns of teacher responses to evidence they picked up of children learning on task. I found it frustrating to compare the evidence I was observing of this consummate skill in assessing and responding to individual learners' progress and needs with teacher inability to articulate the processes they were using. I was irritated by the notion that professional researchers would simply conclude that teachers did not understand the processes by which their pupils learned (Bennett *et al.*, 1984). The evidence I had on tape was that they did, but were unable or unwilling to express that understanding in the theoretical terms that researchers valued. I approached Dr Pat Ashton, who had played a key role in developing Curriculum Action materials, at Leicester University, with a research proposal. The purpose is to devise a framework within which teachers might explore how children learn. The objectives of the project are:

To investigate teachers' understanding of how children learn.

To explore the possibility that teachers' understanding of how children learn affect pupils' strategies for learning.

To explore the possibility that teachers differentiate between different kinds of school learning.

To share information and techniques for classroom-based research with the teachers involved in the project.

To devise inservice material for more general use.

The method I have used is to ask six teachers (teaching from nursery to upper junior age range) to select three groups of children and three learning tasks. In a pre-task discussion the teachers have explained their rationale for the selection of the partiuclar tasks for the particular pupils and identified their expectations of what the pupils will learn on task. The tasks have then been video-taped. The tapes have been used as the basis for a detailed analysis by the teachers and myself of evidence of pupil learning and the teaching strategies employed in response to this evidence. A written response has been elicited and a Kelly grid exercise has been conducted to ascertain each teacher's general understanding of how children learn in his/her classroom. The data has now been collected. The next stage will include a content analysis of the teachers' statements about how children learn and a discussion of its relationship to current theories of learning. Finally inservice material will be devised based on the insights and experiences gained from working with the teachers on the project.

Three of the sample teachers work in the nursery/infant school where I was then the headteacher. The other three were personal contacts. As a classroom-based researcher I did not have to spend a great deal of time building up an atmosphere of trust between us. Yet even those teachers whom I knew well tended to opt for 'safe' tasks for the first sessions we recorded. They were invariably hypercritical about the quality of their teaching in some of the sequences. Nevertheless, they enjoyed the 'luxury' of spending time working with small groups and of the opportunity of using the video-tapes to analyse pupil responses in depth. They also found reviewing the tapes a useful way of identifying recurring patterns in their teaching strategies. They became more critically aware of what worked and what did not. They also began to analyse why certain strategies they used were more effective than others. These were very personal insights providing a potent source of self knowledge. However across the six teachers common issues are detectable from an analysis of the transcripts, such as time given for response, risk-taking, response to errors, pacing, control, use of humour, response to pupil type.

Whole School Involvement

Three teachers in the school were already aware of the value of observations in classrooms, but I wanted to encourage other members of staff to learn the skills required to observe effectively. We were planning to introduce some method of assessing children's progress in mathematical thinking through the school. Already alerted to the negative implications of using commercial tests − teaching to the test, imposing minimum expectations, the gap between pupils' ability to record and their ability to reason − I wanted the staff to design their own testing procedures. We asked the teachers if they would devise two tasks on a specific area of the maths curriculum − sorting into categories − one practical and one recorded, taking into account the general level of development of the age group they taught. We were also keen to identify issues about teacher expectations. We asked the teachers to group all the children in their class into three levels of mathematical competence. We asked them to select one target child from each ability band and make detailed observations of them working on both the practical and recorded tasks. The insights gained from this exercise were apparent in lively staffroom discussions. Field notes indicate that the following issues were discussed in depth as a result of analysing the data collected by the teachers: teacher expectation, motivation to learn, match of task to ability, transfer of learning, risk taking, the gap between practical competence on task and the ability to record; progression through the acquisition of key mathematical concepts. Informed by these discussions, the staff are now planning to try various methods of assessing mathematical competence by observing children engaged on purposeful, practical tasks such as building with a range of different sized and shaped blocks, planning and preparing a simple meal, and designing and constructing a model.

ISSUES

I now find myself suspended uneasily between the roles of researcher and practitioner. From this uncomfortable position, I perceive two major issues that the action research movement must confront: the monitoring of the effectiveness of this type of professional personal development in changing classroom practice, and the formulation of a pedagogic language for meaningful discussions about the processes of teaching and learning.

Monitoring Effectiveness

In an earlier section of the chapter I argued against the effectiveness of traditional input models of inservice. The model assumes that the teachers are passive receivers of pearls of wisdom. The *Curriculum in Action* approach is fundamentally different in design. It involves teachers as active learners. They must seek to improve practice by developing the ability to analyse critically their own role in the classroom and the awareness of how that affects the learning of their pupils. In that sense it is a reflection of the more broadly based quest for self knowledge and a critical awareness of processes that characterizes the whole action research movement. In my experience, thinking teachers respond with unusual intensity to the challenge presented by the *Curriculum in Action* approach. What is more important they are highly motivated to modify their practice to accommodate the insights they have gained from a profoundly personal learning experience. Since they have been involved in the process of identifying the need for change, they have a strong commitment to implement them. There are examples of personal testimonies of changed practice as a result of this kind of learning experience in the Classroom Action Research Network bulletin (e.g. Day, 1984, Henderson and Perry, 1981) and from reports of the work of Kemmis at Deakin University of Australia. What we need now is a more systematic attempt to monitor changes in practice over several years. The movement cannot afford to be lightly dismissed as another bandwagon.

Finding a Language

The major stumbling block, however, is the difficulty teachers seem to have in articulating their understanding of how children learn and of presenting their views about the processes of teaching and learning within a coherent framework. This is hardly surprising since they have traditionally been expected to shut up and get on with what other 'more learned people' told them to do. Most teachers were simply never trained to reflect on their own practice in any depth. The critics who accuse the action research movement of wasting time as simply 'reinventing the wheel' perhaps forget that for teachers it is an entirely new experience to hypothesize, collect data, analyse and evaluate. It is also a new experience for them to present their thoughts to an audience. They are still amazed that they are being taken seriously! Lawrence Stenhouse saw the teacher accounts as providing a pack of specialized case studies, as in medical practice, to which other practitioners faced with similar 'symptoms' might refer. In this context teachers' accounts are valuable in their own right. From diffident beginnings some teachers will perhaps want to adopt more rigorous frameworks within which to examine practice such as those outlined by Elliott (1981) or Kemmis (1981). More significantly they will perhaps move from specific accounts to generalized theory. This is the point at which a new language must be systematically hammered out. At present it is the researchers who take on the role of providing pedagogic theory. In so doing, they often adopt the kind of jargon that has become second nature to them, but which teachers find elitist and irrelevant. It is equally unhelpful for teacher/researchers to defiantly reject the notion of referring to existing research models. What point can there be in ignoring existing sources of information and expertise? Polarizing practitioners and researchers as Them and Us is counter-productive. We can learn from each other. We need each other. Somehow we must find a way of expressing ourselves in a common language which bridges the gap.

6

Teachers' Perspectives on Matching: Implications for Action Research

CHARLES DESFORGES, ANNE COCKBURN and NEVILLE BENNETT

'A perspective is a way of seeing. By the same token it is a way of not seeing.'

It is a truism that to foster learning, it is necessary for pupils to work on tasks appropriate to their attainments and abilities. In the jargon of education this facilitation is called matching.

In 1978 HMI published a report in which they claimed matching, or more accurately mismatching, to be a serious educational problem. It was concluded that for high attaining children in primary schools underestimation in mathematics was evident in almost half the classes observed and in geography, history and science this figure rose to more than two thirds. HMI noted that whilst high attainers were extensively underestimated, teachers fared much better in assigning appropriate work to lower attainers.

Unfortunately, HMI did not make it clear how they had made their decisions on the match between a child's attainment and his assigned work. Neither did they state the model of teaching and learning which had guided their observations and interpretations. For these reasons it was a moot point as to whether matching was a problem or not.

A more recent research project (Bennett et al., 1984) set out to explore the incidence and origins of mismatching in infant schools. The research was conducted within a clearly articulated theoretical framework and permitted the comparison of researchers' judgements on matching with those made by teachers. Whilst not strictly an action research project the work was carried out in close collaboration with participating teachers and, it will be argued, the results have some implications for action research work.

The project, entitled *The Quality of Pupil Learning Experiences* (QPLE) comprised two phases, (1) an initial observation phase and (2) an intervention phase in the form of an inservice course for teachers. The inservice course was designed in the light of problems exposed in phase one. Space does not permit the detailed description of the design and theoretical background which are reported elsewhere (Bennett *et al.*, 1984). Only sufficient details for the present purposes are reported here.

The first phase of the research took place in sixteen top infant classes in schools scattered across the northwest of England. Each teacher involved was a volunteer and highly experienced with this age range. None of the teachers had any problems in the control and management of children or materials.

The focus of observation was on six target children in each class (two high, two middle and two low attainers). However, only one target child was observed at any one time. Data were collected by six experienced infant teachers who had been specially trained in interview and observation techniques. Detailed records were made of more than 400 maths and language tasks.

Before each task the research worker told the teacher which target child was her (the researcher's) selection for that lesson. She then interviewed the teacher to ascertain her objectives for the tasks to be set that child and the kinds of problems she expected to meet. After this the observer made herself as unobtrusive as possible in the classroom and recorded all the teacher's instructions to the class or to the target child in setting work. Attention was then focused on the target child and as much as possible was recorded of his manner of work or his conversations whether on or off task. All observations were recorded longhand in a log book. When the child had finished his work, or when the teacher's set period for the work ended, the researcher interviewed the child in order to establish the enjoyment and interest in the task and also to ascertain his degree of understanding of the work. This she did by setting the child a series of small tasks related to that set by the teacher. If the researcher suspected the child was in difficulty, these small additional tasks were easier than that set by the teacher, the objective being to find a task the child could do. If the suspicion was that the teacher's task was too easy, the researcher's tasks were set to be increasingly difficult with a view to finding the child's limit.

At the end of the day the researcher interviewed the teacher again to find out the teacher's appraisal of the child's work and her view on its degree of suitability for him or her.

To decide whether the set work had been appropriate or not, the research team examined the log of each entire lesson and interpreted the child's work in the light of the post task interview. Using criteria based on modern learning theory, tasks assigned by teachers were judged to be too hard, too easy or, if no good reason were found otherwise, to be matched. Tasks were judged too hard, for example, if children did not have the basic subskills to carry out the work. Tasks were judged too easy, for example, if children could do in their heads what they were being asked laboriously to record.

In the research team's judgement, 44 per cent of tasks were matched, 28 per cent were too hard and 26 per cent too easy. In contrast, in the teacher's view 30 per cent of tasks were too hard, 70 per cent matched and none was too easy.

This striking difference of interpretation was examined by sending complete logs of 24 tasks out to some of the participating teachers. These logs were from the lessons and child interviews in other teachers' classes. No teacher was sent a log from a task she had set. These teachers were told that the research team had selected the tasks as being examples of assigned work perceived as too hard, too easy or matched and they were asked to make their judgements as to which tasks fell into which category.

Whilst there was almost total agreement on identifying tasks which were too hard, there was no agreement on judging tasks too easy. Of the eight sent out only one was seen to be too easy by the teachers: the rest were seen as matched. This confirmed the view that for these teachers at least, the problem of mismatching is highly visible when it takes the form of work which is too difficult but that the problem of underestimating was almost entirely invisible to them.

The problem of the match may now be seen to take three different forms depending on the perspective of the observer. HMI were seriously concerned about underestimating children, teachers see only overestimation, whilst a research team saw both aspects of mismatching.

IMPLICATIONS FOR ACTION RESEARCH

Different perceptions of the problem of the match have led to different proposals for solution. HMI has argued that teachers do not extend the thinking of able children because they lack the necessary subject expertise. Bennett *et al.* argued that teachers need to develop the skills of rapid diagnosis to gain insight into the strengths and weaknesses of children. Left to teachers to interpret and remediate the problems, only that facet perceived would be likely to receive attention. This is not to say that teachers are wrong in their conception of the problems of the match: on the contrary they could be entirely right. Teachers' conceptions however are deficient in a way which is fundamental to the whole notion of research and development. That is, their conception is not based on a clear and explicit framework of judgement. In this respect at least they are in common with HMI.

Since solutions to problems depend on the perception of the problem and since perceptions arise from interpretations and not merely observations it becomes crucial to identify the interpretative framework which defines the nature of the problem. Perhaps the most critical function of action research is to articulate the interpretative framework in which an issue is conceived. In this instance, for example, what is the teachers' view of learning and teaching which throws overestimation into such sharp relief whilst casting underestimation into the shadows?

This is not to imply that such cogitations must, as a matter of procedure, come before intervention. Indeed it is probably more practicable for cogitation and action to proceed in concert. The important point is that if action research is to go beyond local trouble shooting and for the record to show an accumulation of knowledge from this endeavour, the articulation, analysis and justification of the grounds of action must be made explicit.

Such analysis, it is claimed, is unlikely to be spontaneous. Professionals – especially those involved in intensive decision making – have their interpretations as part of the warp and weft of practice. Interpretations are best exposed when thrown into juxtaposition with alternative interpretations of the same events. There is nothing new in this view – indeed it is simply a re-expression of the adversary model of research traditional to British scholarship. What it provokes, however, is the question of the course of alternative perceptions and the matter of their juxtaposition. Typically at this juncture the notion of a collaborator as a 'critical friend' is invoked as a suitable, and suitably low key, non-directive adversary. Working in a friendly, circumspect way, this collaboration induces, it seems, the development of at least reservations on interpretations if not alternative perspectives. We would like to suggest an alternative model for collaboration – that of respected and credible enemy.

THE ROLE OF ADVERSARY IN ACTION RESEARCH

Teachers engaged in action research are typically conducting a full teaching programme whilst at the same time examining some aspects of their impact with a view to improvement. It might seem that the last thing they want is an adversary. Before justifying this apparently odd proposal it is worth repeating that at the roots of action are deep-seated interpretative frameworks which can so readily blind us to alternative forms of behaviour or analysis. It was argued above that the most critical function of action research is that an adversary will be much more useful than a friend.

A particular kind of adversary is required. It is crucial that the opponent is committed to understanding and embracing the *same* conditions as the researcher, that alternative perspectives are based on strongly held grounds which go beyond mere debating strategy and that the adversaries hold each other in considerable esteem. Exchanges should produce insight rather than controversary. Additionally, the relationship would ideally meet frequently and on demand. Curiously such an ideal adversary is readily available: it is oneself.

IN RESEARCH YOU ARE YOUR OWN BEST ENEMY

Perhaps the best account of a working self adversary is provided by Charles Darwin. On setting out on his voyage on the *Beagle* he was an orthodox Christian given to using the authority of the Bible to make moral points to seamen. His extensive observation and analysis of wildlife continually provoked him to examine the Old Testament account of the origins of species and the descent of man. In this he claimed no special intelligence. 'I have no great quickness of wit or apprehension . . . I am therefore a poor critic; a paper or book when first read generally excites my admiration, and it is only after considerable reflection that I perceive the weak points. My power to follow a long and purely abstract train of thought is very limited . . .' He found great difficulty in expressing his thoughts in writing, 'I have as much difficulty as ever in expressing myself clearly and concisely and this difficulty has caused me a very great loss of time. . .'

However, he capitalized on these limitations. Recognizing his problems with writing he noted that 'it has had the compensating advantage of forcing me to think long and intently about every sentence, and thus I have often been led to see errors in reasoning in my own observations or those of others'. In exploring self delusion he developed a critical strategy in that he 'followed a golden rule, namely, that whenever a published fact, a new observation or thought came to me, which was opposed to my general results, to make a memorandum of it without fail and at once; for I have found from experience that such facts and thoughts were far more apt to escape my memory than favourable ones.'

In Darwin's self analysis he saw his main skill in terms of a questioning attitude. 'I have had the strongest desire to understand or explain whatever I observed . . . and great patience to reflect or ponder for any number of years over any problem.' These self-acclaimed attributes were matched, of necessity, to research with extreme humility. He acknowledged that 'If I lived for twenty years or more . . . how I should modify the *Origin of Species* and how much the views on all points will have to be modified!' In short he epitomized the questioning spirit which is not easily satisfied with its own answers.

For the present purposes it is important to emphasize the central object lessons provided by Darwin. The first is that research requires no great intelligence. It does however demand a deeply questioning attitude and a desire to understand. Research does not simply seek different ways to manipulate people or situations. Secondly, research may be expected to be a long or very long process quite ill-suited to the typical project or thesis time-scale. Third, writing is a crucial thinking process long before it is a public communication process. Projects which absolve participants from writing run the risk of absolving them from thinking.

There is a danger that some approaches to action research avoid or subvert these lessons. With the best intentions, and in recognition of the teacher's major professional activity, collaborators are often lured into a supporting role which might, from another perspective, be seen to be patronizing if not indeed manipulative. A false image of research and its difficulties and rewards is generated. Worse, when the support moves out the research frequently ceases.

If action research is to play a more enduring role in teachers' professional lives it seems essential to make it part of every teacher's job description and its successful prosecution part of the teacher's career structure. Such a general commitment to research and the development of a body of objective professional knowledge might be expected to enhance not only the efficiency and responsiveness of the profession but also its status within the community. However, since the demands on teachers' time seem to be increasing from all directions this proposal could be examined only within the context of a debate on the general issue of what teachers might be legitimately expected to undertake in their professional work.

SECTION B

CASE STUDIES: STARTING WITH TEACHERS' CONCERNS

───────────

This section contains six small-scale case studies showing action research at work in a variety of contexts and pointing up a variety of issues.

The first three concern the individual teacher in his or her own classroom. John Groarke, feeling strongly that his habitual methods are inappropriate for the new, mixed ability junior class he is teaching, experiments with different forms of organization and timetabling, monitoring their effects closely. Jim Nind, concerned about his primary pupils' hostile response to non-literal art, engages in a deliberately provocative action, with the dual purpose of challenging pupil perceptions, and monitoring their responses. In Eileen Booth's work with deaf children, she notes a lack of understanding of the nature and purpose of literacy, devises multiple strategies for a six-week interventionist project, and observes the results.

These three studies could be described as action research in the classic sense. In each case, the teachers perceive a problem or difficulty in their daily classroom experience. Investigation suggests a line of action, which is pursued and monitored more or less systematically. Observations of the effects of these changes in routine suggest further action. Thus, analyses of the existing situation, and experimenting with alternative approaches, are part of an exploratory and developmental cycle.

In each case the motivation for the action research is personal, the methods simple, and the intentions practical. The teacher's sense of dissatisfaction or frustration with certain aspects of the existing situation is the starting point. John Groarke speaks of 'my worry that children seemed to be wasting a lot of time in activities peripheral to or unrelated to the work which I wanted them to be doing', and confessed that 'I became more and more dissatisfied with the way in which I was running my class'. Similarly, Jim Nind 'felt that my current teaching at that time . . . was inadequate to deal with the issues that pupil responses to art raised'. Eileen Booth's problem was that her pupils 'did not seem interested in reading, and did not perceive reading as if it were a useful or relevant skill'. The need for this sort of self-critical refusal to be complacent about one's work is a common thread running through all the contributions to this section.

The methods used by these three teacher researchers to monitor the effects of interventions and strategies are simple and easily accessible. Daily diaries, observation schedules and journals, tape transcripts and structured interviews may lack methodological sophistication in certain conventional research terms, but their practicality is obvious and their potential versatility in recording the subtleties of qualitative data is apparent in these studies. The procedural blueprint credited to John Elliott in the first study (General idea – Reconnaisance – General Plan – Action Steps – Monitoring of Implementation and Effects) seems to have been instinctively followed in the others.

The practical intentions of the research are stressed throughout. The introduction to Groarke's study speaks of 'a personal search for understanding of his own teaching', and Booth probably speaks for all when she states that her piece of action research was 'designed not to offer formal proof of anything, but to help the teacher reflect on what was, for her, a problem of teaching'. Central to the whole question of the role of action research is the principle she adopts from Elliott (1981, p. 1) that 'in action research "theories" are not validated independently and then applied to practice. They are validated through practice.'

There are other features of these three studies which it is worth drawing attention to. First, all three represent some form of collaboration or contact between individuals working in differing sectors of the educational system. All three studies have been shaped up in part according to the collaboration involved. It is probably no accident that Jim Nind displays so strongly the concern for children's understandings; a concern which dominates the contribution in Section A by Stephen Rowland. John Groarke's study is modelled clearly on a John Elliott paper from the Schools Council TIQL project, and Peter Ovens and Margaret Hargreaves were associated with this project through an 'outer network' group. We do not get a strong sense of the precise nature of that collaboration, although the impression is gained that the comment from Peter Ovens and Margaret Hargreaves holds for all three: 'All an outsider could do was to extend his range of interpretation and ideas for action.' There seems a close parallel here with aspects of what Ebbutt (1983) calls a 'critical friend'. What might also be of interest to know more about is how these collaborating 'critical friends' have themselves had their own 'range of interpretations and ideas for action' extended. John Elliott has addressed this point with regard to 'facilitation of school based action research' (1983, p. 26; 1985).

All three studies also seem to have led to unanticipated discoveries and developments, some of them very tangential to the original concern. Certain of these are discoveries in the sense that Glaser and Strauss (1967) identify: through comparisons grounded in detailed observation ideas have been generated about some aspect of these teachers' classrooms and children. These ideas have then fed back into the study. In addition, all three studies raise questions and open up later strategies for future action, whether it be in terms of linked career moves, continuing use of monitoring techniques, or teaching strategies. Finally, the three teachers involved seem to feel that their work here has been beneficial for them; they have moved forward in terms of personal and professional development. We would argue that such outcomes are strongly associated with the commitment of these teachers to idea-generating and strategy-generating approaches, rather than using only an idea-testing or validating methodology. In particular, using action as a probe has led to ways forward. This leads us back to the issues raised earlier in Section A, but more immediately it leads us on to Diane Tranter's contribution.

Diane Tranter's study moves beyond the confines of the classroom using, she would claim, action research methods to focus on the personal and professional problems experienced by a teacher in adapting to the cultural climate of an inner-city comprehensive school to which she has recently moved. Again there is the sense of dual purpose; her intention in conducting the research is to help her to 'build a new scheme of reference' which will help her to integrate professionally, as well as to contribute to a more general understanding of such changes. Field journals and focused interviews are used, but these simple methods are not, in this case, indicative of any impatience with theoretical perspectives or methodological rigour. Tranter is obviously as concerned with the theoretical underpinnings of her project as she is with its personal relevance to her own progress. Her familiarity with the literature, and particularly with the principles and methods of the symbolic interactionists, lends weight and structure to her observations.

Action research writers at times almost seem to go out of their way to avoid reference to what some might see as very relevant theoretical and methodological conceptual frameworks. One argument is that practitioners' problems become reformulated in terms of, and subservient to, theoretical problems rooted in the disciplines of the social sciences. In addition particular problems for 'me' in this situation become diluted through the concern for general understanding. Diane Tranter attempts to ride both horses. She explores in depth certain aspects of the theoretical and methodological literature, feeling that this approach is necessary from the point of view of her requirement for rigour and for some detachment. Clearly, she feels that the study has benefited her 'both as a teacher, and as a person too'. She does, however, settle for a mode of presentation which reads very much like a sociological case study and, as reported here, we get little insight into the moves she in fact made over time within the school into the process of integration as it developed for her. We do see that she adopts an open and developmental methodology as regards data-gathering techniques, but some readers will feel unhappy about viewing the study as action research. It may be useful to distinguish between the more general notion of the 'teacher as researcher' and the 'teacher doing action research', and regard Diane Tranter's study as an example of the former but not the latter. In our view, however, her approach and her results do seem to have provided her with the capacity to get a grip on her situation in the new school. In this sense, her initial worries, after an earlier unhappy experience of changing schools, do seem to have been eased. John Elliott notes that action research involves 'review, diagnosis, planning, implementation, monitoring effects' and that this total process 'provides the necessary link between *self-evaluation* and professional development' (Elliott, 1981, p. ii). It is our feeling that her study does involve this total process, albeit in relation to a very distinctive problem. It is however a problem which many teachers face and a problem which, as addressed by Diane Tranter, may give middle and senior management in schools some food for thought.

Diane Tranter's study also serves a useful function within the book by making explicit some of the links between the 'interpretative paradigm' in the social sciences and the ideas and practices associated with action research. For example, in settling for an approach emphasizing qualitative data she joins with the first three studies in this section. We would however ask the reader to bear in mind the discussion in Section A about the emphasis on qualitative data.

The focus of the section broadens still further with Tony Cassidy's article. It describes his work in two comprehensive schools, over a period of several years in instigating, co-ordinating and maintaining action research across the curriculum, involving large numbers of teachers in examining critically their own practices. Classroom-based action research is being used here as a vehicle for staff development and inservice training, as well as a means towards improving the quality of learning experience for pupils by altering the ethos of the school. The attitude of self-critical inquiry, and the methods of journal-keeping and use of transcripts, which we have seen in earlier studies, are apparent again, but a new dimension is added: that of co-operative discussion and action between teachers from many different subject areas and professional backgrounds. As well as providing some insights into pupils' experience of the curriculum, this study highlights some of the obstacles encountered when generating action research in schools, particularly those of teacher resistance through misunderstanding, insecurity, or entrenched attitudes.

There are, however, other ways of viewing this study and in particular the imposed large-scale intervention of 'talk day' and the 'curriculum survey'. We have in the study what might be regarded as an uneasy mix between a systems approach and an action research approach to school focused INSET (see Elliott, 1983). It will be interesting to place this study alongside the full reports from the TIQL Project. Some case studies have emerged from this project, focusing on the work of school-based co-ordinators (Ebbutt, 1982) and one of the central concerns of the project has been to identify the conditions and approaches which facilitate action research within the school. The reader of Tony Cassidy's study might raise some legitimate questions as to whose problems counted, and to what extent collaboration is in fact visible. The study stands perhaps as a good example of the need to know more about what a facilitator needs to know. Most of all, it may be that a commitment to generating action research amongst colleagues requires an adequate conceptualization of what it is to be a teacher, what the practical concerns of teachers are, and how these practical concerns can be related to within particular institutional structures. The inclusion of this study and the next contribution (by Lilian Street) are indicative of some ways in which action research has shifted focus over the last few years. The study by Tony Cassidy relates to questions as to how a community of practitioners can be established within a school. Lilian Street's contribution raises questions as to how award-bearing courses, and the tutors involved, could or should connect with action research. In both cases, there is the clear danger of senior management in schools or course constructors using action research rationales as a convenient vocabulary and not much more.

Lilian Street describes the central role of action research in the M.Ed. course for serving teachers at Manchester Polytechnic. Departing from the traditional insistence on research based on the disciplines of psychology, sociology or philosophy, the course emphasizes peda-gogical research, seeking to integrate theories developed by teachers through their own practice into the main body of educational theory. She believes that the cyclical nature of action research links the pragmatic and the theoretical, contributing to and enriching both.

She sounds a cautionary note, pointing out the danger that action research can make the individual teacher overly introspective or self-critical to a destructive degree. But overall, the immense positive benefits of the approach are emphasized.

Lilian Street's contribution is interesting in three other particular respects: the reliance placed on Kemmis *et al*.'s *The Action Research Planner*; the references once again to the unintended and unanticipated outcomes for the teachers involved; and the emphasis placed on a collaborative sharing of the individual experiences of the projects as they developed. This point connects with what Jean Rudduck notes as a particular strength across her studies of inservice collaboration (Rudduck, 1982). The strength lay in a structure which enabled focused discussion and moved beyond the exchange of opinions. More generally, the article raises questions concerning the extent to which action research is constrained, or can be fostered, in the context of an award-bearing course. Difficult questions emerge here, where an assessment relationship is involved, but one major resource for addressing such questions must be noted: the series of conferences organized by the Cambridge Institute of Education (see in particular, the reports from these edited by Jennifer Nias, 1983a and 1984a).

The contributions to this section demonstrate the versatility of the action research approach to teaching and learning and its potential as an agent for development and change. The professionally analytical and self-critical attitude which it embodies should ideally be the hallmark of all good teaching, but this attitude is unlikely to flourish in an atmosphere where demands for accountability, performance appraisal, self evaluation and the like, are couched in language and presented in contexts which suggest distrust and accusation, rather than mutual collaboration in the pursuit of professional development.

7

Towards a More Open Classroom

JOHN GROARKE, PETER OVENS
and MARGARET HARGREAVES

An action research study of the development of classroom organization in a primary school by John Groarke, a teacher of fourth year junior children in a Stockport primary school, and Margaret Hargreaves and Peter Ovens, who were tutors at the City of Manchester College of Higher Education at the time of the study.

Part One is written by Margaret Hargreaves and Peter Ovens and it provides an introduction to and commentary upon John Groarke's account of his work, which is Part Two.

PART ONE

John Groarke's account of the action research undertaken in his classroom describes how his research stems from his real need to know more about his teaching situation and how his progressive focusing on the changes he made clearly matched the model presented by John Elliott in his Working Paper No. 1 (Schools' Council TIQL Project 1981).

The need to find out more about his classroom was, for John Groarke, very urgent as it arose from a feeling of inadequacy and a fear of failure. He recounts his experiences of learning how to organize a primary classroom starting from a point where he knew how to teach within well defined limits of school and class organization. He taught very effectively and felt secure knowing that he met the demands of the school. On finding himself in a school with very different teaching going on around him in other classrooms he was confronted by questions related to 'good primary practice'. He sought answers from a course for primary teachers, he visited other schools and he read widely, but although the concepts of openness, child-centredness, individual learning, etc., could direct John's thinking about his problem, how was he to know which changes to make in order to get maximum learning in a mixed ability classroom? What were the first moves to make towards what he saw happening in the other classrooms in his own school and in those he visited?

His first step was to talk to an observer who discussed his situation and helped him to focus on areas for exploration. He had first to let go of his class teaching and organize groups. This was a tremendous step and the fear of failure was uppermost in the factors which pushed him to find out whether the groups were working. Initial insights gained from tape-recordings often surprised him, as when some children were allowed to work in friendship groups the 'chatter', which had seemed worrying, proved to be about the task in hand most of the time and only occasionally about last night's TV programme!

Each change in John's classroom was kept within his ability to teach competently. Many stages produced a feeling of elation and only close monitoring revealed the need for further investigation and change. Each stage emerged as a 'discovery' on John's part although any experienced primary teacher would recognize it as a stage in his evolution. He had developed his own theory of teaching; he was not testing out for an 'expert'. He set himself towards gradual understanding – not a pre-set goal of an 'open' classroom, and integrated timetable or individualized teaching – not to test the formulae for 'good' practice but to understand what could make his classroom work for him.

Throughout his research John kept a diary which was the result of his contemplation of his jottings during each working day. This diary illustrates perfectly how difficult it may be for some teachers to arrive at where many teachers have actually started. School experience shapes a teacher's learning and many of us have to 're-invent the wheel'. The metaphor implies that time should be spent upon finding the wheel which already exists and is in use by teachers, and having found it one should immediately embark upon learning how to use it for onself. Furthermore it assumes that innovations in teaching are comparable with innovations in technology and that it is a matter of working from a blueprint and applying set procedures. It represents a view of professional learning which is blind to the fact that over twenty years of 'innovation' contained in curriculum development packages and educational research prescriptions have failed to produce change.

Many would see the outcome of John's work as comparable with a stage which they achieved without difficulties, but closer reflection on both the starting point and the stages of his development would show that there was throughout a personal search for understanding of his own teaching. This relates to the true nature of classroom action research in that it is much more akin to research than is the unthinking implementation of a ready-made 'answer'. At each stage he genuinely thought his latest chosen strategy would work completely and it was only with hindsight that it could be seen as one step among many steps towards the improvement of his organization for learning. How this was to be achieved was beyond his understanding at the outset. His organized searching and willingness to learn from his findings led him towards making the most efficient use of himself and the available resources of which 'time' was the chief concern.

Only John, with his existing beliefs and his knowledge of himself, the pupils and the school, was able to choose which ideas could enable him to make sense of his most recently collected information, and only John could decide which course of action was practical for him to try next. Anyone else would be unable to make those choices and decisions for him simply because they would come to the situation with a completely different complex of ideas, knowledge, abilities and experience, and these would produce different perceptions of John's situation. All that an outsider could do was to extend his range of interpretations and ideas for action.

PART TWO

I decided to study the organization of my classroom and its effect on the quality of learning for several reasons. First, I knew that in order to provide the best possible learning situation I needed to make some systematic study which would give me insight into the present organization and how it affected the structure of learning. Secondly, having taught previously in large junior schools where streaming and setting were the norm, I felt that I needed to revise my ideas and practice to suit the needs of a mixed ability class in a small primary school. Thirdly, I wanted to find out which methods worked best for me; so many (apparently) conflicting theories and exhortations as to how best to teach were, to say the least, confusing. There were other, sub-sidiary reasons stemming from the three broad ones above. In particular, my worry that children seemed to be wasting a lot of time in activities peripheral to or unrelated to the work which I wanted them to be doing.

My previous experience was of two large 'three form entry' junior schools which were considered 'formal' in that there was a timetable which had to be adhered to and class teaching resulted in all children in a class working at the same subject at the same time. Both schools were streamed: one by ability, the other by age with sets for language and maths. My appointment to a smaller, one form entry primary school with mixed ability classes meant that I had to consider making changes which from the start included arranging my own timetable. In order to meet the challenges of this new situation I started an inservice course which led me to investigate my teaching and embark upon classroom action research.

During my first two terms at the school (I started in January) I became more and more dissatisfied with the way in which I was running my class. I had grouped the children by ability for maths and English work but then more or less allowed them to proceed individually. They had to complete certain maths and/or language tasks before they went on to project work or art and craft. Many of the other lessons were class lessons in which I attempted to teach the class as a whole. I was still 'bound' by the restrictions placed upon me by my previous schools and by my lack of knowledge as to the alternatives available and I felt that I was not getting to the heart of the problem for the children at both ends of the ability range. So, at the start of the new academic year (1980), I decided that I needed to make a definite break from the way in which I had been teaching for the previous five years. I did not want to rely solely on intuition – I felt that more objective evidence was required upon which to base any changes I might make. Hence my interest in classroom action research when it was introduced during one of the lectures at college. I was introduced to John Elliott's Working Paper No. 1 as part of the Schools Council project TIQL and whilst not contributing to this enquiry I found the model on page three helpful as the basis for my thinking. This is the formula adopted for the report of the research undertaken in my classroom.

(1) General idea

Any previous changes in the organization of my classroom had been made on the basis of guesswork, experience or intuition. Any subsequent changes I wanted to make should be made on the basis of a close examination of what was actually going on in the classroom. The changes which would be made should aim to relieve the pressures on me (e.g. with all children doing maths there was a constant demand for my attention – for help, for marking, for telling children what to do next . . .) so that I could stand back from time to time to see what was going on and thus use my time to best advantage. The changes should also result in a better match of the task to the child, obviating the boredom of the more able children and the frustration of the less able.

(2) Reconnaissance

I wanted to use a portable cassette recorder to 'listen in' to what was going on in a target group of children. Before doing this I told the children what I was going to do and that it was for my 'night school'. They accepted this without question as many of their parents go to night school. To accustom them to the presence of the tape recorder I left it around (recording) for several weeks. This ensured that, by the time I came to make the recordings which I would transcribe the novelty had worn off and the children would be behaving quite naturally.

I observed and recorded the target group for half-hour periods during which I made written observations of five-minute intervals, noting down what each child in the group was doing. As an aid to my memory, and to give a more general impression of the classroom, I kept a daily diary in which I jotted down anything which might give me a clearer insight into the workings of the classroom.

One or two problems arose which I had not foreseen. First, it can be very difficult trying to observe a group of six children at regular intervals when there are thirty others in the room – just as you are about to write down your third observation a mini-crisis develops at another table! Second, small portable cassette recorders pick up a lot of unwanted noise as well as the interaction of the target children. Perhaps more sophisticated equipment would have overcome this; as it was, it made transcribing the tape recordings very difficult at times. A valuable insight into the workings of my classroom was obtained from an observer with wide experience of primary schools who helped me to realize that certain aspects of the classroom could be investigated more deeply.

My findings were interesting because, although (to my surprise) most of the talking (which I had assumed to be 'time-wasting') was 'on task', it tended to be very superficial. The children were not really involved in their work. They appeared to be interested only in completing the task in hand. Some of the children were rushing to finish work to get on to 'more exciting' tasks. The children with difficulties were penalized as they could not finish their tasks (in maths or language) and get on to art and craft or project work and they were relying heavily on other children nearby to help them. Instead of motivating them to complete their English and maths, this method of organization seemed to be counter-productive (i.e. realizing that they would not finish in time, they gave up and became bored and disruptive).

(3) General Plan

I would abandon the system which had specified maths/language tasks followed by more creative work and introduce a 'rotating timetable'. This would, I hoped, relieve the pressure on me and also the pressure on the children. They would know that, at the end of a particular group period, they would change activities, so that even if they disliked what they were doing they knew that there would be an end to it in the not-too-distant future. They would all get a turn at art or topic work, as well as maths or language.

(4) Action Steps

(a) Reorganize furniture and materials. I made several resource-cum-work areas in the classroom, starting with a library area and an art area, then introducing a maths area and a project area. I tried to arrange the desks and chairs so that there was a variety of environments available – large group, small group, pair and individual.

(b) Reorganize the timetable. Instead of subject areas I wrote 'group work'. During these periods the children would be doing one of the specified activities with their group. The times were quite long (on average one hour), though I still had to accommodate class lessons such as PE, music, games.

(c) Reorganize the curriculum so that each of the six groups had a particular curriculum area to work at. These were: language, maths (number work), practical maths (measuring, etc.), project, art and craft and music. Subsequently, when the school adopted a better-balanced maths scheme the number work and practical maths were integrated and I added creative writing.

(d) Organize the children into groups of approximately six. These were friendship groups so they were mixed ability groups. The maths and language work, however, was set according to ability. So, for example, for six children working at language during one 'group work' period only two or three might be doing the same work.

(5) Monitoring and Implementation + Effect

I immediately noticed a reduction in the pressure on me, the children and (something which I had not considered, though it seems obvious now) the materials. If only six children were engaged in language work at any one time it did not matter if we only had twenty-nine dictionaries, for example: previously it could have caused problems. I also found that the curriculum had broadened for the children at the lower end of the ability range. Whereas before it had taken them so long to complete their maths and language task that they could rarely spend any appreciable time on other areas of the curriculum, now they spent the same amount of time as everybody else on the different curriculum areas. The time spent changing from activity to activity was not as long as I had feared.

(6) Reconnaissance

Although this system worked far better than the previous one I had used, it was not without its drawbacks, as I found after a few months. I was still keeping the diary and so I decided to narrow the focus again on to a small group of children to confirm or contradict the conclusions I had drawn from the wider observation. I used the same techniques as before (with the same inadequate equipment!) and my findings were as follows:

(a) the system was too inflexible. One hour might be too long (far too long!) for a group to practise percussion instruments in the stock room; it might be too short for a group engaged in research for a topic.

(b) Some children needed a lot of supervision and encouragement from me or they would sit back and let the time pass until they could get on to something else.

(c) My time was still not being used to best advantage. I found that I was repeating instructions to group after group; the same problems kept cropping up as each group came to work at a particular 'subject' so I would have to leave the group I was with to come and explain.

(d) I was still tending to mis-match tasks to certain children.

(7) **Revised General Idea**

I would achieve more flexibility by altering the organization.

(8) **Action Steps**

(a) I revised the timetable so that there were a large number of shorter (approximately half-hour) group periods in a week.

(b) I gave the children more responsibility for organizing their work in that they could decide when they would do a particular activity (as long as they did a certain number during the course of a week). This means that they could spend half an hour at something then change, or they could carry on and spend an hour, an hour and a half, two hours, depending upon their interest and the demands of the task. The children kept their own daily record of what they had done. These were collected by me every Friday so that I could see how much time each child was spending on the various activities to ensure that there was not too much emphasis on one area of the curriculum at the expense of others.

(c) I devised a timetable for myself, distinct from the children's, showing the 'group work' periods as blanks, during which I could work with a particular ability group, or friendship group, or with an individual. This was to be as flexible as possible, being filled in from day to day.

(9) **Monitoring of Implementation + Effects**

This system produced a good response from the children who seem adapted to it and made good use of its flexibility. It seemed to make the best use of their time as they had quite a large degree of control over its use. I was able to spend more time with individual children or with small groups, and so I was able to discover their needs and cater for them. The work I set the children tended to be a better 'match' and therefore there was a better chance of its seeming meaningful to the children who would then complete it. So in changing the organization of my class I had also improved the motivation of the children. The atmosphere in the classroom was more relaxed and informal, but the quality of the work and the attitude towards the work had improved visibly.

The study highlighted ways in which I needed to grow as a teacher and helped me to become aware of certain steps I could take to achieve this. When I moved to a new school as deputy head I found myself in a situation where I had to re-examine my practice, taking into account the different ethos of the school, the different expectations of parents, children, colleagues and the head and the previous experience of the children. I could not start at this new school where I had left off at my previous school, but because of my experience of action research I was able to undertake close scrutiny of *this* classroom and make the changes I thought necessary much more quickly and confidently then would otherwise have been the case.

I still keep a daily diary and value the cassette recorder (with all its limitations) as an 'ear' into what is happening in the classroom. I anticipate that this kind of questioning will continue throughout my teaching career – nothing ever stays the same, the teacher changes, the children change, and consequently one's perception of oneself in the classroom changes. I now know that there is a process by which I can investigate my classroom and initiate improvements in my practice whenever I perceive the need.

8

An Enquiry into Pupil-Responses to Non-Literal Art Objects: a CRISES Case Study

JIM NIND

Working in primary school classrooms over a period of years, I had noticed that many children expressed strong opinions about art. For instance, a number of children that I had taught appeared confused by, and often derisive about, art works which they referred to as 'modern'. For some the use of this word seemed to indicate a degree of historical awareness in their thinking about art. In other instances the word 'modern' appeared to be a term of abuse inherited from parental views about art. Young though they were, the individual and collective views of art that children held appeared to be rather complex. I also felt that my current teaching at that time, which was largely geared toward the production of art, was inadequate to deal with the issues that pupil-responses to art raised. I therefore sought to re-structure my teaching in a way that would help me interpret and respond to pupil understandings of art.

After some searching around I drew upon the philosophic perspective of phenomenology to help me develop a framework. I noted the following points as relevant to my aims. First, the ideas children expressed and the words they chose to express them in could be taken as ways of making sense of the world. Secondly, art education might be furthered by constructing and focusing upon social situations in which pupil understandings about art become apparent. Thirdly, those areas which children most took for granted would become major starting points. A primary task for the art teacher appeared to be that of highlighting pupil experience of art by making their assumptions problematic and, thereby, raising the level of their understanding.

A key problem in my teaching became that of interpreting pupil assumptions about art. A prior task to this was to stimulate pupils' statements, questions, comments and opinions about art, or about particular instances of it. However, in the classroom I quickly found that the best means for eliciting pupil-responses were also those which tended to challenge pupil assumptions. Attempts to understand and develop pupil attitudes and understandings became parts of a reciprocal process. Teaching and researching into these attitudes were reciprocal activities using joint strategies.

I had been puzzled over a period of time by pupil questions concerning non-literal art objects. The primary question among these appeared to be 'what is it?' The enquiry seemed to carry the expectation that a simple and literal reply would be forthcoming. The question apparently begged a reply which began 'It is a . . .'. It seemed possible that a lack of literal content was contrary to the expectations that children had of art and that this resulted in problems of orientation. The children were apparently unable to ascribe a literal meaning to these objects and could not therefore orient themselves towards them. The expectation that art was primarily concerned with the representation of literally readable items would constitute a major and far-reaching assumption.

To explore this matter I decided to initiate a situation which would provoke any need for orientation toward non-literal art objects that existed. I therefore planned to build a large non-literal art object in the centre of the open-plan area in which my children worked, and note those responses which were aroused. Pupil responses in the form of questions or statements would be construed in terms of the attempt to ascribe meaning to this event. I sought to elicit statements that would both inform me as a teacher, and enable me to help children in their attempts to come to an understanding of what I was doing. The building of the art object thus had two sets of intended consequences. It would challenge any 'everyday' expectations that pupils had regarding the literal content of art objects. It would also be informative for me as a teacher concerned with pupil constructions of reality.

The painting was formalist in conception. Four doors were hinged together to form a shape approximating the dimensions of a telephone box. One corner of this form, however, was left unhinged so that the surfaces could be repositioned, and the enclosed space varied. A continuous line, on average seven centimetres in width, was drawn to cross the four internal and four external surfaces of the box. These lines emphasized horizontal, vertical and diagonal directional qualities. The two and three dimensional qualities of single and joined surfaces were stressed by the lines and colours used. Red and green, and blue and orange colour combinations were used as complementary pairs to lend emphasis to the lines and surfaces.

The painting was made in the midst of children engaged in a variety of endeavours of their own. In the course of its making, many individuals watched, thought about, talked about, laughed at, questioned and commented upon what I was doing, some of which was public enough to reach my notice.

Nic. W.	What's it gonna be?
Me	A painting.
Nic. W.	A painting of what?
Me	What do you mean 'a painting of what?'
Nic.	What's it gonna be?
Me	A painting.
Nic. W.	Oh. (He walks away shrugging).

A variety of factors appeared to influence pupil responses. The fact that I had, in order to provoke responses, chosen to make rather than present an existing art object to the children, appeared influential. The children were in this instance responding to an artistic process rather than merely a product. They were also presented with the problem of adjusting to my additional role of 'artist' rather than simply that of 'teacher'.

Some children did not appear to conceive of what I was doing in terms of making art at all. Others construed my activity in relation to past events.

Nic. Y.	I want to know what you're painting this stage for – or what you're painting it into, if it is something.
Richard P.	It don't look like a painting to me – it's an object.

The fact that I had previously constructed stage sets, display boards and storage screens, in the teaching area, obviously influenced some attempts to ascribe meaning to my present activity.

David B.	Mr Nind what are you building there?
Me	Got any ideas?
David B.	To pin drawings on.
Jason P.	I know – like a theatre, dressing up things, where you dress behind. You could use it as a stage.
Me	No, I'm making a painting.
Jason P.	A big painting for it?
Me	For what?
David B.	To fix on it – to fix tools on.

Other children appeared confused by the physical nature of the object I was making and were surprised to hear me call it a painting, even though I was actually painting while we talked. Some children appeared to have the expectation that a painting was flat and was hung on the wall, rather than three dimensional and free standing.

Having observed the process by which it was made, and finding no readily conferrable literal interpretation of the object, other children appeared to be over-concerned with the materials used. This seemed to indicate either an inability to suspend the practical reality of those materials, or a return to this reality when its suspension proved problematic in terms of attributing meaning.

Martin	There's three bits of wood with paint over it.
Me	There's four bits of wood.
Jason	Four doors stuck together and painted.
Nic. Y.	Yeah, but you don't want them to be shown as doors do you?
Me	When I look at them the fact that they are doors does not even strike me.
Joint Cry	They are doors.
Nic. Y.	Yeah, they're real, but you're changing them from doors into an abstract.
Me	Yes I've taken what were doors and I've made them into an abstract painting. But having done that I don't think about them as doors anymore. Some of you seem to be stuck with the thing that they're doors.
Martin	You know that they're doors but you try and think of what they could be, and then you go back to them as being doors because you know they're doors.

I was struck both by the variety of possible meanings the children attempted to give to the object, and by the complexity of the problems they had in doing so. The object seemed most essentially characterizable as 'enigmatic'. This term began to feature in my teaching notes and was indicative of my own thinking at this time.

> Is it a Portaloo, what is it?
> It looks like a Tardis don't it?
> Do people sit in it or something?
> . . . tunnels on the London Underground.

Whilst some of them may have been tongue in cheek, many pupils either attempted to ascribe a literal meaning to the object or appeared baffled and confused by difficulties in doing so. Their 'what is it?' questions, rather than merely indicating an orientation toward the literal, appeared to be aimed at alleviating general confusion. Whilst the reply 'it's a painting' was often accepted in that the children often enquired no further, it did not appear to provide the necessary clarification. Possibly because of limited experience, language, or intellectual immaturity, more probing questions were seldom received. By asking the children what their questions meant, telling them that I did not understand what they were asking me, I tried to encourage them to re-phrase their questions and explain what their concerns were.

Jenny   What is it?
Me   What do you mean?
Jenny   What's it meant to be?
Me   I don't understand the question.
Jenny   Is it meant to be something?
Me   What do you mean?
Jenny   Is it an abstract?
Me   Yes.
Jenny   Oh . . .

The term 'abstract' appeared potent as a means of explaining the object I was making. Having found a literal interpretation of the object problematic to achieve, some children appeared to use or accept the use of 'abstract' as a means of explanation. I mistrusted the usage this word was put to, however, because it appeared to conclude rather than initiate phases of pupil enquiry.

Jason   It's an abstract that can be moved into different positions.
Michael   It can be used for all sorts of things though can it? It can be just for show or used as a cupboard, or shutter, or store.
Jason   Is it like modern art, abstract? It's got a green line round there to make it like modern art. It's got a red line on the other side – like opposite.
Michael   There's a middle green line and then it goes to two blue ones. I just think it's an abstract.

I remained intrigued by pupil usage of the word abstract for some time. Some children seemed to use the word in a descriptive way to denote modernity. Others, it seemed, expecting a painting to have a literal content, appeared to use the word abstract to describe its absence. To one child, at least, an abstract was not conceivable as a painting because of this lack of literal content. A painting, to this child, had to be 'of something'.

Jeanette   What is this, a painting or an abstract?
Me   What do you mean?
Jeanette   A painting is more or less a picture of something, but an abstract can be almost anything.

The appearance of two lads who asked me if they could make an abstract gave me the opportunity to watch them working at their task and ask them about what they were doing. They appeared to share a view which contrasted 'pictures' and 'abstracts'.

James   You can do lines or shapes and things . . . they're not sort of, pictures or anything.

Jason   If you do a house and a flock of sheep that's a picture, and if you do lines and things, that's an abstract.

In this view, pictures were considered to be 'of something'. On the other hand, abstracts were not thought to be 'of anything'. This dichotomy seemed to echo many of the statements that had been made to me. I decided to try and gauge how common this use of these terms was. In order to do this I asked twenty five children to write brief replies to the questions 'what is an abstract?' and 'what is a picture?' The replies suggested that pictures were largely characterized by their ease of recognition in representational or literal terms. Abstracts, however, were apt to be described by reference to formal qualities such as shape, colours, lines and textures, or by their lack of recognizable literal content.

A picture is a thing that I can recognize as something I know or that I have seen or something that is really in real life.

A picture is something realistic and you can see around you and you can put it on the wall.

A picture is an illustration of something that you can recognize.

The children appeared to lean toward the view that meaning in art was primarily related to the depiction of things in the external world. My painting, emerging from an interest in formal relationships, was not understood by the large majority to have any meaningful content.

An abstract is a sort of picture but it's not of anything in particular.

An abstract is something that isn't recognizable, like all shapes put together, and sometimes coloured in.

An abstract is not a picture, it is made up and not an actual object as such.

For the majority of children who appeared to adhere to it, the dichotomy of art objects into 'pictures' and 'abstracts' seemed to represent a blockage to further exploration of art objects in general. Non-literal work appeared to suffer in particular, however, since the description 'abstract' seemed to foreclose further possible meaning-attributing activities. In many instances the polarization between the two kinds of art appeared extreme, value laden, simple and unquestioning.

> Absolutely anybody can do an abstract.
> The artist just plops the paint on any-old-how.
> Because it's an abstract you can call it anything.
> It could be anything an abstract can.
> It's harder to draw a picture than an abstract.

The reactions I had provoked became multiple starting points for continuing processes of discussion, action and interaction through which I aimed to encounter such 'everyday' notions of art that became apparent. Encountering these 'taken-for-granted' understandings was, in many ways, just a beginning. It was a necessary point of departure in the process of understanding pupil experience and a pre-requisite to any changes that might be brought about. These processes of encounter, understanding and development continued far beyond what I have been able to record here.

Immediately following the period of teaching described above I was given the opportunity to spend a year researching into art education in connection with the CRISES project (see Rowland, Section A). I decided to continue and to develop my concerns to clarify, interpret and challenge pupil assumptions about the nature of art. In order to do this I decided to step outside the conventional role of 'teacher' altogether and, finding a school and children similar to my own, I presented myself as an 'artist'. Over a four-month period I made paintings in the school, using photographic, audio-tape and field note methods to record events and the subtle nuances of pupil responses. I made regular presentations of my notes and transcript material to other teacher researchers who helped in the endeavour to interpret them.

The findings of this further enquiry are too rich in detail to report here. One or two things, however, are worthy of note. First, in this other school the word 'abstract' was not in common use. However, the children here used the word 'patterns' in a similar way. I realized on reflection that the word 'abstract' was in usage in my own school largely as a result of my introducing it, though the children coined it for their own purposes. I found also that the kinds of things children say vary from context to context. Their assumptions are dynamic rather than static and, for this if no other reason, they are difficult to interpret and challenge. For all this, there were recognizable similarities between the children in the two schools and I learned much that could be of use in my usual teaching circumstances. The 'what is it?' strategy for understanding art appears to be extremely common within our western culture, passed on from adult to child as an item of socialization. I even, to my own chagrin, catch myself using it. I believe we must go beyond this predominant tendency to 'identify' things as the content of art if we are to develop in children an appreciation of its more qualitative dimensions. Pre-requisite to this, we must treat the artistic manifestations of our culture as worthy of serious consideration. And in the classroom, the first step is to treat children's opinions about art with the seriousness that they, also, deserve.

9

Making Sense of Literacy

EILEEN BOOTH and NIGEL HALL

INTRODUCTION

Some years ago John Downing published a paper (1970) in which he set out some fundamental ideas relating to the teaching of literacy. Essentially he was making a claim that in order to learn to read and write successfully a person must have some idea about the nature and purpose of literacy. Failure to possess this understanding, either through an absence of prior experience or being subject to a methodology which places structure above meaning, can leave a child believing that reading is some kind of mystical school ritual.

No individual, whatever age, will learn anything easily if the purpose of the learning activity is obscure. Indeed, as adults our first line of defence when asked to do something we do not understand is to ask 'why?' or 'what for?'. There are many areas of school life, the purposes for which can be obscure to a young child. If that child has a further handicap related to the subject being taught then that purpose may be very obscure indeed. A child who does not understand that literacy, like oral language, has communicative purpose may find that learning to become literate is an activity that cannot be invested with real meaning.

Downing (1970, p. 9) claimed that 'we should reject materials or methods which may give children a false impression of the purpose and relevance of reading and writing'. Equally a claim must be made that teachers should set out to provide materials or methods which facilitate a young child's developing understanding of the nature and purpose of literacy.

In much education of the hearing-impaired neither the methods nor the materials are always as helpful as they might be in encouraging children to see literacy as something of interest and value. Too many methods are structurally based rather than giving an overall demonstration of the communicative purpose of written language. Even when the movement is made to reading schemes, such materials often do little to demonstrate that reading is a purposeful activity (Hall, 1983a).

It may well be unavoidable that in teaching the hearing-impaired to read there has to be some emphasis on structure. However, this does not mean that attention cannot also be paid to helping a child understand why literacy is useful and interesting. It is the teacher's responsibility through methods, materials and behaviour to convey the message that literacy is necessary, valuable and pleasant. Methods which begin with decontextualized materials are unlikely to carry positive messages about literacy.

In recent years a considerable amount of research has been demonstrating the extensive knowledge about literacy held by normally hearing pre-school children (Goodman, 1980; Harste, Burke and Woodward, 1982; Ferreiro and Teberosky, 1983; Heath, 1983). Children who have such understandings usually come from literate homes and will have been involved with all kinds of real, and pretend, literacy activities. One of the biggest influences in the development of literacy knowledge is 'language about literacy'. By being able to ask questions about literacy phenomena, and by receiving answers, children build up perceptions about the nature and purpose of literacy (Teale, 1982). It is these language-mediated literacy experiences that many deaf children will have missed. Because of this gap their understanding of the nature and purpose of literacy is unlikely to be as well developed as that of hearing children. If there is a failure to comprehend what literacy is then what sense can be made of learning to read and write? There is clear evidence that normally hearing children who lack literacy knowledge, experience considerable problems when learning to read (Francis, 1982). As far as we are aware no one has considered whether such lack of understanding of the nature and purpose of literacy could be a contributing factor to the poor reading performance of most hearing-impaired readers. If hearing-impaired children become confused or bewildered as a result of exposure to literacy teaching, then their attitudes towards, and interest in, literacy are unlikely to be positive.

The role of knowledge about literacy in facilitating the reading and writing of hearing-impaired children is something that seems largely neglected in books about teaching hearing-impaired children to read. Even in an article titled 'Developing a taste for reading', Peyre (1981) paid no attention at all to the possibility that understanding what literacy is, and what it is about, might influence the development of a 'taste for literacy'. There is at the moment no answer to the question of whether possession of understandings about literacy would improve hearing-impaired children's reading ability. However, the small investigation reported below does suggest that it might be possible to help hearing-impaired children see more relevance in reading and writing.

THE NATURE OF THE INVESTIGATION

The investigation was a classroom-based action research project in which some strategies to encourage interest in, and awareness of, print were developed. Being a small action research project it was not designed to offer formal 'proof' of anything. It was designed to help one teacher reflect on what was, for her, a problem in her teaching. The investigation is reported here not as evidence that such strategies will inevitably work, but as a resource so that other teachers can try out the ideas and develop them for use in their own teaching situations. As John Elliott (1981, p. 1) says, 'action research aims to feed practical judgement in concrete situations and the validity of the "theories" it generates depends not so much on "scientific" tests of truth as on their usefulness in helping people to act more intelligently and skilfully. In action research "theories" are not validated independently and then applied to practice. They are validated through practice.'

The problem for this teacher was that the children in the class, although beginning the school's reading programme, did not seem interested in reading, and did not seem to be reacting to reading as if it were a useful or relevant skill. The class involved in this study was a group of nine children whose ages ranged from four to seven at the beginning of the investigation. All the children had been placed in the class on their admission to this school. Five of the children were from homes where English was not the first language. All the children had profound hearing losses.

After considering the evidence relating to the way normally hearing children develop concepts about literacy, it was decided to devise a set of strategies that together would form a short intervention programme to increase interest in and awareness of literacy. It was felt important that the programme was not a set of facts about literacy, but a programme of experiences which featured literacy in purposeful contexts. Thus the children would be introduced to situations where literacy had genuine communicative purpose. The aim was that in a relatively short period of time the children would, in an intense form, experience some of the situations to which many normally hearing children would have been exposed over a long period of time.

It was important to attempt to establish the state of literacy knowledge of the children before the intervention period began. However, determining such knowledge is difficult even where hearing children are concerned. Therefore the assumptions had to be based on somewhat general observations of the children's behaviour in relation to literacy phenomena. Such observations indicated that the children hardly ever chose, of their own volition, to look at books and never looked at books for very long. They paid no attention to magazines and newspapers placed in the classroom. They seldom noticed any changes in classroom labelling, and on walks in the environment around their school never gave any indication of attending to environmental print.

THE INTERVENTION

The programme lasted six weeks and had a number of objectives:

- to help the children become more aware of the existence of environmental print
- to help the children understand that print conveys messages
- to help them understand that print is useful
- to help them understand that print can be interesting

STRATEGIES AND RESPONSES

(1) Directed walks around the school's immediate neighbourhood were undertaken. Each child was equipped with a clipboard, paper and pencil. As the children walked the group stopped at major items of environmental print (mostly signs). Each one was drawn and a photograph was taken. A discussion took place about the meaning of each sign. Back in the classroom a street painting was begun and the children created signs for it. The photographs were developed and printed overnight and the next day the children repeated the walk, matching the photographs to the signs. Photographs had also been taken of many of the road signs and street names and the child searched out the actual name-plates. All this work was, of course, accompanied by discussion.

(2) Directed walks were taken around a shopping precinct – the emphasis this time being on print for selling rather than on street signs. Again drawings were made and discussions held. Back in the classroom the children began making what they felt were important signs for the class. Trips were made around the school looking at signs and notices.

The directed walks and accompanying activities were, for the most part, quite successful. Certainly the older children quickly seemed to grasp the significance of the signs and notices they saw. They began to search for new signs and to run ahead looking for street names. Most of the children had no trouble matching the photographs to the street names. The children began to point out notices and signs around the school. One child pointed out the 'exit' sign on one of the classroom doors. No child (even in previous cohorts) had ever indicated any awareness of the sign. Signs began to appear in their spontaneous drawings. The children had copied some of the street and shop signs. This was a useful diagnostic exercise in that it revealed those who had some awareness of letter and word position. Several of the younger children broke words at any point in order to get them on the sheet of paper. In general it was felt that the walks and associated activities had helped the children become more aware of the extent to which we are surrounded by print, and that much of that print is very important in communicating messages.

(3) A number of trips were made during the six weeks to large local children's libraries. Each trip was made by minibus, thus giving opportunities for searching for other significant signs. At the libraries the children saw other people using the book collections and they were allowed to select a number of books for themselves. These were read to the children when back in the classroom.

These visits helped the children appreciate that books were not something valued solely by schools. The very fact that enormous quantities of books had been collected together impressed the children. The cumulative effect of these and other activities was that when some of the children's book choices were read, some of the children indicated clearly that they looked ahead and understood some aspects of the story. None of these children had ever done this before. The journeys to the libraries reinforced the belief that directed walks had been successful. While on the minibus going to the libraries several children spontaneously began to identify items of environmental print. One pair of boys matched bus numbers to the bus stops and followed the route as long as they could.

Again it tended to be the older children who made the most of the journey, but all of the children (except one four year old) enjoyed the library visits.

(4) Regular newspapers and magazines were introduced into the classroom. Pictures of interest to the children were identified (usually the Royal baby or football). The children collected photographs and played games searching for words they knew. The children were introduced to the TV schedules and each day children pointed out the things they had seen. Adults in the classroom made a point of reading the newspapers themselves.

This was one of the most interesting parts of the intervention. During pre-intervention observation hardly any of the children had reacted to the introduction of non-book materials. Even those who had looked gave items only the most cursory of glances. However, once the children had witnessed the adults reading and talking with each other about the newspapers, interest developed. One child brought in a newspaper cutting which initiated a whole batch of similar responses. One child brought (without his mother's permission – she had successfully prevented him from doing so three times before) the *Radio Times*. Together with other children favourite programmes were examined. This led to regular perusal of the TV pages of newspapers.

(5) The children were actively encouraged to identify changes in the labelling in the classroom. Each day a couple of labels were changed. When they had been found discussions took place about the purpose of the label. All the labels were whole sentences which actually conveyed information.

(6) A café was set up in the classroom. Real items were made for it using, of course, recipes and instructions. Notices were made for the café, as were menus. A stock of order pads was supplied. At first the activities were modelled by the teacher and her assistants. The assistants looked at the menu and gave their order to the teacher who wrote it down. The teacher collected the food and gave it to the assistants who ate it. After this demonstration the adults served the children, then the children served each other and finally the children served visitors. The café ran for several weeks.

The success of this venture is indicated by one particular incident. At one point a child getting an order forgot which items were to be collected. Instead of going back and asking, the child looked at the note pad – a clear indication that the significance of print for recording events had been appreciated. This was an extremely popular project and was reintroduced once the official intervention period had ended.

(7) As many opportunities as possible were made for the children to receive and write letters. Invitations to parties were received and sent. This was an activity which ran throughout the intervention period. Usually the letters received were unexpected, so the communicative nature of the letter was emphasized

All the children participated in, and enjoyed, writing letters and receiving letters. The whole school co-operated in this and the class frequently received invitations to attend small events. Communication through writing was given special significance when one of the class went into hospital for open heart surgery. The parents agreed to send notes and messages to the class to keep them informed. It was remarkably successful in helping them understand where the child was and what was happening to her. Naturally all the letters received replies.

(8) Where possible the adults in the classroom emphasized through their behaviour that literacy was personally important to them and that it wasn't just an instructional ploy to inflict work on the children. The adults read and talked about the newspapers and journals; they also did any administrative work in the classroom in front of the children.

Too often the demonstration of literacy behaviours by teachers is extremely weak (Hall 1983b). The varied nature of the activities in this project enabled the adults to present a varied and purposeful set of models of literate behaviour.

In addition to these specific strategies other more general ones were in operation. There was an increase in the amount of story telling and attention was given to orientation of books, order of pages, and the print contained within the books. The level of book stock was increased and many opportunities made for the children to select and look at books. Collections of print items were made both by the adults and children. Inevitably many other activities could have been included but this would have led to a quite distorted curriculum for six weeks. As it was, although there was a strong emphasis on print-related activities, they were balanced by the continuation of all other normal curriculum activities.

Clearly quite dramatic changes had taken place in the apparent literacy awareness of some of the children. As indicated already, it tended to be the older, more mature children, who changed most. At the end of the six-week intervention period there was a wholly different sense of literacy activity present in the class. This has not changed with the finishing of the project. Indeed some of the most spectacular effects have occurred after the conclusion of the project. A lovely example happened a few months after the project. The class went to see a pantomime. At one point during the performance one of the children became very agitated; a character on stage had lit a cigarette. The child kept waving to the character and pointing to the dimly lit 'No Smoking' sign. His sensitivity to, or even awareness of, this dissonance would have seemed quite magical before the project.

In another example a mother jokingly complained to the teacher, 'I can't fool her anymore'. Apparently the parents had been in the habit of telling the child that a particular TV programme wasn't on anymore so that they could prevent her watching it. Now the child searches the newspaper and finds out for herself.

In both cases literacy had become something purposeful to the child. It was no longer a school-based instructional activity. It was something that had relevance to their lives.

Six weeks is a short time to record significant changes in levels of awareness of a phenomenon such as literacy. It is hardly surprising that it was the more mature children who seemed to gain the most immediate benefit from these strategies. They may well have been 'ready' to make such moves. Where the younger children are concerned it may well be that a more sustained but gradual set of strategies would have been beneficial.

GENERAL POINTS

Inevitably a number of questions need to be asked about this apparent increase in awareness of some of the children as a result of the intervention.

(1) *Has the children's level of literacy awareness and understanding increased or has the teacher simply become more sensitive to the children's literacy behaviour?*

Almost certainly the teacher's sensitivity to literacy responses will have increased as a result of conducting this piece of action research. However, to argue that the results were solely attributable to such a cause would be unreasonable. The teacher certainly had a degree of sensitivity prior to the study or it would not have been identified as a problematic area. Equally the small size of previous classes and the good level of assistance mean that close attention had always been paid to the children's responses to any subject. The sheer number of appropriate responses during and after the intervention strategy could not have been missed if they had occurred in earlier years.

(2) *Would the children, as a result of previous reading–teaching practices, have achieved a similar level of response?*

This seems very unlikely. No other group of children had ever demonstrated such a spirited and sustained interest in literacy.

(3) *Has anything else occurred which might have contributed to such a set of responses?*

Again this seems unlikely. No other major events occurred within the school and contact with the parents leads to the conclusion that in the first instance nothing had occurred outside of school. It was however apparent that the parents had noticed and in many cases responded to the children's interest in literacy. This may have increased the momentum behind the intervention strategy, but there is no particular evidence to support a belief that it would have happened if the intervention had not been initiated in the first place.

(4) *Were the children really understanding something about the nature and purpose of literacy or were they just performing tricks to gain teacher interest and approval?*

It is difficult to be too specific about the answer to this point as almost certainly some of the early responses would have been made because the teacher appeared to want them. However, even if such responses happened at the beginning the momentum and style of the intervention period made this kind of behaviour less likely as time went on. It seems unlikely that some of the responses outlined earlier could have taken place without understanding of the concepts involved.

(5) *Is the apparent change in interest and understanding likely to be permanent?*

It is easy to forget arbitrary sets of skills or lists of words. It is almost impossible to unlearn something which has resulted in a change in the way one understands something about the world. Certainly the children have, since the end of the intervention period six months ago, shown no signs of forgetting that print has communicative purpose, or that it is interesting. The way the children now respond to print seems to represent a difference in the way they think about print. Such changes do not come about through learning tricks or copying. They are changes in understanding; such changes do not fade away easily. The nature of this change also supports the answer to (4).

(6) *Did the children understand the nature and purpose of literacy in the first instance, but not actually manifest their knowledge?*

This point, like some of the others, is difficult to answer. The observations made prior to the intervention were not very precise, but more accurate measures are not available for such children. It may, in future, be possible to adapt elements of the Linguistic Awareness In Reading Readiness Test (Downing, Ayers and Schaffer, 1983) but this had not been published at the time of the study. The best that can be said is that neither the specific observations, nor the more general observations, made by the teacher during the eight months prior to the intervention justified, in any way, a belief that the children had anything other than a most crude awareness of literacy phenomena.

CONCLUSION

The results of this study do give support to the idea that it would be worthwhile making a specific effort to assist young hearing-impaired children make more sense of the activity of learning to become literate. The results are not 'proof' that these strategies will work for all teachers with all children; they simply suggest somewhere to start. Like all interesting studies it raises more questions than it answers and it certainly indicates an area which has been rather neglected by the field of deaf education.

The strategies outlined above are not in themselves new or unique. What gives them power is their utilization in a coherent way in order to teach explicitly about the communicative nature of print. It is this 'explicitness' which distinguishes this programme from a 'Language-Experience' approach which, in some respects it resembles. The central feature of a 'Language-Experience' approach is that literacy arrives gradually by using the interests of the children through their language. The strategies outlined above are definitely interventionist; they do not mean waiting until interest occurs – they exist to create interest. They do so by using literacy in real communicative contexts and by illustrating that people in that child's world view literacy as being of functional and personal importance. It is, in essence, a demonstration to children that literacy is necessary, valuable and pleasant.

Unfortunately for many hearing-impaired learners literacy can appear as anything but 'valuable or pleasant' and 'necessity' is the necessity to satisfy school requirements, not directly a social or personal necessity. The strategies discussed in this article are not the kind, in themselves, to effect dramatic changes in the literacy interests and knowledge of hearing-impaired children. They do, however, represent a positive step in the attempt to make literacy a more purposeful and meaningful activity. Only time and further investigation will reveal whether changes in attitude and understanding could result in improvements in reading ability; it is not a simple step. However, at the very least we believe that the results of this study justify further investigation of the area.

As a piece of action research it has certainly resulted in significant changes in the understanding of the class teacher. There is no doubt that future groups of children will be taught by a teacher who is extremely sensitive to their needs to understand the nature of written communication. It would be arrogant to claim that these strategies have been 'validated through practice' at this moment in time. However, these strategies will inevitably become an intrinsic part of this teacher's classroom practices. Perhaps at a future date it may be justly claimed that extended use of these practices has consistently yielded positive results.

10

Changing Schools

DIANE TRANTER

INTRODUCTION

This study is concerned with a particular stage in the career of the teacher. In the narrowest sense, it focuses upon my movement from one school to another and my perceptions on being a new member of staff. There are however more general issues. The problems that probationary teachers encounter during their first year of teaching are well documented (Taylor and Dale, 1971; Hannam, 1976; Lacey, 1977). The incumbent difficulties, processes of integration, adjustment, etc., are, although to varying degrees, taken for granted, even expected, as part of what it is to be a probationary teacher. But what of the experienced teacher who moves to another school? 'Moving school' is a reality that many teachers have to face, for many reasons, and this is a reality that I too have become familiar with. That there is little research into the effects on teachers of changing from one school to another is not only worrying, but a point of interest in itself. It appears to be yet another taken-for granted aspect of teachers' careers and indeed the careers of schools themselves.

My concern in this area originated from my own experience on moving to another school over two years ago. It was not a smooth transition. In gaining a new post and in anticipating my move, which was to a position on the same scale point but in a very different school, the notion that I could monitor my initial term in order to investigate and even generate some ideas about being in this position, became strong enough for me to decide to use this personal situation as a suitable case for enquiry. The 'pay-offs' from such a study, I felt, could also have implications far wider than its subjective interest value. The notion of the 'self-monitoring' teacher is one that interests me greatly. Elliott and Adelman (1975) have explored this method with the result that various projects, e.g. Ford Teaching Project, and individual teachers (Cummings, 1982) have used this technique with a view to improving practice. This study, though taking on board the central ideas of self-monitoring, must view the notion of 'the teacher as researcher' (Stenhouse, 1975, pp. 142–65) and what it involves, as something slightly different, because it touches upon aspects of the self and others that in most action research, one may take account of, but not necessarily use as the substance of one's investigation. Now to the context in which the research was to take place.

The school to which I had been appointed and which I shall refer to as school X, is an inner-city, multi-ethnic, 11–16 comprehensive of approximately five hundred children and forty staff. It has had problems. These include a low level of achievement in external examinations and poor discipline. I had also been told that the school was still suffering the unsettling effects of secondary reorganization. The post I was to take up was that of teacher of Personal and Social Education (PSE). I had never worked in a multicultural school, nor had I taught PSE across all the age range. I did possess over six years' teaching experience, which included a secondary school in a social priority area and a rural comprehensive. This latter school, my previous place of work, drew its children from a wide area. There were few black children on roll and many of the children came from middle-class backgrounds. My feelings on working at the school ranged from indifference to abject misery. My move to an inner-city comprehensive was seen by some of my colleagues there as a drastic step – a sign of my desperation to 'get out'. My reasons for moving were reasonably simple. I wished to find a school where I could operate as the teacher I feel I am. I wanted to discover if my feelings of inadequacy and worthlessness were ephemeral and linked to my situation, or whether these were truths I would have to accept.

So, at the start of the spring term I entered school X as a new member of staff. Like an actor entering a play with an already established cast I had a notion of the scenario but no definite knowledge of the plot. Like Schutz's (1964) stranger I would be 'the man who has to place in question nearly everything that seems to be unquestionable to the members of the approached group' (p. 34). This article vividly describes the processes that operate in adjusting to 'a culture' of which one has no prior knowledge. Schools do have their own cultures, they are different, and some of Schutz's central ideas of the stranger entering a new culture seemed to have particular relevance to my situation. These ideas provided a focus not only for what this study is concerned with, what it is about, but also some of the methodological issues involved. First, entering school X as a newcomer and wanting to become a member of that 'culture' would involve me in experiences and interactions that in themselves would not seem problematic to the members of the in-group, i.e. the staff and the children, but they would be problematic to me as a new teacher. Building a new scheme of reference would take time. Secondly, the objectivity that I would possess as a stranger in a new setting is something that might allow me to observe this setting in ways that the in-group could not. In the dual role of teacher/researcher and new member of staff investigating my inception to school X I would be a stranger in the real sense of the word. Not a transient observer/researcher, but one very much immersed in the reality of my situation. This suggests a dimension to this study that is not only of interest as regards its substance, but also the means employed in investigating the various aspects of the 'reality' concerned.

METHODOLOGY AND METHODS

The way forward methodologically seemed to be linked with what has been called the naturalistic or interpretative paradigm. Empirical research which reflects this paradigm and adopts an interpretative stance is largely concerned with the collection of qualitative data. Rather than beginning with a theory which is then used and applied to observations of human behaviour, theory is something that emerges, that arises from the data (Glaser and Strauss, 1967). In order to get access to that data, the researcher must get close to the area of life under study, become a part of it and enter into the sorts of interactions that her subjects encounter.

One of the major criticisms levelled at this approach is that it lacks scientific rigour. Strategies such as participant observation, unstructured interviews, field notes, have been cited by some (Odum and Jocher, 1929; Blalock, 1971) as methods more akin to journalism than social science. Such methods have been used for many years by anthropologists, and indeed some symbolic interactionists (Delamont and Hamilton, 1976), describe their research activities as just that. Because the interactionist is concerned with exploring the taken-for-granted aspects of social life, and seeking to explain subjective realities rather than objective reality, there is the danger that the researcher's interpretations of those realities will be affected by the very fact that she too is susceptible to the same influences she is observing in others. Problems of bias can arise. By becoming immersed in what one is studying, the danger of being absorbed into that culture, is always apparent. (Hammersley and Atkinson, 1983, have criticized Willis, 1977, for doing this).

That one paradigm or method is better than the other is not an argument to go into here. Differing approaches have important parts to play in increasing our knowledge of social activities. The overriding principle is one of suitability. To gain access to the inner perspective (Bruyn, 1966) of human and social relations, the need for an approach informed by symbolic interactionism seemed to me to be the way forward. For me it was also important to sort out some of the key ideas informing my approach as a teacher/researcher. I needed to legitimate my sense of what Lawrence Stenhouse (1975, p. 165) intended in his notion of 'A research tradition which is accessible to teachers and which feeds teaching'.

My central concern stemmed from a personal and professional interest in my own circumstances, namely moving to another school. Alongside this there were certain notions of career, self, socialization and institutional culture which fed my curiosity and influenced my decisions on the methodology and methods of data collection used. In many ways my stance as a researcher could be likened to a pivot, moving from the reality of my situation experienced by me, as me, and that of the detached observer entering a new setting. For although I was researching into a situation I had experience of, I was also entering into a new social arena of which I had little knowledge. The 'ability to take the role of the other, like any potential skill, requires cultivation to be effective'. Blumer (1969) makes reference to a very interesting point here and one central to the methodological position employed by this study. 'Taking the role of the other' as a skill is one that is tested in the individual no more so than in initial interactions with others. As a teacher I had knowledge of what it was to *be* a teacher, but not at school X. The interactions that were to take place there between myself and staff and pupils, were to be of immense significance in my monitoring those first few weeks. As an almost covert participant observer, the need to interpret those interactions and record my perceptions was, I felt, vital. I was to be involved with investigating my own subjective reality, but in doing so drawing on the subjective realities of others. Another concern was to be that of getting access to the objective realities that exist in relation to this situation and setting. The notion of 'career' exemplifies this dual reality factor. 'Career' implies something that takes place over time, objectively it appears to be structured. However 'career' can be interpreted subjectively in many different ways. Clearly this concept was one I needed to pursue in some depth although there is not space to do that here. The decision then to opt for a qualititative approach to this research stemmed from not only a belief in symbolic interactionism as a means of viewing and understanding human and social behaviour, but also the nature of the concern being investigated. The methods employed as a result of that decision are described next.

Field notes are the means by which much qualitative observational data is recorded (Hammersley and Atkinson, 1983, p. 145). The form these take depends largely upon the time one has to write them and the setting one is working in. Many researchers (Bogdan and Taylor, 1975) use a diary or journal to supplement their field notes. This can provide not only a running account of the conduct of the research but also the personal feelings and thoughts experienced by the researcher. In combining the two into a 'field journal', where perceptions, observations and emotions are all recorded on a daily or regular basis, I felt that this would provide a realistic method of collecting a substantial part of the data necessary. In addition to this the use of analytic notes or memos, jotted down at intervals, as necessary, as a result of some reflection, would also be important as a device not only for sharpening awareness, but as a means of 'preliminary analysis'. These techniques would provide 'a constant interplay between the personal and emotional and the intellectual' (Hammersley and Atkinson, 1983, p. 166) and also enable a 'natural history' of the research to develop. Another method of acquiring data, which might overcome questions of rigour, aid analysis and to some extent balance the anticipated effects of 'going native' became part of the research design. Therefore triangulation in the form of focused interviews (Merton and Kendall, 1946), with a small theoretical sample was envisaged.

It is important to note here that the methods outlined above should not be seen in isolation. The process of applying those methods, the context in which they were used, the way in which they evolved and indeed informed, to enable other means to develop, accentuated the temporal nature of this form of empirical research. As such, reference to that process is as necessary as a description of the methods themselves. Glaser and Strauss (1967) have emphasized how the generation of theory 'demands a broad and eclectic reading of textual sources' (p. 132). Recording personal data can after a certain time become an unwieldy task lacking any semblance of direction. So, it was in turning to relevant articles of both a theoretical and empirical nature that I, in a sense, was able to narrow down and define more clearly what I as a teacher was researching. This 'reflexive' process' enabled me not only to clarify the past but inform the future – the areas to concentrate on as regards my own personal perceptions and observations and the procedures for implementing other methods. There were action steps at various stages but they were somewhat different to action as identified in the classroom.

In devising an interview schedule for the sample of what became three teachers plus one 'outsider' (a Post-Graduate Certificate of Education (PGCE) student), the themes that had emerged through my data and from literary sources served as a means of focus. The perceptions I wished to discover were tied to the areas that had already 'surfaced'. That is as worries, interests and concerns for me as a teacher to the school. An originally unplanned source of data came from discussion with a group of pupils. Because of (1) my developing a good relationship with this group and (2) some of the categories that had emerged from the literature and from the focused interviews, a sample of fourth year pupils agreed to discuss certain questions, e.g. 'How do you think it feels to be a new teacher at this school?' This added a different perspective, which only became available due to factors that are as much a part of what this study is concerned with as the processes involved in empirical research.

TWO THEMES

What is presented here is an attempt to summarize two particular themes which emerged for me during the course of my study. They are presented very much along the lines of a traditional piece of research on education and do not capture the actual process of the research in terms of the steps I took and the moments when particular ideas began to emerge. Apart from the limitations of space, there are however two reasons for my wishing to present the materials in this way. The first is that such a form of presentation may appear to be more generalizable and relate more easily to the experiences of other teachers. The second is that I did in fact attempt to adopt throughout the study a third person writing mode, as if I were at times an outside researcher. This approach helped me to detach myself in ways which I thought were necessary, and the mode of presentation adopted here reflects this strategy.

Socialization and the Influence of Groups and Sub-cultures

Teacher B   One of the things I found the most difficult to accept when I first came to school C, was that the children I was teaching were not operating to my already established standards.

Teacher A   I was shocked by the different set of standards here, as compared with my previous school. The staff here accept and expect different things from the kids. They're not my standards.

Teacher C   What amazed me was that there was no standard within the school as a whole, only in pockets within departments. There appeared to be no general ethos.

It seems that in the case of these teachers it is not only desirable that standards exist, but that they should be acceptable to them. Being somewhere with different standards or where there are no identifiable standards, not only provides the newcomer wtih a dilemma in the form of acceptance or rejection, but also poses the question as to whether one's personal standards are appropriate and if not what are the alternatives. The following diary extract illustrates the problem clearly:

Diary extract   I have been getting nowhere with my 1st year
English group. I decided on a new tactic today.
Lined them up outside the classroom – very
regimental. K, on his way to his class, came over
and said, 'You're on the right lines here, love'.
A few days later . . .

Diary extract   A disastrous afternoon, I feel I made a mistake
insisting upon the 1st years lining up. They
disturbed all the other classes on the corridor. K
came out of his class and shouted at them. He
offered to take a couple of them off my hands. I
felt a complete fool.

'Lining a class up' outside their classroom is a procedure that many
teachers adhere to, indeed it may be one of a number of procedures that
make up the stock of 'recipe knowledge' (Schutz, 1964) that the new
teacher brings with her. It may though be a procedure that does not
travel well, particularly in a setting where (1) other staff seem to allow
children to enter the classroom freely and (2) the children make it clear
that 'lining up' is something they are not used to doing. To add further
to the newcomer's problems, as the above extract shows, is the
conflicting advice or ways in which approval or disapproval are shown
to and interpreted by the newcomer, whilst still struggling with the
question 'Am I doing things right?' This mis-matching of standards, or
realization that one's 'recipe knowledge' is inadequate or inappropriate,
is even more problematic when the new recipes, as it were, are far from
obvious. Teacher C, who referred to school X as having 'no general
ethos', in a sense identifies the nature of the problem, which can in
effect be related to an assumption that many new members of any new
culture they are entering may be expected to make. That is that the
culture or organization has stability. Not recognizing that there is
instability can mean that the search for clues becomes a mammoth task,
complicated by conflicting pieces of information and advice.

Diary extract   Conversation in the staffroom on my third day at
school X:
T   Had a bad day?
D   Yes, you could say that.
T   Don't think it'll get any better.

Teacher B   Somebody said to me when I first came here.
'Some of the kids may be unruly, but they're not
all like that, and they're not all like that all of the
time. When you do get something from them –

don't blink, because you might miss it.' There is
something in that. I think probably him having
said that to me, I probably looked for it.

Diary extract   W to D
'All people have problems here. It's OK to talk to
anybody about it, no one will think the worse of
you.'
B to D
'I felt like I was being watched all the time when I
first came here, not for positive reasons either.
You've got to be careful who you talk to, they
could hold it against you.'

Unfortunately it is only over time that these contradictions emerge and
instability reveals itself.

Diary extract   The last three weeks have shown school X to be
far from stable.

What one learns is not only the diverse and complex nature of the
institution, but that groups exist within it, which may be fulfilling
different needs and performing different functions for different
members. Critically this can lead to self doubt.

Diary extract   A to D
'I felt so cheated when I came here. I couldn't
understand why I was having problems. The
Head (then) seemed to imagine everything was
alright in the school. It must be me, I thought. I
started asking other people and discovered that all
the new staff felt like me. I felt better then.'

According to Becker (1970, pp. 282-3) 'where the response to
problematic situations is collective, members of the group involved
develop group loyalties that become part of the environment they must
adjust to'. The teacher above had joined the school as a result of
secondary reorganization, along with twenty other new members of
staff. 'Being new' as a group may well provide a form of support that is
denied the lone newcomer. Teacher B who also joined School X due to
reorganization, commented:

There was and to some extent still is a closeness among the staff,
which I feel is due to us realizing that there existed or exists a
common enemy, as it were.

However the perceptions of Teacher C, who entered the school in
different circumstances, seem markedly different.

The staff generally seemed a bitter and insecure group of people who took a long time to know. I didn't like the way some of them discussed the children and I made a point not to enter into these conversations.

The observations of a student teacher who was on teaching practice at school X, provide here another contrast which may shed further light on the ways in which standards and groups are perceived by individuals according to their circumstances and past knowledge.

Student Teacher   At school Y, where I did my last teaching practice, on the first day I was presented with a file containing rules, regulations, etc., almost a work pack. After the first day I knew quite a lot about how the school operated. At school X there was nothing like that. Fortunately the department I was attached to was very good, but I didn't know anything about the school, its rules, etc. I had to find those out as I went along. At School Y no one discussed children publicly in the staffroom, only at staff meetings. At School X, I got to know some kids very well, by reputation, though I never taught them or even met them.

This student teacher paints a contrasting picture and one which identifies the sorts of cultural standards and behaviours that can exist in two different schools. However, being 'new' together as a group may have the effect of reducing some of the factors that normally are at work on individual new members of staff. Corporate support can be translated into such items as 'discussing children openly in the staffroom' because it provides a common reference point to which all can relate. The very things that are of importance to a group of newcomers may be an anathema to someone who lacks that common group identity. Added to which previous knowledge may count far more for the individual newcomer, because her investment in this possible future may be greater because she has chosen to move. Those who have been reorganized, are, as it were, refugees who have to make the best of their situation. It is possible that the latter do not make quite the same assumptions about the stability of the school, because there may be recognition of their movement being a symptom of and a contributory factor to what must inevitably be instability.

Teacher B   It's not a question of the standards here being lower or worse than . . . it's just that they're different. You adapt to them.

This teacher who had been 'reorganized' expressed the least dissatisfaction about how the school was run and did not criticize standards or staff nor express a feeling of lack of support. This process of adaptation and acceptance of things within the school cannot be wholly attributed to this teacher's alliance with others who joined due to reorganization. However it does raise the question of which persons and which groups new teachers, particularly those who join as individuals, do relate to, come into contact with, and are influenced by.

Teacher C	I feel that I have been and was necessarily influenced by my head of department . . . I consider myself lucky to be a member of such a supportive department.
Teacher A	I think you're very much on your own here.
Diary extract	I feel so lost, so out of my depth at times. Although there are other staff on my corridor I can relate to, I still feel cut off, I'm like a poor relation to the English department. They make decisions and don't tell me. I think the Head of Department thinks I'm psychic.

In secondary schools the organization of the school in terms of houses, year groups and departments can determine to some degree the contact that new staff members have with established staff. One's department in particular can, in the early days, provide the newcomer with a reference group that is identifiable with something – an area of the curriculum – which carries with it some common elements which the newcomer may recognize. If, as at school X, there is no general or formal induction policy, then the department may act as a filtering agency in that certain items and 'facts' are made more explicit to the newcomer, via the department, than through the headteacher or deputies. That these items become changed or altered due to this process is highly dependent upon the department in its role as a subgroup and how it sees itself in relation to other subgroups and the wider structure of the school. The data above show how different teachers perceive their membership to a department.

But schools are more than just departments. The staffroom often provides the setting for informal interactions between individuals and groups which demonstrate the cohesive or fragmented nature of the institution, and which again may provide reference groups, support and 'recipes' which the newcomer can 'pick up'.

Diary extract	Week A
	It has become clear to me now where I feel the most comfortable, as regards where I sit and who

I mix with in the staffroom. There are two
obvious groups and the group I am drawn to
consists of the younger members of staff. There is
more laughter going on, more jokes, more
swearing where they sit. It's more legitimate to
use expletives at that end of the staffroom.

One of the identifiable characteristics of the group described above
was its unpredictability. The function that it served for the writer and
for others in the group was that of escapism. (Woods, 1979, has made
reference to this in his study of staffroom humour at Lowfield School.)
Problems would be treated lightly, a crisis would become a joke and
anger would soon turn into laughter. However it was at the same time
the source of much stimulating debate and discussion and could, when
required, be the provider of sympathetic support and advice. The
cohesion within the group, despite its unpredictable nature, was its
most attractive feature. At the same time, though, it had its own
methods for excluding those who did not fit into the group.

Diary extract   Thursday – E who has just joined the school,
spent most of the lunch hour with our group. The
conversation was exceptionally bawdy, thanks to
various characters. E looked very shocked and
actually said about one member – 'Isn't he rude!'
Friday
Today E sat at the other end of the staffroom,
however she looked unsure.

R   Oh, you're sitting with us today?
E   I don't really know where to sit, I feel in
the middle.
R   Oh, stay here.
H   Yes, I think I will, I'm staying here, they're
so rude at that end.

The group also had methods for testing acceptability of possible
members.

Diary extract   One person on the staff, it transpires, is disliked
by many of the members of the group I sit with, I
became drawn into this and indeed although I feel
G is a little odd, at the same time he has been very
supportive and kind to me. I really don't see him
in quite the same way as the others. Part of my
being accepted though, was to join in this
discussion. I found this situation very difficult.

According to Schutz (1964), there are two basic traits which may explain a stranger's attitude to an approached group (1) the stranger's objectivity and (2) his doubtful loyalty. The former is a result of the stranger's 'need to acquire full knowledge of the elements of the approached cultural pattern and to examine for this purpose with care and precision what seems self explanatory to the in group' (p. 32). Because the newcomer to a group has had no part in its history, the group's 'thinking as usual' is viewed in a discerning way and as such becomes, as in the above extract, a matter of acute concern for the newcomer and one which can be identified as threatening her conception of the group and her place in it. The trait of 'doubtful loyalty' is often one 'that originates in the astonishment of the members of the in-group, that the stranger does not accept the total of its cultural pattern as the natural and appropriate way of life' (p. 32). Testing that loyalty is in a sense a necessary procedure, not only for the group but also for the stranger, but this is far more problematical and much more of a consequential factor for the latter.

What has emerged from the data is that becoming a member of the school also involves membership of subgroups within the school, and that the choice of groups may be much wider than the two that have been mentioned already. Learning the ropes is not a straightforward matter, because as some of the data have shown, the newcomer has to decide on whose ropes.

The one group in particular that the new teacher is in contact with most of the time is that of the pupils. Initial encounters, as described below by some of the teachers at school X and the writer, reveal some interesting features:

Diary extract	I was taken up by K to meet my tutor group. They were quiet and listened to him introducing me. However, as soon as he left the room, there was uproar. They were noisy, troublesome, would not sit down or listen. They acted as though I wasn't there.
Teacher C	My initial impression of the children was that they were noisy, lively and demanding of your attention . . . they seemed afraid of anything new . . . their attitude towards me ranged from being very aggressive to non-committal.
Teacher B	The major thing I remember was the constant never-ending challenge to practically anything you asked the children to do. You can accept incidents, but it was their constant denial of your presence, their ignorance to your wishes – that was the wearing thing.

The main feature of these statements is that initial encounters with pupils were difficult and full of conflict. Another interesting feature is that of ignoring the teacher's presence. Possibly the pupil sub-culture is the most exclusive club within the school that the new teacher can seek entry into. Pupils' perceptions of initial encounters reveal their almost ritualistic initiation of new staff.

D   Why do you think you take advantage of new teachers?

P2   Well you've got to . . . you know . . . check them out.

D   What do you mean by 'check them out'?

P4   Well, you got to see if they're going to get stricter, 'cos you only get used to them once they get strict.

This group of fourth years appears to have attitudes that are not exclusive to them, nor school X. Ball's (1980) study showed similar attitudes amongst pupils, and indeed 'trying it on' is something that most new staff expect.

Teacher C   At first with some groups, I felt I was teaching in a vacuum, until they started testing me out.

But the process by which teacher and pupils eventually arrive at a mutually acceptable existence within the classroom can be a hard one and often more so for the teacher.

Diary extract   They (the pupils) seems almost schizophrenic – I feel a bit like giving up. I think I'm too soft for this place.

Teacher C   When I first started here, I used to go home absolutely exhausted. I couldn't relax though, even when I got home.

Teacher A   I don't think I'd ever been as 'uptight' in my life as I did then. I found it hard to relax.

'Not knowing the children' was something that all the teachers interviewed referred to as being the biggest cause of their problems, hence their emphasis on 'building relationships'. This was something that was emphasized recently in a TES article about an inner-city school in London (16 March 1984).

Pupils and teachers may appear to be striving for different things, different goals in their initial encounters, but their time perspectives are in many ways similar.

P3   You think that at first a new teacher isn't going to stay, but then after a bit when the newness wears off . . . you don't think of them as a new teacher and you know they're not goin' to leave.

Diary extract   I can't help feeling that this is all temporary – that
                 I'm temporary, but I'm not going to be here much
                 longer. There's no sense of permanence.

The new teacher's short-term perspective may be to 'get through the
day', the pupils' to give the new teacher 'a hard time'. But their longer-
term perspectives match up better, because both in the end are working
towards a setting for social interaction which is conducive to both.
What that ultimately develops as depends on many factors and as
Riseborough (1983) has pointed out, may not even occur. It may not be
as simple as 'the invader' becoming one of the natives, but all the
teachers the writer interviewed and the majority of those spoken to
informally, felt they had come through the worst.

Diary extracts   P The first six weeks are hell, but it does get
                    better.
                 W You may think you're going mad, but it does
                    get better.

The notion of matching self and situation

There is only one issue which I can give adequate attention to here,
but it is one which was particularly illuminating to me. Nias (1983b), in
her study of primary school teachers, notes that where teachers could
not find within their schools reference groups or social groups which
seemed to match with their own values, there was a tendency for those
teachers to use their pupils as reinforcers of their identity and as
respondents to their values and ideas. It doesn't matter that I don't
agree with the rest of the staff. I can cut myself off from them by
working with the kids (p. 24).

Nias refers to pupils in this context being 'the joker' in the hand of
these teachers. They could be used 'to defend any number of beliefs and
practices' (p. 24). This leads us beyond the function that groups have
for socializing individuals, to their role as confirmers of values and
ideals that are held by individuals. In a sense, seeking out 'confirming'
reference groups and 'learning the ropes' from different subgroups can
be viewed as a closely interlinked process. However achieving a match
can be difficult.

To return to some of Nias's data:

It's easier to find teachers you wouldn't want to be like, than ones
you would . . . you don't meet many teachers who make you feel
'that's the sort of person I'd like to be'.

The search for 'like-minded' people by a new teacher can in itself be an extension of the search for 'a school where I can be the teacher I am'. The reasons for moving, then, may be a vital indicator for understanding why this search is important.

> Diary extract   First impressions: I felt this was somewhere
>   where I could fit in, where I could be me and
>   not worry whether it was right or not. The
>   school seems more concerned with kids as
>   people rather than packages to fill with
>   knowledge. I hope this is so.

Nias's (1984b) findings do to some extent connect with this. The teachers in her study, once they had become aware that they could 'survive', 'needed to satisfy themselves that they could become, somewhere within the profession, the sort of teacher I would like to be' (p. 4). This search often involved movement. Its purpose according to Nias, was to achieve a match between 'the deeply held values and attitudes of the substantial self and the behaviour expected by significant others of the situational self'.

The sample of teachers interviewed for this study moved school for a variety of reasons to do with seeking experience, security, or as a result of reorganization. In trying to discover how much these reasons were to do with finding a match there did seem to be a link between the views these teachers hold about themselves and the circumstances surrounding their movement to school X. Nias (1983b) has said that many teachers seek reference groups that confirm the values teachers held when they first entered the teaching profession, and even use negative reference groups to confirm their views. She believes they have an important function in sustaining the match between substantial and situational self.

By seeking out reference groups which confirm one's own values, Nias believes that this can result in teachers being less open to new influences. The data produced from this study suggests that although this may be so for some teachers, there are those who have been influenced and as a result have changed not only as teachers, but as people.

> Teacher C   My educational ideals and principles have become
>   more fervent, it has reinforced them. I think I am
>   now more liberal and more aware of problems. I also
>   feel that as a person I am now much harder.
>
> Teacher A   I think I'm a much more caring sort of person now,
>   mainly because the school has allowed me to be –
>   my teaching methods have also changed because of
>   working in an integrated department.

But are these changes real changes or 'optical illusions' (Becker, 1970)? Teacher B is more caring, because the school has allowed him to be, Teacher C is now more liberal and 'much harder'. Could it be then that rather than just seeking and finding confirmation from reference groups, individuals also find parts of themselves, discover new values, which past situations or other groups have suppressed?

| Teacher A | At my last school you had to maintain a 'macho hard' image in order to have credibility with the rest of the staff. |

Indeed taking this further, an individual may be one sort of person in one setting or place and another in another.

| Teacher A | At my last school I was considered something of a 'trendy' by the staff who were nearly all reactionaries. Here I feel like a reactionary looking at the trendies. |
| Diary extract | I feel so different here, in fact I'm quite moderate in comparison to some of the staff. Such a contrast from school Z, where I was viewed as a subversive, left wing, progressive. |

Becker (1970, p. 279) has said that 'the individual turns himself into the kind of person the situation demands'. But in viewing her situation, particularly if it is one that is relatively new or unfamiliar, the individual may also discover something about herself, in the ways in which she responds or reacts to that situation. It may not just be a matter of sustaining or finding a match between situational and substantial self. It is possible that if one is seeking 'experience' for example one is more open to influences, and as a result is more likely to become a different person or someone who changes. This, in particular is one issue which struck me as the research developed, the ways in which for some teachers at least, we can gain radically different perspectives on ourselves as people through the process of moving schools. Perhaps it is only through a close monitoring of this process, that one can note these changes in oneself, can discover new aspects of the relationship between self and the job of teaching, and can feed these discoveries into one's present and future.

CONCLUSION

This study concentrated on the experienced teacher and her perceptions on being a new member of staff, supplemented with the perceptions of others who have undergone the same experience. The two broad themes that emerged from the data as described previously, illustrate the differences and similarities between people's perceptions; their subjective definitions and meanings reveal 'realities' that are grounded in their own individual experience. This experience cannot then be ignored or discounted when observing the ways in which individuals 'learn the ropes', discover new recipes, and become members rather than strangers.

What the experienced teacher may have to face, though, is that making the grade once is not the ticket to instant success.

Diary extract   E to D
                     'I can't understand it. Is it me? I've been
                     teaching all these years and I've never met a
                     class like that before . . . someone of my
                     experience shouldn't be having these
                     problems.'

But does this mean 'starting again'? Referring once more to Schutz and his article 'The Stranger', where he comments on the 'environmental character' that new cultures take on for the stranger, he draws attention to the fact that one's closeness to and one's desire to be a member of that culture, demands a reshaping of one's thinking and restatement of the concepts that before, in one's past, existed without question. But in reshaping her thinking, the individual is not necessarily abandoning her past, she is using her past to make sense of her present situation. It may not provide ready made 'recipes' as we have seen and it may produce feelings of inadequacy, but it does exist. This is, as I see it, where the problem lies in being an experienced teacher, yet at the same time, a new teacher. It is a problem because the teacher in this situation is confronted by a range of expectations, by a set of assumptions which are related to her objective career to date. The school she is entering sees her only as a teacher, sees her experience as her curriculum vitae. Salaman (1979) has noted that selectors search for candidates with a 'predisposition towards the organizational culture' and the school does have evidence of her 'predisposition'. She *is* a teacher and the qualities she displays at interview are taken as part of that evidence.

The precarious nature of 'moving schools' is taken for granted by teachers and schools alike. However, if it were to be viewed as the problem which I believe it is and which it certainly was for me, then the ways in which teachers are selected and the support and guidance provided by schools could be improved in order to serve the teaching profession more adequately.

Moving to another school was something I had experienced before and it was something I viewed as problematic. Moving to school X was not problem free, as the reader will observe from the diary notes, and that others had similar perceptions of their situation adds further validity. In an indirect and perhaps unintended way, by monitoring my initiation and subsequent progress at school X, by being a teacher/ researcher, the reflexive process I consciously adopted helped serve me in my endeavours to become a member of the school. Because I feel I managed to maintain the objective stance necessary, methodologically, for this study, my situation became a 'field of adventure', not only in the sense that Schutz has described but also intellectually. It has been said elsewhere that the purpose of the teacher as researcher is to improve practice. I feel this study enabled me to improve at being a member of school X. What this suggests to me is that more studies of individual teachers, their careers, their personal development need to be undertaken. More needs to be discovered about the whole process of teacher socialization, not only at the start and end of teachers' careers, but also the different stages that teachers go through. Lacey (1977) has also expressed these views in relation to greater collaboration between teachers and researchers. Although this is something I would endorse, it is clear to me that teachers need to collaborate more with one another – that the implicit, taken-for-granted aspects of teaching, of what it is to be a teacher, need further investigation by those whom it most affects. Findings from such investigations would not only be of value to headteachers and teachers in charge of staff welfare and development, they would also be of value to teacher educators in their preparation of future generations of teachers.

Jennifer Nias at the beginning of her paper *A More Distant Drummer: Teacher Development as the Development of Self* (1984b) seems to state the obvious when she refers to teachers being people too. But this is something that certain perspectives in sociology do not always take cognizance of, and indeed Nias has pointed out the generalized nature of much of the sociological literature produced about the lives and careers of teachers. This has been a small-scale empirical study from which no vast generalizations can be made. However, I believe it has captured the essence of Nias's words, which I feel succinctly describe what this study is basically about. As such, it has been of value to me, not only as a teacher, but as a person too.

11

Mathematics, Teachers and an Action Research Course

LILIAN STREET

In 1981 a team of tutors at Manchester Polytechnic particularly interested in early childhood education, began to teach a Masters degree course in the education of young children four to eight (M.Ed.Y.C.4–8). The starting point for our planning had been the major aim of facilitating and encouraging children's learning, promoted by helping teachers to develop their professional expertise in that part of the course which deals with the teaching of mathematics to young children.

Although teachers are said to be resistant to and suspicious of educational research and theory, nevertheless, certain theories seem to have affected teachers' thinking, though they may not be recognized or attributed to their source. The word 'theory' is normally used to mean the body of educational research and writing. The theories of teachers have not been seen as material for study, yet only if this happens can their validity be examined and their effects understood. Certainly, the theories which teachers have affect very much the way in which they teach mathematics. Recent evidence from research projects like Bennett's reported in *The Quality of Pupil Learning Experiences* suggests that teachers think of mathematics as facts to be learned and as skills to be mastered by practice. Practice activities are those most commonly found in the classrooms studied by Bennett.

Classroom method is also affected by theory in other ways. The influence of psychological theories, mainly Piagetian can be clearly seen in the published schemes of work in mathematics for infant schools, particularly in the activities suggested for the learning of environmental measures. For example, certain Piagetian test results showed that in the test situation he devised children concluded that larger meant heavier, that a tall, thin container held more liquid than a short, wide one and so on. All infant mathematics schemes suggest that children should have structured experiences which demonstrate that the largest parcel is not necessarily the heaviest, and that containers of different shapes may hold more, the same, or less liquid than another, and that the only way to be sure of relative size is to measure. It is not the intention to dispute the value of these activities. It seems likely that they are useful, but the research in this area is by no means conclusive, and little has taken place in the classroom situation. Some teachers contribute to these schemes by suggesting activities which they have found useful, or by trying out the materials in their classrooms, but these contributions are rarely submitted to the kind of rigorous examination that they would receive as part of a research programme, because teachers are not seen as researchers.

The unthinking acceptance of theory, and its reification into a basis for classroom practice have undesirable side effects. Teachers are led to feel that these schemes are devised by experts, so tend not to question what is proposed. It is also forgotten that the basis for these activities was theoretical so it is likely to change, as in this case, for in the meantime mainstream psychology has moved on. Although Piaget's research results are still held to be valid much of the interpretation based on his experiments is now under attack. There is a growing feeling that children's understandings are greater than Piagetian findings would suggest and taking a positive view of what they can do would be better than stressing what they cannot. We are left with maths schemes which enshrine a particular view of children's activities.

These case histories of research in practice are not reassuring, and it is clear that a different approach would be helpful. How can teachers be helped to teach mathematics more effectively? Recently there have been developments in research which could be an answer to some of the problems highlighted here. These create a bridge between the disciplinary research of psychologists and the practice of teachers in their classrooms by using the mathematical classroom as an area for data collection. In addition, we suggest that within the umbrella term 'pedagogical research' there must also be a place for research done by teachers. Who is better placed than teachers to collect data towards the solution of teaching problems in mathematics, from easy questions like 'What do children find easy/difficult?' to more probing ones like 'Why?'

Action research seemed to us to offer most in this direction because it is meant to be undertaken by practitioners, that is those involved in a social situation, rather than by outsiders. Therefore it is normally small-scale and manageable in a classroom setting: the data arising from normal class activities, or the context within which the teacher works. Because it is organized and carried out internally by the teachers themselves it should be congruent with school practices, the methods used being chosen to fit this situation. Participatory observational techniques are more likely to be used than experimental ones as, for instance, many teachers find the use of a control group unacceptable. A creative approach to methods is encouraged using any discipline and any technique thought appropriate, providing the flexibility to cope even with the unforeseen. Teacher initiated action research projects are beginning to be reported but it is too early yet to assess their effects. They can be seen to answer some teacher reservations about traditional research projects.

However the M.Ed. was not designed to produce a body of knowledge about mathematics teaching but to help its students to teach mathematics more effectively. Both the Cockcroft Report and the HMI paper *Matters for discussion: Mathematics 5–11* quote from much earlier papers all of which have recommended similar courses of action towards a more investigatory approach, yet mathematics teaching in primary classrooms remains very formal. Imposing set schemes and applying research from allied disciplines has not changed matters. If the theories which teachers hold affect the way they teach mathematics this teaching will not change or improve unless those theories and attitudes are changed, and there are particular facets of the action research process which we believe will promote this.

Beginning with the classroom and examining teacher theories seems more likely to have an effect. There are unlikely to be major and unmanageable shifts of emphasis because the experimenter is also the manager. Changes which are made are likely to be maintained and even extended. The collection and analysis of data confronts the teacher with the actuality, rather than the rationalization, of the teaching and this alone can shift perceptions dramatically. Whatever happens the teacher should gain an insight into how her mathematics teaching is being received by the children and this is the first step to improving it. The teacher also begins to challenge the theories and practices of others, making the unthinking acceptance of research findings less likely. Action research approaches theories from the standpoint of the practitioner asking 'what will enhance your insight?' and so encouraging the generation of hypotheses which can then be tested out where they have real meaning. Action is suspended while accounts are constructed. These accounts are investigated or tested in the next cycle. This cyclical quality of action research proceeds by subjecting practice to evaluation, providing further data for reflection followed by action and thereby helping to link the pragmatic and the theoretical. The expectation is that this will develop the teacher's self awareness and analytical powers. As stated earlier the theories which teachers hold affect the way they teach mathematics. Those teachers who have a blind faith in the value of practical activity, and also those who do not value it at all, need to confront the personal theories which generate their teaching methods and hence improve them. The testing out of theories should also help to make teachers more critical of the activities suggested in published schemes and develop their ability to appraise and use the more valuable ones.

Action research lends itself well as a research method for teachers' dissertations because it is easier to carry out in the classroom while teaching than traditional research, yet has many of the strengths of traditional methods. It takes a similarly critical stance, processes data systematically and seeks to arrive at coherent and justifiable conclusions, but because its conclusions are practitioner-based rather than discipline-based the teacher does not need to maintain laboratory type methods. Proving or disproving theories or providing generalizable results is not necessary. The centrality of the practitioner to the research is seen to provide a much needed emphasis on pedagogical research.

Collaboration with other teachers is an integral part of the package because the discovery that others see classroom events in a different way can mean a confrontation with the hitherto taken-for-granted knowledge normally used in an unreflective way. This can help in the process of testing and refining personal theory and can also give confidence to pursue and develop new approaches. The course seeks to encourage this co-operation by providing 'a critical community' within which teachers are helped to rationally defend and evaluate their ideas and submit the ideas of others to reasoned criticism or support. It is hoped that the experience will help teachers to continue to do this by creating similar groups in their own schools.

THE MATHEMATICS UNIT IN THE M.ED.

The rest of this chapter aims to describe the mathematics teaching unit of the Master's course, showing how this unit exemplified the reasoning and beliefs of the course team and illustrating the reasons why action research became the main vehicle for the development of the teachers' expertise by drawing on some work done by teachers in their mathematics lessons.

The mathematics teaching unit is described as follows in the M.Ed. handbook:

Mathematics
Your practical experience of teaching mathematics to young children will be the starting point for a critical examination of theory and practice in schools, both manifest and hidden. You will share your experience with the other students, helping each other to investigate and analyse a range of ideas in the classroom situation. In this way you will extend your understanding of the process of mathematical learning in young children, and develop

your ability to plan, apply, and evaluate curricular policies in school. To help in this we will also examine the methods used to investigate the learning of mathematics, the general nature of mathematical learning in our infant schools, and the various ways in which mathematics curricula may be implemented and evaluated. It is anticipated that you will find many areas where research evidence is limited, or non-existent, and we hope you will rise to the challenge this offers.

Teachers are given an assignment to carry out and write up based on the *Action Research Planner* (Kemmis *et al.*, 1981) and they work through it over a period of several weeks bringing in their data for discussion at each stage.

M.Ed. (Y.C.)   *Assignment 4*
A small action research project in mathematics
(1) Plan
(4) Reflect   (2) Act
(3) Collect Data

Complete the cycle twice, then write a report.

This assignment was designed to satisfy two purposes: to help teachers to analyse and improve their practice in maths, and also to give some rehearsal to action research skills which will be needed for the dissertation.

More detailed aims for the exercise were as follows:

To develop:
- the ability to identify an aspect of teaching or select a problem for investigation
- an awareness of the multi-dimensional character of most teaching and learning so that the issue chosen can be put into context
- the ability to negotiate and collaborate with colleagues, headteachers, parents or others, so that classroom events can be related and affect school policies and goals
- the ability to recognize the implicit theories used in explaining classroom events
- the ability to search out and use professional literature to enhance understanding
- knowledge of a range of methods and techniques for gathering and processing data and criteria for the choice of the most suitable for a given purpose
- ability to carry through the action research cycle, to review teaching, to diagnose probable or possible factors affecting the situation, to

plan a course of action, to monitor and understand the implications for the next cycle of that monitoring, until a conclusion is reached.

– ability to draw conclusions for practice
– ability to use the benefits for immediate gain in teaching
– ability to compare experiences with other teachers to their mutual benefit.

Examples from the Teacher's Research Assignments Related to the Aims of the Unit

The following pages draw on the work done by teachers in response to the assignment set, using examples to show how far the aims were realized in practice and pointing out difficulties which arose. There were no problems in identifying an area though at the end of the exercise it was felt that some topics, e.g. division, were unsatisfactory because advisory texts were found to be less helpful in the chosen area than in other cases. There was some discussion over the setting up of 'special' situations in order to study them. One teacher felt strongly that the exercise should be undertaken on the 'normal' work of the class so that any findings would relate to everyday professional practice and since this is where it is hoped to gain insight it would be foolish to plan anything different or special. In practice it is difficult to set up and maintain something so special that it has no significance for everyday practice, though many of the teachers did try to set up an 'ideal' situation, devoting a lot of time to the initial planning. All of Section 1 in Kemmis's *Planner* needed much discussion before teachers could state their intentions, reasons and predictions for the chosen task. Some of the difficulties seem to arise from a feeling that all of this is not significant enough to be of interest. Is this an inevitable feature of tackling the teacher's everyday taken-for-granted practice? Perhaps it would be better simply to record present practice without the prior preparation, and then aim to improve the quality of the interaction.

Many of the teachers were led to contextualize issues raised in their search for explanations. 'This opens up frightening questions of how to plan learning activities which are useful to children whilst still satisfying the teacher's need to justify the role of the teacher and the paymaster's requirement of proof of learning and records.' The pressure which teachers feel to produce written evidence of the work in mathematics was often debated in the group, and led to the treatment of many wider issues about schooling and about society. In a smaller way most of the teachers chose to look at more than one child because a necessary social element was thus introduced, which is always present in the normal teaching situation.

The opportunity to collaborate in school with other teachers did not really arise in this deliberately limited exercise, though one teacher did work with another member of staff to mutual advantage.

The unintended and unanticipated data often confronted teachers with hitherto implicit theories of classroom practice. One teacher found himself provoked to question the use of structural apparatus on finding that his pupils failed to link what they did with the apparatus with the solving of set problems. His purpose in using the apparatus had been to increase understanding, yet these children were unable to transfer understanding from the manipulation of the blocks to more formal number work and were in fact using their rote knowledge of tables in order to manipulate the material to his satisfaction. They arrived at the answer, then arranged the apparatus to fit the answer. The teacher realized that he had internalized, without thinking, the idea that structural apparatus is intrinsically good at promoting understanding, when its use is far more problematic.

Another teacher found that a lack of ability to attend, to 'tune-in' to what was going on, was a great problem for the children. A successful gambit proved to be the making of shapes with the apparatus (straws and pencils). 'How many triangles can you make with 21 straws?' proved easier to answer than 'How many 3's can you make with 21 straws?' This kind of discovery can be said to be obvious with hindsight, but is not so easy to predict. The teacher had felt that the making of shapes might prove just an additional complication, rather than a motivational device and was surprised to find otherwise. He also found a change of pace necessary. He concludes 'the large steps originally envisaged were not made' and 'unintended and unanticipated consequences occurred, particularly the difficulties the children had in reading the work cards and in maintaining interest and concentration. The most important positive aspect resulting from this short series of experimental lessons was that there was no question but that teacher and children learnt more about each other and about problems both encountered.'

The next teacher had problems with a child she knew to be able but who was reluctant to work. She explored possible reasons and felt that the Cockcroft Report over-simplifies when it suggests that children vary greatly in the amount of time which they take to move through the stages. She went on to describe the tactics which she employed but commented, 'The ability to match the task, the quality and quantity of teaching and the scope of the learning situation to the child in an intimate situation proved very difficult which indicates that it must be a very hit and miss affair in the normal class.' She concluded, 'When we turn mathematicians into doers of sums is perhaps the moment we destroy pleasure for those who cannot and limit the horizons of those who can.'

Another problem was the use of reading to broaden thinking and support a line of argument in their essays; at least so the teachers claimed. Certainly it is not easy to use reading in the traditional way, as a source of quotations to support points. I felt that the difficulties they had stemmed from the nature of the task; it is hard to link practice and theory. All the teachers read widely but were dissatisfied with the usefulness of much of what they read. They showed considerable powers of discrimination between expository and explanatory texts, preferring books and articles about the processes of mathematical thinking to those which gave ideas for what to do. They had no time for 'tips for teachers' which 'didn't tell you anything'. General dissatisfaction was expressed with the kind of activities suggested in current schemes to develop children's understanding. Most schemes of work gave few details about why certain activities were suggested and this is the kind of detail which is needed if teachers are to judge whether or not the activities are successful. All this supports my view that they used their reading very well, in a much wider sense than simply backing up their opinions. I would claim that this 'theory' really did improve their practice. If it did not advance their thinking, they had no time for it.

Tape-recording of lessons proved the most popular methodological tool. All the teachers were very conscious of the need for an unbiased record of what actually happened, alongside other more anecdotal data-gathering procedures. The ease with which data can be collected this way is its main attraction. Other methods proved cumbersome if you had to teach at the same time, or were less reliable because written after the event from recollections. Even though transcription is tedious, the very repetitive nature of the task can bring its own insights into what is happening. These teachers were concerned to put the insider's case, backed by the careful collection and evaluation of data. Only one of the teachers used a third party as part of the investigation. There were difficulties in finding an appropriate third person, and it can be a very stressful procedure. Perhaps that is why the others shied away from it. The teacher who did have a colleague to help found her comments particularly useful, and was struck by the way the children confided in her, realizing for the first time that they were rather timid in their response to him, and that he needed to do more to put them at their ease.

Another interesting aspect of his report is a comparison between an anecdotal account, written immediately after the lesson, and a later analysis of the transcript of the tape-recording done at the time. The teacher says that his response in the first lesson ignores the possibility that the children might not understand the concept. He goes on to say 'analysis of the transcript appears to show a deep misunderstanding of the division task involved' and 'child misunderstandings are often easily missed, disregarded or misinterpreted'.

The teachers were certainly able to carry out the action research cycle but there were difficulties of several kinds. First, there were those of a practical nature, often concerning the need to isolate children so that an effective recording session could be arranged. Even in action research, where the nature of the situation is taken into account, research methods are not easy or straightforward and teachers always feel guilty about the rest of the class who may not be involved and who may be suffering as a result. There were also worries about the danger of the teacher becoming over-involved, with such a vested interest in the results that they might be altered disproportionately, or of becoming overly introspective, reading too much into situations, or of becoming so self-critical that it becomes destructive. Certainly, having carefully planned a session, the detailed statement tended to become a strait-jacket. Nearly all the teachers found themselves getting through the programme set regardless. Making the children fit their predictions became the most important guiding feature of the work though this was not usually realized until a stage later than transcribing from the tape-recording. Is this what happenes regularly in mathematics lessons when teachers are following set schemes? The fact that the hoops are there perhaps encourages teachers to feel that all the children must jump through them, and in a particular order too.

All the teachers said they had learned a good deal from this exercise, and that action research does improve teaching. The insights they claimed ranged from 'teachers stop children learning by their urge to teach', 'my manner which I believed would inspire confidence, bordered on harassment', and 'my language presented a barrier to the children' to 'I have greater understanding of the problems which children have and of the stages of development in mathematics' and 'I have been looking outward rather than reflecting more on my own performance, with a generalized "model" of what should be achieved rather than where the children actually are'.

In reading through the essays of these teachers and in talking to them about their work it is hard to think of other approaches which could have been as productive. All that we discover about learning suggests that we need to change our teaching methods and that what comes naturally as a method of teaching (tell them) is not the most helpful. The move from a recognition of this to the implementation of more helpful techniques is far from simple and the guilt feelings which arise from placing more responsibility on the learner do not help. There is this reluctance to stop teaching and observe instead, and an underlying unease derived from the belief that learning only occurs when direct teaching is going on, both of which have their bases in a praiseworthy desire to teach more effectively. How can we leave, apparently to chance, the learning of vital concepts? These doubts afflict the teacher educator too. Was it right to spend all those evenings discussing when they could have been spent 'teaching'? When I read the assignments the teachers have completed I am considerably reassured. I am reassured because they are good by any standards and also because they read as if they had meaning for the writer; they are far from being 'academic' exercises.

Within the group, experiences were shared to mutual benefit. An awareness of and confrontation with other beliefs and practices is an excellent way to become more aware of one's own stance. But in addition, conscientious teachers need a great deal of support when undertaking this kind of analysis. It comes much closer to home than many others, and all the teachers were grateful for the opportunity to talk with others who were sharing similar experiences.

It is impossible to say whether or not this leads to 'immediate gain in teaching'. The accounts make impressive reading, and it is hard to believe that such insights could be gained without an effect on practice. We intend to continue and as the teachers collect evidence about their teaching we tutors will do the same about ours, and perhaps in time will be able to report more confidently about such effects.

12

Initiating and Encouraging Action Research in Comprehensive Schools

TONY CASSIDY

Educational research is largely ignored by teachers. While many teachers are aware in a generalized way of recent trends in psychological, sociological and economic research into the theory and practice of education, the impact of this work on classroom teaching is minimal. In the case of more direct studies into teacher–pupil behaviour in the classroom, few teachers take the time to read them, and even fewer modify their own practice as a result.

Cynics may blame the anti–intellectual, anti–theoretical bias of many staffrooms, best characterized as 'its all very well for these researchers/lecturers/educationists, they don't have to take 4C last thing on a Friday'.

However, much professional pedagogic research is undeniably of little direct use to the teacher. Conventional criteria of rigorous methodology, formality of language, the search for verifiable and generalizable results, and adequate control of variables, result in published findings which are either so specific as to seem banal, or at a level of generality which seems hopelessly remote from the teacher's everyday experience.

For several years now, in two comprehensive schools, I have been involved in encouraging and co-ordinating teacher-based action research; first as a Scale 4 teacher with a responsibility for promoting effective learning and communication across the curriculum, and currently as a senior teacher with fairly wide responsibilities, including the professional development of staff, and the promotion of good classroom practice.

That action research could play a central role in the discharging of these responsibilities became apparent to me though my involvement with the Schools Council Project: Teacher–Pupil Interaction and the Quality of Learning (TIQL). I became a founder member of an Outer Network group based at Manchester Polytechnic in 1981 and through our work with tape transcripts of lessons I became aware gradually of the far-reaching applications of the teacher-as-researcher approach, especially when it involved a sizeable group of teachers in one school working on co-operative ventures and sharing their experiences and problems.

This paper is a brief summary of some of the projects in which I have been involved. It is intended as an indication of the potential for action research methods to go far beyond the classic model of the single teacher in the classroom, developing or testing strategies to deal with a particular problem. In my experience, co-ordinated action research can be a powerful tool for generating school-wide curriculum change, the professional development of staff, and quite radical changes to the ethos of a school.

In 1980 I set up and chaired a school working party containing teachers of English, physics, chemistry, history, geography, mathematics, craft, home economics, French and religious education, and with a cross section of seniority from heads of faculty to Scale 1 teachers. Our brief was to examine current classroom practice with regard to language: the role of written work, question and answer techniques, pupil talk, group discussion, reading for research, etc. In short, all the aspects of interaction which the HMI report, *Aspects of Secondary Education* (1979), had identified as contributing to the 'language climate' of the school.

After a meeting to clarify aims and methods I decided, fairly arbitrarily, on pupils' written work as our first area of enquiry. I had a suspicion that pupils spent an excessive amount of time writing, and that much of the writing was in itself fairly pointless. This suspicion was confirmed by our first piece of research as a group, which showed that an 'average' pupil, during the fourth and fifth years leading up to examinations, wrote nearly 320,000 words, plus about 400 pages of mathematical exercises. An average paperback book is about 60–70,000 words. Moreover, about two-thirds of the staggering volume of written work, excluding mathematics, consisted of either notes which were dictated, copied, or listed from a single text-book, or mechanical exercises testing recall or simple comprehension.

To my surprise, many of the other members of the working party did not share my dismay. Many of the teachers seemed to feel that the value of such written work was self-evident, since it kept the children quiet, made sure the syllabus was 'covered', and provided the pupils with the necessary factual information, which was seen as the teacher's primary responsibility. The statistics summarized above simply proved that the pupils were 'working well'. The pressure of external examination syllabuses was cited as ample justification for this approach to learning.

In an effort to counteract what I personally viewed as complacency, I began furnishing items for group discussion drawn from recent research and theoretical publications. These stressed such matters as the usefulness of purposeful writing with a clearly defined audience and communicative function; the use which can be made of personal discursive styles as opposed to the impersonal 'transactional' style so ubiquitous in schools, yet so alien to most children; the need for practice in such neglected areas as re-drafting, synthesizing and interpreting data instead of single-source copying, and the marshalling of opinion and argument.

These outside sources met with polite, momentary interest, or simple rejection as irrelevant to the day-to-day exigencies of 'getting through the syllabus' or 'making sure they've got all the notes'. The inability of conventional academic research and theory to influence classroom practice, was brought home to me most forcibly.

Attempts to supplement these outside sources with some minor work of my own were similarly unsuccessful. I had experimented with getting some pupils in an English lesson to write up an experiment from their previous chemistry class, using spontaneous personal language instead of the passive-voiced, 'objective' style usually demanded of them. A subsequent questionnaire to the pupils had revealed that they found the 'expressive' style much more useful for generating understanding of the chemical processes involved. The science staff on the working party were unimpressed. Recording the facts was paramount; it was even maintained that 'understanding' was a superfluous luxury, at least until the sixth form.

The discussions of the working party were published to the whole staff as a document, which they, in turn, discussed in groups and in plenary session at a staff meeting. Reactions ranged from mild, detached interest, through bafflement, cynicism, to downright hostility. A chemistry teacher reacted in outrage to the discussions on expressive versus transactional writing: 'It's my job to train scientists; I have to stamp out any personal reactions or opinions.' My inquiry as to what proportion of his comprehensive pupils went on to become practising scientists met with a snort of indignation. My attempts to bring educational research and current theory to bear on our everyday practice was summed up by a history teacher as 'just a lot of extra work dreamed up by [the author] to justify his scale point.'

It became obvious to me that any attempt to influence classroom practice which relied on a strategy of exposing teachers to educational research was doomed from the start. I decided to try direct intervention.

A clear implication of the vast amount of written work being done in class was that precious little talking was taking place. I had been committed, as an English teacher, to the value of small group talk in lessons, both for its intrinsic value in the personal development of the child, and its instrumental use in the acquisition of new concepts, skills and information. This commitment had been strengthened around this time by my involvement with the Schools Council project (see later). The lesson transcripts we had analysed and discussed demonstrated quite vividly that the limited amount of discussion which is allowed to take place in lessons is often of dubious educational value, mainly because of over-domination by the teacher.

There was, of course, nothing new in this observation. For many years, and particularly since the Bullock Report (1975), educational theorists and researchers had emphasized the point that the development of 'pupil talk' was a vital, but neglected area.

Yet relatively few teachers, certainly in the school where I was working, seemed prepared to take the apparently logical step of organizing pupils into small groups, and devising tasks where interactive talk is the main feature.

I decided to organize a 'Talk Day', on which *every* teacher in the school would organize their lessons around small group talk. The purpose was to focus attention on what was actually taking place in lessons, largely unquestioned, every day; to generate ideas for alternative methods as approaches to learning, and to make the whole school more talk conscious.

The key to the whole strategy was the active participation of all teachers in departing from customary practice, and monitoring and evaluating the results. In other words, each of the eighty members of staff would be conducting a small piece of action research, and then comparing findings.

All staff were issued with a handout explaining the venture, and the thinking behind it. An Inservice Training Session was organized, in which small group activities were experienced by the participating teachers. This was followed up by Faculty meetings, at which staff could discuss the possible application of these activities to their subject area. Each member of staff then selected a particular day during one designated week, planning all their lessons for that day around small-group talk activities. A questionnaire was issued afterwards to gauge teachers' responses to the experiment.

Throughout the organization of 'Talk Day', the small group of staff responsible for planning and execution had to overcome considerable resistance to the idea from their colleagues. Misunderstanding of the intention, and suspicion as to the value of pupil talk were very prevalent, and many teachers obviously felt defensive about this invasion of their classroom privacy. A combination of patient explanation, diplomacy, and the discreet pressure that could be applied because of the headmaster's enthusiastic support, was eventually sufficient to carry the scheme through.

The effect of the 'Talk Day' itself on the school was dramatic. Response from teachers was overwhelmingly positive. The tenor of subsequent staff discussions on the role of talk, and of small group work in general, was significantly different. More tangibly, results from the follow-up questionnaire were highly encouraging.

The questionnaire asked for brief details of (1) the most successful lesson, (2) in what ways was it successful? (3) the least successful lesson? (4) why was it unsatisfactory? (5) will this exercise affect your teaching in the future?

Forty-six questionnaires were returned completed. It is impossible to summarize the wide variety of lessons described in the responses. This response fully vindicated our belief in the potential versatility of small group talk.

Similarly, a detailed summary of the other responses is beyond the scope of this chapter, but very briefly, most teachers were impressed by the high level of enjoyment and commitment from the students, the fact that all, or nearly all students had contributed, even those who never normally participate in lessons, that the discussions were relevant throughout and showed a good degree of organization and group discipline, that there was clear evidence of teaching taking place, that group co-operation and 'teamwork' factors were high, and that often the discussions had taken off in new and unexpected directions, yielding new 'creative' insights and perspectives. Many of the comments summarized above were couched in terms of some surprise, and several teachers commented directly that the positive benefits of the lesson were unexpected.

Perhaps most significant in the context of the general thrust of this chapter, was that a clear majority stated unequivocally, even enthusiastically, that this experiment would have an effect on their teaching in future.

In my view one of the most useful by-products of the exercise had been staff discussions, in which teachers from different disciplines had begun tentatively to shed some of the privacy of the classroom, and to describe and compare with some frankness their habitual methods and approaches. The potential of this sort of co-operation was the starting point for my next piece of action research across the curriculum.

As I mentioned earlier, I had been involved, with research at Didsbury, in the study and discussion of lesson transcripts. It seemed that this could be a useful approach within school, so I assembled a group of volunteers interested in close examination of classroom interaction.

Our aim was to examine our own lessons with some degree of objectivity. The keeping of journals or lesson notes seemed insufficient for this purpose, since a teacher's perception of what has occurred in his lesson is inevitably coloured by a whole host of distorting factors. For example, the existence of a syllabus means that the teacher has an overall scheme in mind, a chain in which this particular lesson is but a single link. This perspective is usually denied to the pupil, who therefore has a very different perception of what is taking place, and acts accordingly. The teacher can become blinkered by his intentions, judging that today he has taught, or failed to teach, element two in a progression, while being blind to what has *actually* taken place; what messages have been communicated, what meaning created, in the hurly-burly of classroom interaction. This distorting conflict between intention and actuality becomes particularly acute when we are teaching concepts, skills and attitudes, rather than simply passing on information.

Transcripts of tape-recordings are a rich source of objective data, which, as well as being more reliable than teacher recall, and less artificial than observer's notes, also offer the possibility of analysing at leisure and in detail the qualitative aspects of interaction.

Our research group contained teachers of history, mathematics, art, English, vocational preparation and religious education. We established a pattern of regular meetings, at which we would discuss a transcript or transcripts, produced by a group member of a recent lesson. After the initial embarrassment at such self-exposure, the discussions became a rich source of insight and analysis into classroom practice. We discussed more than a dozen quite lengthy transcripts (Payne and Cuff, 1983). The following is a very brief summary of some of the issues raised in discussion over a period of several months.

Lesson openings were examined, particularly where the teacher was attempting to introduce a new topic. Apart from the organizational difficulties which were obvious in the transcripts, and the central problem of gaining and focusing attention, we discussed at some length the artificiality of the orthodox lesson opening, the hermetic 'sealing off' from all that has immediately preceded the pupils' entry, the centralized, authoritarian structure of the interchanges, and the ritualized behaviour. In transcripts, these features become clearly visible.

Pupil resistance and refusal to become involved seemed to be compounded of several elements, including quite often embarrassment at the seemingly pointless nature of what they were being asked to do, or uncertainty over what was required of them. Behind the apparent bloody-mindedness of the pupils, and the rather nervous and increasingly desperate questioning by the teacher, it was not difficult to detect embarrassment at the lack of a clearly discernible purpose or context for activities demanded of them. Teachers rarely made their overall intentions explicit to the pupils.

Indeed, much progressive teaching in recent years, in its concern to move away from the teacher-as-instructor model, and its emphasis on eliciting ideas as responses from pupils, and involving them in discourse, is vulnerable to this sort of mystification. Its classic symptom is the 'question and answer' session, of which we studied several.

Some bizarre features were noticeable in these interactions. The style and structure of discourse were of a type commonplace in the classroom, and yet it would be difficult to conceive of any other social situation in which they would be considered normal. There was evidence that pupils were often fully in possession of the necessary concepts and vocabulary to answer the teacher's leading questions, but were simply in the dark as to the meaning and direction of the questions. A well-meaning attempt to avoid dry, *ex cathedra* statement from the teacher had become an elaborate, ritualized game of 'guess what teacher wants'.

Over-domination of discussion by the teacher was obvious in other ways. The sheer quantity of teacher utterance, and the meagre amount of pupil contribution in contrast, was a feature of all the transcripts, in spite of the fact that most of the lessons had been characterized by the teachers as 'teacher–class discussion'. A feature which particularly interested the research group was teacher domination of content, and rejection of contributions by pupils which were not perceived as relevant. When studying the transcripts, teachers were often surprised and dismayed at the number of pupils' contributions which had been ignored or dismissed, because they had not fitted into the teacher's pre-conceived plan. We speculated on the long-term effect on pupils of this type of rejection.

Lessons often seemed structurally to resemble a game, the object being to guess what the teacher wanted; approval was the reward and rejection the punishment for any deviation from a narrow concept of relevance. It is hardly surprising, therefore, that like all games, they sometimes became competitive and aggressive. Several members of the research group, who as a matter of principle aim to make their lessons co-operative in style and supportive in atmosphere, were startled by the amount of competitive behaviour found in transcripts of their lessons. While some of this can be put down to personality clashes or universal human instincts, we discussed at some length the extent to which its origins are deeply embedded in the structures of classroom interaction.

These are some of the main issues which were raised by discussion of our transcripts. None of the preceding observations are particularly original. We could probably have culled theoretical approximations to most of them by reading up on educational texts. But to arrive at them by observing the particularities of our own lessons had a psychological and professional impact which no book could equal.

The next step seemed to be to unleash some of this on to the staff as a whole, to encourage them to take a similarly hard look at their own lessons. The school's Autumn Inservice days were devoted to a two-day conference on evaluation. The headmaster requested that our transcript group contribute two ninety-minute sessions for the whole staff.

We decided to dramatize our work, rather than simply to lecture. Using the transcripts like play scripts, we presented a talk on our observations, illustrated by members of the group reading edited highlights, taking the parts of teacher and pupils. The presentation was highly successful. The dramatic and particularly the humorous aspects of this approach were very useful in overcoming all the usual resistance and hostilities which one encounters when a large body of teachers suspects that one is telling them how they should teach.

Feedback was highly positive, both from the follow-up structured discussion groups, and informally from a large number of colleagues. As a result of the interest generated, our research group gained another five members, including the heads of chemistry, business studies and English.

After the wide-ranging, unstructured approach of our previous research, it seemed time to focus more directly on specific issues. Each member of the group was invited to nominate a particular area of interest, and then to involve at least one other member of staff, from outside the research group, in his/her research. In this way about twenty teachers (one quarter of the staff) would be involved in action research and evaluation, using data derived from lesson transcripts, interviews, questionnaires, etc. The aim was still to generate thoughts for discussion amongst staff, rather than to publish definitive results. The topics chosen were: the effect of pupils' conversation on the performance of individual tasks in art; pupils' perceptions of their classroom roles, and the origins of competitive and unco-operative attitudes in class discussion; difficulties in class question and answer sessions; conceptual and language problems in sixth form economics; communication difficulties arising from ambiguities in teachers' language; history with a mixed ability third year group – problems; sex-role factors in contributions to class and small-group discussion; comparison of different approaches to 'comprehension' work in English.

Unfortunately, I left shortly after this to take up a new post as senior teacher in another comprehensive school, and at present I have no information on how these initiatives are progressing.

In my current job, encouragement of action research is a specific part of my job description. So far this has proved problematic. Starting again from scratch, many of the familiar resistances and misunderstandings, have again been encountered. In addition, we are currently involved in our second lengthy period of industrial action in twelve months. Action research involves extra work outside the classroom, and involvement in evaluation and self-appraisal. Neither of these are popular in the current climate.

However, one interesting piece of research has been concluded. The aim was to get a picture of the real curriculum for second years, i.e. the sum total of experiences and activities undergone by a sample group of pupils through a week picked at random. Questionnaires were issued without warning, to teachers of the group at the end of the week, asking for precise details of who did what and for how long in each lesson, and what the aim of the lesson was. Several of the pupils were interviewed each morning throughout the week, asking for their impressions and recollections of the previous day's lessons. Longer interviews were transcribed at the end of the week. Heads of faculty were asked to provide details of faculty aims for second year pupils.

All this data has been condensed and summarized in various ways. For example, the following represents a percentage breakdown of pupil activity in lesson time, for the week under scrutiny.

Pupils' writing exercises	26.43%
Teacher talking, pupils listening	17.7%
Class question and answer	9.61%
Class question and answer (in French)	9.31%
Pupils doing practical work individually	9.0%
Pupils writing: copying notes	5.71%
Practical work in groups	5.41%
Admin: Giving out books, etc.	5.41%
Other input, e.g. tape, film, etc.	5.1%
Pupils' continuous writing: poetry	1.8%
Pupil input, e.g. reading out, addressing class	1.8%
Teacher reading with/to pupils	1.8%
Pupils' continuous writing: prose	0.6%
Other	0.3%
Pupils discussing in pairs or groups	0.0%
Pupils reading	0.0%
Pupils writing: making own notes	0.0%

Other charts summarized the skills and abilities which the week's lessons were designed to develop, the lesson content, and the features of the lesson recalled by students the following day.

The data provide powerful critical ammunition for those who would argue that our curriculum is fragmented, lacking any overall coherence, that it emphasizes *ad nauseam* a narrow range of skills, and that it has little genuine impact on pupils. When the data were discussed by staff at an inservice day there was considerable dismay and some fairly radical reappraisal.

As a result, a small team of teachers are currently working on designing an integrated, skills-based course for lower school pupils, starting in the first year.

This chapter, based on personal experiences in two comprehensive schools, hopefully illustrates the range and versatility of classroom-based action research in promoting evaluation, reappraisal, co-operative working amongst teachers, and innovation in curriculum and method. Viewed in their broadest sense, the methods and principles of action research can make a significant contribution to solving many of the problems with which schools are beset. Current emphasis on the need for constructive evaluation of teaching effectiveness, and supportive professional development of staff, can only begin to lead towards real progress where the specifics of classroom interactions are analysed by the participants themselves, using methods that promote genuine change. These initiatives rarely occur spontaneously, however. There is a need for committed research leaders in schools, who are willing and able, whatever their official designation, to set about the difficult and often frustrating task of persuading teachers to open up their work to scrutiny.

The role of research leader or co-ordinator is vital, but extremely delicate. For action research style ventures to succeed, the active and honest participation of staff is essential. So their perception of the role and status of the research leader is crucial. Someone junior to them in professional ranking is unlikely to carry sufficient weight to persuade teachers into irksome and sometimes threatening tasks. On the other hand, a member of the traditional hierarchy of senior teachers and deputy heads, is likely to be treated with suspicion and defensiveness, by teachers worried that the sort of appraisal I have described here might have more sinister overtones. Perhaps a role such as 'Professional Staff Tutor' might strike the right balance.

Current developments in the area of teacher appraisal are likely to throw these problems into much higher relief. There is a real danger that the potential usefulness of the action research model, the applications of which we are only beginning to explore, will be lost amongst demands for cruder, superficial methods of appraisal, externally imposed upon reluctant teachers.

TWO LARGE-SCALE PROJECTS: EXTERNALLY INITIATED CONCERNS

At the end of *Inside a Curriculum Project*, Shipman (1974, p. 177) notes that 'The way to effective curriculum development may lie, not in more efficient projects, but in narrowing the distance between schools and the agencies in education that administer, advise and train, or generate new ideas.' This final section consists of contributions from people involved in two relatively large-scale projects in the Manchester area, and it is our view that these materials do serve to raise some further questions about collaboration between schools and other agencies. The central purpose, however, is not in any sense to overview these two projects, or to compare them, but rather to provide some additional resources which document interesting action research practices, and which raise questions about action research.

The first of these projects was jointly directed by Alison Kelly, a sociology lecturer at Manchester University, and Judith Whyte, an education lecturer at Manchester Polytechnic. Starting in 1979 it received joint funding from the Equal Opportunities Commission and the Social Science Research Council for the first three years. The project directors have written extensively about the project, particularly as regards its action research character, (Whyte and Smail, 1982; Kelly, 1985) and a useful way into the project is provided by Judith Whyte (1984, pp. 75–6) who notes that:

Girls into Science and Technology (GIST) is a project based in mixed comprehensive schools in the North of England. Its aim is to improve girls' attitudes to science and technology and to increase female participation in physical science and craft options at school. We are not only investigating causes of female under-achievement in science and technology, but simultaneously trying to change the situation. This 'action research' approach requires us to combine traditional research concerns with practical school-based activity. We have, for instance, brought women working in science and technology into schools as positive feminine role models while attempting to evaluate the impact of these visits on pupils' attitudes (see Smail, 1982). We also work with teachers to sensitise them to the nature and effects of gender stereotyping in the school and the classroom.

(Smail et al., *1982; Whyte, 1983)*

The action orientation of GIST means that we do not just aim to investigate inequalities but to inform teachers about our findings, and help them to devise appropriate intervention strategies in the immediate school context. For example, the evidence gathered about girls' poorer opportunities to engage in 'tinkering activities' such as using a saw, mending a bicycle or playing with Meccano was fed back to teachers, some of whom then decided that it was both desirable and justifiable to run single sex craft clubs to compensate girls for the experiences they lacked.

Our practical aim was to help teachers become aware of the way gender impinges on classroom interaction with presumed effects on learning outcomes for boys and girls. We also hoped to cast some light on whether laboratories and workshops are more male dominated than the classrooms in which other subjects are taught, the concrete processes which make them so, and also how far it might be possible to promote positive change.

The problem was to devise an observational tool which could quantify the variable participation of girls and boys with some degree of objectivity, and at the same time operate as a training technique to increase teachers' awareness of interactions. Ideally, we hoped to be able to feed back the results of observations to a teacher almost instantaneously, and so involve him or her as a collaborator in reaching a solution to the problem we had set ourselves. In this, our approach resembles the Ford Teaching Project, where the researcher John Elliott developed a method for self-monitoring of classroom questions in order to assist teachers in evaluating how far their questions contributed to an inquiry or discovery approach to learning.

(Elliott & Hurlin, undated)

As a project, it was particularly interesting in its attempt to engage in research both *on* schools and teachers along largely traditional quantitative lines, and also to generate collaborative action research with teachers. It was felt that the two strands would be complementary by displaying that there was a problem, a cause for concern, which teachers could and should address, together with help from the GIST team. Simply put, this initial combination of targets on the part of the GIST team raises some interesting questions about collaboration between 'outsiders' and 'school staff': to what extent, for example, did the initial thrust of the project serve to identify the project as the GIST team's research project rather than the schools' project? To what extent, also, should participants in the action, i.e. especially teachers, be fully involved in the early planning of strategies for action? This returns us to some of the issues raised in the introductions to section A and section B: issues relating to the need for agendas to be mutually constructed, and for action research facilitators to develop adequate conceptualizations as to what the practical concerns and relevancies of teachers are, and how to relate to these within particular institutional structures.

The contributions here are selected so as to give some impression of the variety within the project. John Thompson provides a useful overview of the impact of the project in one school, and in so doing describes the general pattern of strategies which the GIST team used across all the involved schools. Glenys Ward reports on her experience of the observational tool which Judith Whyte refers to above, and which was one specific strategy used across schools. Sid Slater, as headteacher, and Dave Bowes, within the same school, describe and appraise, from somewhat different perspectives, one quasi-experimental strategy which they decided to explore, but which was not a feature of the project across other schools. Each one of these contributions displays an interesting mix of quantitative and qualitative data. They also provide a range of differing perspectives concerning the contributors' perceptions of their own involvement in the project, and a deliberate choice was made here to include contributors of differing degrees of seniority within the schools. These perceptions can be placed alongside or against the final GIST contribution, by Hustler and Cuff, which draws on an explicit attempt to tap teachers' perception of the GIST project and GIST issues.

The second project also stems from a clear-cut initiative external to schools. At Sheffield in July 1982, Sir Keith Joseph announced a government funded programme to develop a new educational deal for fourth and fifth form pupils who were not benefiting fully from school. Sir Keith commented, 'I believe that in all too many instances we have still not got the mixture right for those pupils who are usually described as lower attainers; broadly, the group for whom pupil examinations at 16+ are not designed.' He went on to say, 'I am announcing this programme on this occasion because you are the providers. But you and I know that good education is made by good teachers. I take it as axiomatic that teachers will be fully involved in the programme. What they bring to it will be crucial to its success.'

Manchester LEA was successful in its bid for a distinctive and ambitious version of this Lower Attaining Pupils project, termed by Manchester: Alternative Curriculum Strategies (ACS). There is no intention here of commenting on the project overall (see, for example, Cockett and Milroy, 1983/4; *Times Educational Supplement*, 27.1.84; Hustler and Ashman, 1985), except to note two points. First, the LEA has relied extensively on schools and teachers to plan and deliver the project. It started by inviting its own schools to bid for funded inclusion in ACS with their own proposals which were to be drawn up in accord with very general criteria of the sort which Mike Cockett, the project leader, identifies in his contribution. Second, a very rapid start to the project was made in September 1983. If much of the flavour of the project for pupils was to be 'learning by doing', then this was certainly also the flavour for teachers.

The key contributions in this section are from Hodgson, Rollins and Davies. Hodgson describes some strategies relating to the involvement of parents and staff development. Rollins focuses on his experience of developing viable relationships with pupils and the lessons learnt between 1983 and 1984. Davies provides a description of the overall curricular structure and particular curricular offerings which seemed to work for his school. Although some may view these materials as further displays of teachers 'reinventing the wheel', we would wish to make two points. In the first place, the contributions convey the conviction that for these teachers it is *their* project, a sense not always conveyed through the GIST materials. In the second place, we happen to agree with Mike Cockett where he argues that there are no outside 'experts' in this area overall. What these materials also display, and what the introductory contributions from Cockett and Hill point to more abstractly, is the capacity of these teachers to appraise situations, take action (often 'chancing their arm'), monitor their experiences and learn lessons from them. The project was not explicitly designed as an action research project, yet there are clearly some, though perhaps not all, of the features which we would associate with an action research stance. We leave readers to arrive at their own judgments here.

It also seems appropriate to close this book with materials which do in our view display that 'good education is made by good teachers'. Here and throughout the rest of this book, it is apparent that good teachers include those who systematically appraise their practice, who use and analyse their actions as teachers to find out more about effective teaching and who are prepared to be explicit about these processes: explicit to themselves and to others. It is perhaps incumbent upon a Secretary of State for Education to recognize more fully the resources which the teaching profession has within it, and make the most of these resources, not least by the appropriate provision of the 'quality time' referred to by Hill and echoed by many other contributors to this book.

13

Some Unseen Effects
of GIST

JOHN THOMPSON

INTRODUCTION

The school in which I teach was involved in the GIST action research project and I was closely involved in my role as Head of Science for that period. I am now Head of Upper School within the same school, closely involved with curriculum planning and pupils' choice procedures.

This article is not an attempt to describe the direct results of the GIST programme as that has been thoroughly explained elsewhere (Kelly *et al.*, 1984). Here I shall attempt to survey the more general, perhaps more covert effects of an action research programme within a department and the school as a whole, looking at staff's individual and collective attitudes and expectations.

THE SCHOOL AND THE PROJECT

The school was and still is an 11–18 mixed comprehensive situated in an urban area of Greater Manchester. It has been comprehensive since 1963 and entry is basically non-selective, being from local feeder primary schools. There is some movement of pupils to single sex schools in the borough – it was 12 in 1980 and is 6 for 1984. The majority of these movements are of girls.

On entry to the school pupils are placed in mixed ability tutor groups and they are all taught in those groups for the first three years. There were 263 pupils in nine tutor groups in September 1980. In science as in other subjects some children were withdrawn into a compensatory education group on the basis of school observation and testings of practical, manipulative and verbal skills in the first half term at school. These children have all participated in all stages of the project.

The local authority was approached by the project staff and the local adviser offered our name as being a school to approach. This approach was in the form of a two-stage talk by members of the GIST project, first to the science and crafts departments, and then to the staff as a whole. They outlined current research into the performance of girls in physical science compared to boys of the same general ability level and other related factors such as subject choice at 14, teacher attitude to girls and pupils' attitude to science at 11. They asked us, if we decided to take part in the project, initially to:

– participate in a series of workshops to be held in the school to increase our awareness of the extent to which sex stereotyping occurs in school;
– conduct tests of children's attitude and knowledge in science and technology for comparison with later choice and performance;
– accept visits to school by women working in scientific and technological jobs who could act as role models for girls.

After lengthy discussion and despite some reservations, the department decided unanimously to become involved in the project. Assorted members of the science and crafts staff took part in workshops in the summer term of 1980 and the project began in earnest in September 1980, with the target group's entry into school.

THE INITIAL PROGRAMME

The testing programme started immediately on arrival at school with an Image of Science and a Science Knowledge test being done within a week of arrival. The co-operation of tutors was invaluable as time was of the essence here to fit in all the early tests before the children began forming opinions of the science they were to meet in school. Throughout the first term the pupils had fairly regular questionnaires/ tests on scientific curiosity, scientific activities and more personal background and school attitudes.

It was hoped that the procedure for conducting the tests was uniform for all groups. Staff were asked if the pupils showed any reaction to the tests before, during or after and whether they took it seriously or not. Where possible, absentees were followed up. All marking of the tests was undertaken by the project members. We did receive results but not for individuals. Indeed the project members only know the pupils as numbers. I held the only match to pupils' names. For purposes of analysis the pupils' numbers were indicated only by boy or girl annotation.

As Christmas approached the science department completed its battery of testing and we held another meeting with the GIST project staff for them to outline the next stage of the project. Also at this time the craft department became involved, administering a smaller number of tests on spatial visualization and mechanical reasoning.

FURTHER INTERVENTION STRATEGIES

The second joint meeting between the department and GIST now outlined the strategies for the continuance of the programme. In summary they were:

- a planned series of women scientists visiting science teaching groups to explain their role as scientists in commerce or academic life. It was hoped that this would demonstrate the feasibility of girls doing science subjects and making careers out of science (the VISTA programme).
- Development of pieces of work to encourage continuous writing work in the physical sciences as girls tend to be better at this form of response.
- The distribution of specially prepared posters to indicate the success that women scientists have had in major scientific discoveries and developments.
- The holding of inservice day courses to meet other schools involved in similar programmes and to hear of any current relevant research.

All these strategies took place with varying response from staff and pupils. We still as a science department use the prepared posters. Later meetings with the GIST team led to development of several items, e.g. potted biographies of a number of women scientists. A student on teaching practice at the time of the project began a small-scale investigation into behavioural differences between boys and girls in our classrooms. This investigation was I think beginning evidence of the underlying current that the GIST programme developed in our staff.

The simple observation that arose from it was that several male teachers asked girls far fewer questions than were asked of the boys. Knowledge arising from that observation lead to a small but perceptible change in some teachers, approaching perhaps a beginning of an eye opening for many of us.

The women scientists first visited us in early March 1981 and we had a steady stream of visitors. Each tutor group had at least two visitors by the end of the year and by the end of the project we had at least five. The women visitors had several features in common:

- they had no teaching experience with this age group;
- they were all practising scientists or technologists;
- they were all terribly interested in their own subjects.

This led to a number of problems which were overcome to a greater or lesser extent depending on the personality of the individual speaker:

- the language was too technical
- some of the talk content was not of interest
- questions were asked by the visitors but answers were not prised out of less alert pupils, only the same few tended to answer
- they tended to ask questions and then answer them themselves if there wasn't an immediate response
- they all tended to prefer a more informal atmosphere, e.g. come and sit round me rather than sit where they could be easily seen and heard.

Nevertheless after a few talks most of the women began to open up and several of them became very lively and stimulating talkers to the groups. The children were also now more likely to ask questions. We were surprised at the beginning of the programme how many of the pupils did in fact ask questions of complete strangers.

Some tutor groups were also involved in filming for a television programme devoted to the issue of sex stereotyping in school subjects, especially in the sciences. The programme concentrated on steps being taken to encourage girls into school science courses and then on to engineering apprenticeships. The children reacted by taking the excitement of filming easily in their stride. Perhaps one of the social benefits of the VISTA programme has been the improved reception of strangers by the pupils – not only in an academic sense but also socially.

The visitors that came into school were used on occasion as subjects for active tutorial work within the school's personal and social education programme. For tutor groups who had science teachers as tutors this was an opportunity to develop activities in other curriculum areas, thus using the GIST programme as a trigger for further development.

SOME INITIAL GIST CONCLUSIONS

Soon after the release of these findings we began to plan a new human biology course for the upper school which is now offered to fourth year pupils. I suspect that it hadn't been offered before because the biology course in existence was attracting considerable support and interest, so a new course didn't seem necessary, yet clearly it was because on its first offer it attracted over half the pupils who might normally have been expected to take up biology itself.

The lower school science curriculum has also been re-examined closely recently. The course had originally been based on the Nuffield combined science scheme and had been adapted to our equipment and requirements. It had been re-written attempting to change our approach to incorporate some of the observations inherent in the GIST programme results such as being less didactic, more open ended, more problem solving, and more centred on a child's perception of a topic than a teacher's perception.

The results of the initial testing programme can be found in detail in the Initial GIST Survey Booklet. I shall only deal with some points that when raised seemed more appropriate to the school although many are clearly applicable to all the schools involved to a greater or lesser extent.

On the Science Knowledge Test before the children had experienced formal science lessons, in our school, boys are better on multiple choice and structured questions whereas girls did better on the essay – they wrote more, displayed more knowledge, and handwriting, grammar and spelling were better.

Girls did slightly better on biology multiple choice questions than boys, who did better on physics.

The Science Curiosity Test asked which topics from likely lower school science topics children would like to learn about. Both sexes in all schools were most interested in learning about the human body. In our school, girls were even less interested in physical sciences than the average for girls in all the other schools. They were more interested in nature study than girls in other schools. The boys were slightly less interested in physical science and nature study than boys in other schools.

As a result of these findings, we have begun to introduce elements of human biology as examples wherever possible.

We try to avoid examples which are linked to boys' interests and to use substitute ones based on experience common to both sexes. For example, we used to illustrate the concept of a force by asking children to pull on chest expanders. Now, we use ordinary elastic and expanding luggage fasteners instead.

Observation of lessons by outside agencies taught us the need for care when equipment is distributed. Boys certainly grab the best equipment if given the opportunity – and indeed if allowed they will patrol classrooms for more! Boys tend to answer first and tend to be asked first when there is a teaching class dialogue. More structuring of handing equipment to specific children and asking named children questions enables the girls to get a fairer deal.

Several teachers tried different policies for seating organization in attempts to break down the sex-segregated way in which children usually arrange themselves. The most successful strategy for obtaining mixed working groups has been to announce that during the lesson the class must form groups which do not contain anyone they usually sit next to or work with. If the lesson is a problem-solving one, groups can be built up gradually, starting with pairs working together on one problem then forming fours and eights. Often, when prevented from forming sex-segregated friendship groups in this way the most inventive girls and boys end up working together and producing highly original solutions.

Other teachers started children off in the first year in assigned mixed working groups. In some cases the groups stayed together even after the seating restrictions were lifted, but, in general, they reverted to friendship groups after the first term.

THE SCHOOL AND GIST

The GIST programme which we had embarked upon revealed some gaps in our curriculum both in the lower and upper school. A response was believed necessary by the teachers involved in the management of the science department, but only a response from all the science staff could have produced the necessary positive response.

GIST showed us deficiencies and also suggested some solutions, but its main contribution was to help to create an atmosphere of questioning and intent to develop new ideas amongst the staff.

Lack of satisfaction with the whole school curriculum was an attitude that accompanied some senior staff to an LEA inservice conference in 1982. With considerable desire and enthusiasm to be pointed in new directions we listened to speaker after speaker enthuse about the need to develop the vocational and academic work of the 16+ age group. This led us towards the MSC and associated YTS schemes. We could not involve ourselves in the YTS but we have recently developed a TVEI programme which has demanded considerable curriculum input from teaching staff. The GIST programme has had no direct effect on the development of a TVEI programme but I suspect its appearance in school began a process of awareness and interest that perhaps led to a much easier reception of MSC ideas than would otherwise have been feasible.

Staff during the GIST programme began using the phrase 'being, or been, GISTed'. It was a phrase that implied that somebody had demonstrated some degree of reception or implementation of the ideas of GIST. I wonder if it also meant that staff were becoming imbued with the idea of development and change as a natural process. Had the school been GISTed as a whole, thus being more open to suggestion and change?

We were concerned part way through the project about the effect on our boys. Would emphasis on girls have a negative effect on the boys? If many girls chose science subjects in year 4 would we be able to cope logistically? In fact the pattern of choices has not changed very much at all; this may be more a result of our choice process than any influence or lack of it by the GIST project. The choice procedure has been examined closely, again probably not as a direct result of the GIST project but as a result of its general influence on staff attitude.

Certainly one result of this examination has been on re-structuring of both the process and the phrasing of the careers advice given to pupils. There were areas where advice was not helpful to girls and these I hope have all been removed. A reverse trend has of course been the encouragement of boys to do some subjects not normally associated with them, e.g. boys doing the new TVEI food industries course and child care and development, as well as girls doing design studies.

A re-writing of our guidance programme has enabled us to assess our advice not only to pupils but also parents, perhaps still the main influence on pupils' choices and consequently in some cases a major stumbling block to a pupil making a choice against the normal trend. The guidance booklet is aimed at pupils but hopes to influence parents as well. This will I suspect prove to be much more difficult simply because parents' values are probably much more deepseated and we are not able to give them as much information as the pupils.

Pastorally, two changes have occurred in recent years that may or may not have been influenced by GIST. Did GIST develop a feeling for equality in the school for all pupils, and has this helped create an atmosphere that led to the relaxation of dress rules for girls in that they can now wear trousers, and that corporal punishment for boys has not been used for over two years?

We have developed a school-based work experience scheme for disaffected fifth years as a form of alternative curriculum strategy. Perhaps this has been indicative of a view that when teachers feel something is correct, they go ahead and do it and spend hours arguing about why they should or should not do it later.

CONCLUSION

The teachers at school before GIST would certainly have had particular views and attitudes that I am not sure GIST had measured in a manner which would have allowed any accurate comparison before and after the project. Any attitude changes of staff, individually, or as a whole, may be slight but only a few small changes in technique would I suspect have an effect on pupils.

Teachers as a group of professionals, I believe, do not particularly like being told to undertake a major change in their technique or curriculum content, but they will adapt if the climate is right. I believe the GIST programme helped to create a more suitable climate that was to allow several major pastoral and curriculum changes in recent years. Within the departments the project certainly widened some teachers' views and helped them develop a more global view of school as opposed to a narrow departmental view. It raised questions of the curriculum which led to questions of school and teaching philosophy, perhaps most of all it led some teachers to believe that there is more to teaching than teaching.

On balance, of the three groups involved in the project the teachers, the pupils and the GIST project team, I believe the teachers have gained most. There has not been a dramatic effect on pupils' choice patterns, but teachers individually and as a group I think learnt a lot more, in that we began to ask questions and we have continued to do so, leading to developments that might not otherwise have occurred.

14

Curriculum Innovation
and Evaluation

SIDNEY SLATER

Early in my teaching career I became aware of the under-representation of girls in the physical sciences. This awareness arose when I moved from my first teaching post in a girls' comprehensive school to a mixed co-educational comprehensive school. My interest in this area was reawakened when studying for my M.Ed Degree at Brunel University and again when I was approached by the GIST project team in my role as Deputy Head at Ashgrove High School, Manchester.

There were, of course, a range of reasons for becoming involved: first, to reduce, if not eliminate, sex stereotyping, particularly in terms of science and technology; secondly, to aid curriculum design, particularly in the craft and science areas; thirdly, to improve classroom interaction; fourthly, an opportunity to enhance staff inservice training and finally, the possibility of a limited amount of extra resources.

The experience at Ashgrove High School proved to be successful in changing certain staff attitudes towards girls, particularly in the traditional heavy craft areas, where GIST had run some workshops for teachers. Comment like 'Girls should not really do heavy crafts' changed over a period of time to 'Look what this girl has achieved, it's better than the boys'. However, there was still a problem in terms of the girls' uptake at fourth year option level in terms of both science and technology.

On taking up my new appointment as headteacher, at another High School in 1982, I was again approached by the GIST team to discuss the strategies we were going to employ in the new school. (Manchester had reorganized its schools in 1982 and a large number of new staff were appointed to my school.) The Head of Science, David Bowes, had six classes to judge the effect on the option choices to be made at the end of the third year. I was particularly keen to pursue this area of action research as I had already seen the effect of single sex teaching in terms of option choices earlier in my career. The pressures on a headteacher and staff of a newly organized comprehensive school are great and we decided that we would not pursue other strategies with regard to the craft technology side of projects. This was despite considerable, it seemed like weekly, pressure from the GIST team.

ORGANIZATION OF THE PROGRAMME

The programme in science involved single sex teaching in one half of our third year, the year being split into half-year groups for teaching purposes, group A three classes and group B two classes. It was decided to use only group A and to split the classes into a girls' group, a boys' group and a mixed control group. All the classes in year three were taught in mixed ability groupings. The classes alternated between chemistry, biology and physics being taught by specialist teachers. It was therefore essential to standardize practice and for this reason schemes of work were strictly adhered to. David Bowes discusses the programme in detail in his contribution.

EVALUATION OF THE PROJECT

This action research needed in-depth evaluation if it was to prove useful in terms of future planning. There were, of course, basically two ways of collecting information open to us, first, quantitative research and secondly, qualitative research. The decision to involve both types of data collection reflected the seriousness with which we treated the project. The need also for triangulation to improve the reliability and validity of the research was also a deciding factor. Formative research involved a number of techniques:

- Regular teacher team meetings to discuss the work for forthcoming weeks to ensure standardization.
- Staff teaching on the project kept diaries of the events in the classroom and reported back to team meetings.
- Observation of lessons carried out by my first deputy head teacher.
- End of topic tests, half-year examinations.

Summative evaluation included: pupil questionnaire; individual pupil interviews; teaching staff reports and statistical data re final option choices.

SUMMARY OF RESULTS

The questionnaire and interviews revealed that the majority of girls preferred to be taught in single sex classes for science. The most common reasons were based around the following statements given by the girls.

> I feel that boys mess about more and girls seem to want to work more.
> You get more attention from the teacher in girls' classes.
> Boys make a lot of noise.
> Girls seem to be grown up by this age and boys haven't.
> You can get to the apparatus.
> My work has improved.
> My examination marks are better.

However, it was also clear that most of the girls felt it unnatural to have only girls' groups and did not want this grouping to continue in all subjects.

The boys on the other hand were evenly distributed in their feelings towards single sex teaching, some felt it to be an advantage, others identifying clear disadvantages. The most common advantage given for single sex teaching was that 'girls were always talking' and the main disadvantage was that 'girls will help with difficult work' and 'help boys to behave'!

Teacher team meetings and classroom observations showed that it took some time for pupils to settle down to the new groupings. However, after this initial settling down period the girls' group worked well together. Indeed, the teachers' reports and end of topic tests/ examinations, showed that the girls' work had improved in the single sex class. One teacher reported:

> The amount of work and standard has been much higher in this group than in others. The average half year examination marks are 10–20 per cent higher in this group than in the boys' group.

Another reported that, 'Girls became turned on to science.'

However, it was felt that the boys' group did not achieve as much as they could and one young member of staff expressed it as follows, 'A monster-like boys' group was created.'

The final option groupings revealed that the programme of single sex teaching had been successful in increasing the number of girls taking physical sciences.

FUTURE ACTION

It is clearly unwise to generalize from such a small-scale study.

However, the feeling was that the strategy had been successful enough for us to continue with the programme in the next academic year. The decision to teach all third year science groups in single sex classes was taken and a similar in-depth evaluation of the programme would be undertaken.

THE GIST TEAM

I must thank the GIST team members for keeping us on our toes. They had a difficult job, not made any easier by the reorganization of the secondary sector in Manchester.

The feeling expressed by all the staff involved was that the programme was very worthwhile.

15

Single Sex Science Teaching: a Route to Bias-Free Choices in Science for Third Year Pupils

DAVID BOWES

This action research was begun in 1981 at a neighbourhood comprehensive school which is on a shared use site with a large and rapidly
expanding Open College, a leisure and performing arts centre, youth
centre and old folks' club. It has a reputation for forward thinking and
has been involved in much of the educational innovation which has
taken place in the area in recent years. The staff are aware and keen to
respond to new initiatives where these offer a positive way of enhancing
the learning potential of children. In brief terms this was the
background against which the particular research developed; an
atmosphere of innovation, a staff which was enthusiastic, and perhaps
most importantly an institution where care for the progress of all pupils
was of paramount importance.

There was a well-established pattern within the fourth and fifth
science groups which was a source of genuine concern. It was a worry
for us. The pattern seems to exist in many schools and so will be
known to many teachers. Stated in simple terms it is that girls tend to
choose biology or biologically based subjects in these years in the
secondary school and they seldom choose chemistry or physics. Boys,
by contrast tend to choose the exact opposite, many taking chemistry
or physics, few taking biological studies. Whilst this known and
established pattern may offer certain advantages in terms of class
homogeneity, it may be self perpetuating and based on perceptions
which are erroneous and ideas founded on misconceptions rather than
truth. Clearly the motivation which underlies the pattern of choice was
beyond the scope of this research, but a consideration of these factors
did play a part in the thinking and planning which went into the
project.

The science department had long had a reputation for the open,
even-handed treatment of both girls and boys; there was a blend of staff

who were keen to assist in a scheme which might 'break the circle'. The science curriculum had been developed to give every pupil a sound grounding in basic science skills and concepts in years one and two. Year three was a time to experience those concepts, skill and knowledge areas which are peculiar and special to chemistry, biology and physics. My own view was that each child should be exposed to that subject specialism by the specialist, who would teach with fire and enthusiasm. Children would then have a good idea of what the subject involved when they came to choose fourth and fifth year options.

The two-year 'O' level courses were only part of the science provision. Various Mode I and III CSE courses were also offered which provided possibilities for pupils of all abilities to continue with their science education to a level of their choosing.

Against this curriculum background ran extra curricular activities which were scientifically orientated. Lower and upper school science clubs, for instance, were much influenced by the Girls into Science and Technology project (GIST) and therefore geared to making science as accessible as possible to girls. We were increasingly careful to bear in mind what topics, activities and projects would stimulate and attract girls and boys. Staffing too was important – the need for female role models was considered important. Laboratory work was enhanced and made more appealing to girls by the visits of women scientists. They came in to explain their work – this often fitted into the pattern of lab work. An example of just one such visit was an embryologist joining a first year session dealing with reproduction. Her marvellous aids, exhibits and enthusiasm added greatly to the enjoyment of the work unit.

In sum, therefore, the department was well motivated and aware that if children were to make fully informed choices at the end of the third year some systematic device had to be found to bring about the experiences against which informed choice could be made.

A number of strategies were considered:

– To develop a system of careers advice which would fully inform and lead to more reasoned choices of options.
– To upgrade the systems of consultation and advice at the time of choosing subjects.
– The development of syllabuses which made chemistry and physics and biology more relevant and stimulating. Single sex teaching groups in science lessons.

In fact no single strategy was adopted and an attack was made on a number of fronts. Careers advice was given greater priority and audio-visual material produced by GIST was the mainstay for this. Syllabuses were renewed and through the pastoral system more emphasis was placed on the counselling programme. In the year 1982/3 the experiment which involved single sex groups began.

1981/2

no treatment

1982/3   6 groups in 3rd year

½ year no treatment			Experimental group		
Mixed ability Mixed sex	Mixed ability Mixed sex	Mixed ability Mixed sex	Mixed ability Mixed sex	Mixed ability Males only	Mixed ability Females only
ABC	ABC	ABC	ABC	ABC	ABC

Teacher A = Biology, B = Physics, C = Chemistry

1983/4   4 groups in 3rd year

Experimental group		Experimental group	
Mixed ability Males only ABC	Mixed ability Females only ABC	Mixed ability Males only ABC	Mixed ability Females only ABC

Teacher A = Biology, B = Physics, C = Chemistry

1984/5   6 groups in year

Mixed ability Males AEF	Mixed ability Females AEF	Mixed ability Males DBF	Mixed ability Females DBF	Mixed ability Males ABC	Mixed ability Females ABC

A) Biology   B) Physics   C) Chemistry
D)   E)   F)

Essentially the experimental design was very simple – far too naïve in its approach and consequently not suitable for the parametric analysis of any data which might accrue. If the design was simple, however, so was the intention and that was to find out if the girls and boys altered the pattern of choosing science subjects as a result of the treatment.

As can be seen above, all pupils in the treatment groups of 1982/3 were mixed ability and were taught by the same teacher for each specialism. It was hoped that this strategy would reduce teaching style/personality influences to a minimum.

At the outset all the pupils in the treatment groups were given a very brief idea that the project was primarily to test new curriculum materials which might be expected to work more or less well with either boys or girls. Teacher expectations were altered but not those of the pupils. Staff were expected to use the same course, objectives and teaching methodology with each group taught, trying always to maintain similar standards across the experimental group.

Data on options choice was recorded for the untreated year 1981/2 and followed the observed pattern already mentioned. This was to be used as a base line against which to judge any changes which might arise as a result of the treatment. This was not the only criterion on which results were based. Each week staff completed a diary in which they recorded those details which they considered of interest and importance. The teaching team met each week to discuss these documents. Senior staff interviewed a selection of pupils from each of the experimental groups and finally the pupils themselves were presented with a questionnaire at the year end.

After the first year the team met to consider the outcomes. That a new pattern had emerged was beyond doubt.

3rd years 1981/2 untreated

	Biology	Chemistry/Physics	Other	
Girls	22	5 ＼ 8 ／ 3	43	73
Boys	1	15 ＼ 62 ／ 47	52	115

Using chi-square one can hypothesize that the above difference in frequencies of girls and boys choosing science options is due entirely to chance. If the differences are significant, in this case at the 1 per cent level then the null hypothesis is rejected.

The above frequencies are in fact significant and therefore not chance differences expected in a random sample. The results after the treatment were:

3rd years 1982/3

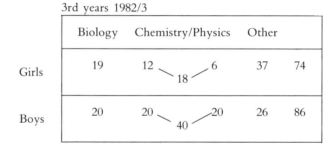

	Biology	Chemistry/Physics	Other	
Girls	19	12 ⟍ 18 ⟋ 6	37	74
Boys	20	20 ⟍ 40 ⟋ 20	26	86

Using chi-square these frequencies are not significant at the 1 per cent level and can be therefore expected to arise from a random sample.

Since the 1982/3 treatment the whole of the year has been subjected to the treatment but the results have been less 'satisfactory' in that a reversion to the original pattern has occurred even though it is lesser in magnitude. Hence the 1983/4 results:

3rd years 1983/4

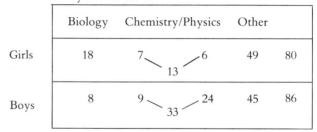

	Biology	Chemistry/Physics	Other	
Girls	18	7 ⟍ 13 ⟋ 6	49	80
Boys	8	9 ⟍ 33 ⟋ 24	45	86

Using chi-square these frequencies are significant at the 1 per cent level. Sex bias seems to have recurred despite the treatment.

What was of great interest was that teachers found the single sex classes were much more difficult to manage in the early weeks than mixed groups. This was a generally expressed view, there being little difference between an all female group and an all male group. With time the groups settled and the staff felt the girls in single sex groups became much more open and confident. They displayed a keenness hitherto seen in very few of their number and they were generally much more assertive than previously. Their own view being that in all science sessions they were taking a much more active part, they enjoyed the class being organized in that way and considered that it gave them the freedom to progress without the constraining influence of the boys.

The boys on the other hand were resentful of the change. They disliked the new groups. Socially they seemed disoriented and therefore much more volatile in the early weeks. They had to establish a new hierarchy which they seemed to find much more difficult without the presence of the girls. That they were unhappy and confused for some time was undeniable but even towards the end of the treatment they were still less than enthusiastic about the change to their ordered lives.

The girls have been quick to see the advantages the new groupings bring them, they have exploited them fully. The boys have always felt disadvantaged and deprived in some unstated way by the treatment.

Teachers have made it clear that they approve of the changes. The pattern of choice which was the cornerstone of the research has become of lesser importance. The pattern may fluctuate but if all pupils are fully aware when they make their options then their choice should be right for them. What has become of lasting value is the notion that the single sex groupings give positive discrimination to girls at a vital time in their school career. They become more self aware, more outgoing and confident. Most girls experience a feeling of worth and identity in the new groups which would seldom be the case in mixed groups. The boys do not suffer academically, they make good progress and are exposed to all the positive and beneficial aspects which the research has generated.

All pupils seem to have gained as a direct result of the extra attention, planning and consideration given to them and their science courses. Their awareness of the career paths open to them has increased and their attention has been focused on the importance of making the best choices at the end of the third year. The research continues undiminished in its scope and intent.

The final word must be with the pupils:

Girls: We get a chance to say what we think.
           We don't get shouted down any more.
           I didn't think much of science but it's not bad now.
           I thought I'd miss them but I don't.

Boys: We used to lark about – it's not as much fun now.
           They do as well in exams as we do now.
           My dad says I should do as well as my sister in science [a twin].
           When can we go back to working in mixed groups?

16

Observing with GIST

GLYNIS WARD

It was by accident that three years ago I became involved in the GIST project. I had never heard of GIST and had no idea of what the letters meant, let alone the aims and objectives of the project. My involvement began when I was told that someone from GIST was coming into my school to follow a first year form/tutor group for one day each week and wasn't I lucky as my tutor group had been selected. I felt pleased that they had been chosen as it was something quite different for them and I looked forward to monitoring any progress involved.

Having been told that Monday would be the day for the observations it was only then that I realized that I would actually be teaching the class. This meant that I would surely become involved to a greater degree than I had anticipated. I then began to wonder what it was all about and what I would have to do. Memories of teaching practice came flooding back, of someone sitting at the back of the room watching and listening. It had been a long time since those days and perhaps this is why I was bothered. The day arrived and the class introduced me to Judith (she had already spent the morning with them). They seemed quite happy about the experience so I thought it must not be too demanding. Judith sat at the front, facing the class, with a name list and another sheet of paper in front of her. Every time I looked across at Judith she was busy marking something down on a sheet. I had prepared the lesson to provide a variety of activities and a fair amount of oral questioning. The pupils responded well and the experience was nothing like the ordeal I had been dreading. Unfortunately lack of time and the need for me to commute to another building prevented Judith and me from talking about what had been going on. It took a week or two before we actually were able to sit down and discuss what Judith had been doing. Apparently, every time I asked a child a question or a pupil made a comment it was noted down on the sheet. Also when I went round the room, note was made of who I helped or talked to. From these early observations in my classroom and others, the classroom observation schedule was developed by the GIST team. When Judith showed me the results of her early observations of my lessons I was rather surprised at what they implied. I had always felt that I had managed to involve most of the class each lesson and that over a few lessons would involve everyone. The results showed that there were in fact some pupils with whom I had no contact either by asking them a question, them volunteering an answer, or asking for help. Another point that emerged was that one very bright girl in the class never volunteered an answer unless forced to by the fact that no one else could answer. Then her answer was so quiet that it could hardly be heard, yet she was nearly always right.

The problem of involvement of all pupils is important and is something which all teachers should be aware of. All pupils whether boy or girl should be included in the lesson in some way, not always an easy task in a thirty-five minute lesson with over thirty pupils. Because the observations were mainly concerned with how girls responded, and mathematics was one of the areas for concern, I was perturbed that many of the non participants in my lessons were girls. When I realized what was happening I decided to try and alter my classroom practice in a way which would certainly involve more girls, and hopefully involve all pupils. I tried to direct questions to pupils and ask another pupil of the same sex for the answer if the person I had asked originally was unable to supply the answer. I had discovered via the observations that although I did this sometimes, more often I asked a question generally and then chose a pupil from those with their hands up. I think the girls preferred the new method because it meant that they did not have to put their hand up if they were uncertain and yet at the same time they were given a chance to answer. When Judith observed my lesson again there were definitely more girl interactions but when the figures were broken down further it was found that about half of the girl interactions were one particular girl. This girl told me later that she had realized what Judith was doing and she was trying to boost the girls' total because she knew that even if I asked some of the other girls a question they probably wouldn't reply. Thus every time a girl failed to reply Andrea provided the answer.

By now we were virtually at the end of the year and Judith asked me if I would like to continue the observation and try and observe some of my colleagues. I said that I would because, despite the reluctance on my part at the beginning, I had by this time become quite interested. I wanted to observe second year pupils as these were the pupils with whom Judith had started the previous year and it seemed sensible to continue their involvement. Up to this point I had not realized just how difficult it would be to actually carry out the observations. Problems were both organizational and situational.

Every time I had things organized I seemed to discover that I had been put down for cover, or that the teacher I was supposed to be observing was absent, or that the teacher requested that I did not observe this particular lesson. This was more common initially and I could sympathize. In addition, because of the timetable, my observations tended to be with the same staff, i.e. those teaching second year mathematics when I had a non teaching period. I was thus relying on their good nature and continued support. I also found it difficult at times to remain detached from what was going on in the classroom, especially if the class were misbehaving, and because of the speed at which interactions sometimes occurred it was difficult keeping the observation schedule correct. Lapses of concentration could not be afforded.

However, despite all the problems I did manage to carry out a few observations although not as many as I would have liked. Before discussing the results of the observations it is worthwhile noting the specific behaviours I was observing. There are eight columns in the schedule. Examples are:

Teacher asks boy, teacher asks girl question.

These columns can show how many times the teacher directs questions to boys as opposed to girls.

Boy answers, girl answers question.

This category can show whether boys or girls are more likely to respond when the question is not specifically directed to one pupil, or when the pupil asked is unable to reply.

Boy comments/girl comments spontaneously

This section shows whether boys or girls are more likely to speak out in class.

Teacher helps boy, teacher helps girl.

Every time there is an interaction in the classroom, the pupil's name is written on the left hand side of the sheet and a tick is put in the correct column. At the end of the lesson each column is totalled. My main concern was with total boy/girl involvement so I totalled the four columns relating to each.

I can only give a brief and selective outline of these results. First of all Mr A. In all the lessons observed Mr A had about 76 per cent interaction with boys and 24 per cent with girls. He knew what the observations were about but did not try to alter the low percentage girl participation in his lessons. In my school we have a 3:2 ratio of boys to girls so numberwise boys would dominate anyway and the girls would tend to feel outnumbered. Despite the 3:2 boy, girl ratio, which I have allowed for in my figures, the boys in this class still had more than a fair share of the teacher's time. Mr A very rarely directed questions at either boy or girl; when a general question was asked it was usually a boy who shouted out the answer. Many of the boys in this class dominated the lesson with their bad behaviour, constantly shouting out and demanding attention. This is where being an observer became difficult as any attempt on my behalf to alter the boys' behaviour would disrupt the interactions. I don't know whether the girls in this particular group knew why I was sitting in their classroom but often they asked me to sit in because they felt it was the only way they received some attention from the teacher. This shows up one of the shortcomings of the observations. You cannot be an observer without affecting the results.

This same problem worried me when observing Mrs C. In most of her lessons she had 50 per cent boy and 50 per cent girl interaction. Mrs C also had this 3:2 boy, girl ratio, so each girl was participating more than each boy to achieve the 50:50 ratio. If this were a permanent situation then maybe the boys in her classes would feel they were being neglected but I think it was more just a particular effort for girl involvement while I was actually observing, knowing that the observations were for GIST.

After I had completed a few more observations, Judith came in to observe my lesson again. This time I managed to involve all pupils. By now the girls in my classes were getting the idea and had more confidence to participate in the lessons. Hopefully I still manage to involve all pupils, especially now as I am constantly aware of this. Recently I asked some of the girls (now fourth year, who had been involved in the observations when they were first years) what their views were of the observations. Below are a selection of their comments.

> I tried to be more forthcoming and answer as many questions as possible.
> I remember that I answered more questions than usual, I think this may have been due to the fact that most of the other pupils became inhibited with their answers.

This comment was from the girl who accounted for about half of the girl interactions in one of the lessons which Judith observed. I was pleased to hear from these girls that the way in which I thought I had altered my practice, with or without Judith's presence had been communicated to the pupils. One such comment was:

> I feel that the only way in which you reacted differently was to

ask slightly more questions of the class, which you kept up even when Judith was not present.

I was interested to find out from the pupils whether or not they felt GIST had affected them in any way. Their main contacts with it having been through the observed mathematics lessons and science lessons.

My involvement with GIST has made me more aware of my capabilities as a girl particularly in the sciences and maths. These are normally considered as boys' subjects but now since GIST I am determined to do well in these subjects to prove that it is the individual's ability that counts, not the fact that they are either a boy or a girl.

GIST is trying to open up more opportunities for girls and I feel that the way we reacted in our class has shown that the aim is worthwhile.

GIST has given girls a chance to show they are equal to boys.

The boys from this original group strangely enough had very little to say about the observations when they were told it was for GIST. I suppose they felt that it did not apply to them. This surprised me as I thought that perhaps once they knew what it was all about they would go out of their way to dominate. However, I was wrong.

Quite recently I observed a science teacher, Mr B, taking a top band third year class for physics (some members of this group were in the original first year mathematics group). Mr B had already had some involvement with GIST and his classes had been visited by the VISTA visitors, but he had never had his lessons observed and note taken of the interactions. The number of girl interactions was very good in comparison with the boys. When I spoke to Mr B afterwards he said that he had altered his technique because I was there and he also felt the pupils behaved differently. I asked him if he could explain the ways in which he felt he had altered his method and also how he felt the pupils were different.

It made me more aware that I should be seen to ask the girls questions.

It made me more aware of the type of questions I was asking.

Those who knew what the observations were about, both boys and girls, responded better.

As far as the pupils were concerned he felt 'they were better behaved and more responsive'.

The comments made by Mr B may well be true for most people who are being observed. The situation is a false one, but if it brings with it an awareness of the situation then the research that has gone on and the observations have served their purpose. This in a way is the central point of my experience and of this contribution.

Personally I feel that my involvement with GIST and the observation has helped to improve my practice. Because I was involved in this way, I talked to the pupils about what I was trying to do and for most of the time I had their support. This was a new venture for both sides and those pupils who helped by, for example, filling in questionnaires felt quite a sense of achievement in having contributed to the research. These discussions and questionnaires came some time after the observations and so did not affect the way in which the pupils responded at the time, but were rather their reflections on the situation. My own involvement began in testing out an observation schedule devised by the GIST team, and time prevented me from going further in observations and trying out different recording techniques. However, I feel that despite feeling exhausted at the time, I think I have benefited enormously from the experience of observing and being observed.

17

Teachers' Perceptions of the GIST Project: an Independent Evaluation

DAVID HUSTLER and TED CUFF

SETTING UP THE EVALUATION EXERCISE

In this chapter we describe how we set about the task of providing an independent evaluation of teachers' perceptions of GIST, the problems we encountered and some of the findings we were to produce. (Reported in Payne, Hustler and Cuff, 1983).

Action research encompasses a great range of different endeavours which vary greatly in scale, scope and complexity. The GIST project was an ambitious project: relative to many other action research projects it was organizationally large-scale, costly, labour intensive, prolonged; academically and socially it was challenging, innovative and, to many, provocative. As we note later, the impact of the project was in our view considerable. A major problem in setting up an evaluation exercise was that evaluation of teacher perceptions was not a design feature of the project, i.e. it was not built into the initial programme as an essential element. This stemmed from the GIST team's view that teacher co-operation might have been endangered. Initially, the GIST team felt that if pupils in the schools subjected to interventionist strategies responded positively and opted in greater numbers for science and craft subjects, then the case would in part be 'proven'. In addition, corroborative evidence would derive from before-and-after studies of pupils' attitudes which would be ascertained by means of carefully designed questionnaires administered by teachers. It was only when the project was well into its second year that the GIST team decided that more evaluation materials were needed from *independent* evaluators.

As part of this newly formulated exercise in independent evaluation, we were invited to participate, presumably because we were handily located on the same site as the project team, knew some members of the GIST team and, as sociologists involved in teacher education, had a relevant background of research and experience to be eligible for the task.

The task itself, however, had still to be defined. Teachers were to be the focus, but what exactly were we to evaluate? After considerable discussion and negotiation, sometimes involving all three evaluators together with the four members of the GIST team, it was agreed that we should focus on teachers' perceptions of the project.

Once the focus of the evaluation was determined, the problem then became how to do it. How could we get at both the current perceptions of teachers *and* somehow contrast them with their perceptions before the GIST project started. For naturally, we and the GIST team would ideally have wanted a before-and-after study.

This problem is far from being novel in social research and there is a large literature concerned with doing such before-and-after studies. Here the problem was compounded by the large scale of the GIST project. With ten schools involved (including two 'control' schools) we were constrained to adopt a one-slice-in-time approach. The constraints derived mainly from time pressures on us as well as on the schools. We would have to construct our before-and-after picture in terms of how the teachers themselves perceived change.

Our approach was the well-tried expedient of the focused interview which we adapted for our purposes. Our intention was to interview a sample of school staff on roughly similar lines which would be achieved by utilizing an interview schedule giving broad headings and a number of 'probes' to stimulate responses. The nature of this interview schedule was the subject of much discussion, drafting and redrafting between the GIST team and the evaluation team.

In these discussions there arose many problems concerning our credibility as 'unbiased' researchers. First, given the ideological nature of the project, involving the need for teachers to change their attitudes to their job, the inevitable question arose as to our own personal suitability. Would we distort the findings? Would we – three males with no overt connection with the study of gender – fail to associate with the work of the project, through, for example, inappropriate questioning? Secondly, and relatedly, the GIST team were far from happy about our proposed methodology. The focused interview, even with an agreed interview schedule, provided us with a lot of freedom. Our response was to point to our own preferred methodology of obtaining 'rich data' rather than compressed and abbreviated data. Thus we wanted to tape-record and transcribe all interviews and build the transcriptions into the report, rather than give edited, and possibly tendentious, highlights. Here we confessed to a methodological bias against methods which refine out real-life events in favour of the researcher's own artefacts and abstractions. We wanted to give a rich detailed picture of school life as seen and related by teachers themselves. By making the transcriptions available, we felt our methods would be transparent, making visible to readers of the report any bias on our part. Here we encountered a further obstacle in that the GIST team wanted judgements and interpretations as to what and how they were doing. Here we assured them that our methodology did not exclude our views, but did make available the materials on which we founded them so that readers themselves could seek to provide alternative interpretations if they so wished.

The final problem in setting up the exercise derived from issues to do with the confidentiality of responses. The GIST team would have liked to have known who was saying what, in order to be able to assess it from the standpoint of their much deeper involvement and experience of that person's involvement with the project in the school. In the end, however, we did agree that individuals should not be identified even for the GIST team. We did accept the nomination by the GIST team of four schools to visit. For each school, we were supplied with a list of names of all GIST contacts from which we were to make our own sample. We were not able to utilize a fourfold GIST categorization, reflecting degrees of involvement as perceived by the GIST team, because in view of the overall size of the sample, there was only one name in some cells, making identification of an individual certain for anyone with a little background knowledge. Of course, with our 'open' approach regarding the publication of transcriptions, there was plenty of material for some readers to make informed guesses, even though we edited out give-away pieces of biographical information. We felt, however, that there was a great difference between guessing, albeit informed, and providing information that made identification a certainty.

On going into the schools, we found that some staff were very appreciative of the guarantee of confidentiality, while others were not concerned. With few exceptions, staff seemed to express themselves freely, not refraining from critical comments which might concern aspects of the school's organization as well as of the GIST project.

We interviewed 32 of the 65 staff nominated by the GIST team as being connected in some way with the project. Within each of the three categories we used, i.e. (1) science staff, (2) craft, design and technology (CDT) and (3) others (including the four heads) we interviewed approximately half the staff nominated. All staff were helpful and co-operative and all but three consented to have the interview tape-recorded.

All four schools were so well organized that the interviewing programme went smoothly, although some names within a category were substituted at the last minute (one because a teacher's horse was unwell).

PRESENTING THE REPORT

In presenting the report, we were hoisted by our own methodology. By the time agreement had been reached concerning methodology and the final version of the interview schedule produced, we had a calendar year (1983) to do everything else. Consequently, we produced only six transcriptions from the earliest interviews, of which five were reproduced in our Report – taking up no less than 51 pages.

Although we had a small budget, we discovered that it could not run to a cost of something like £7 a page for commercial transcription. Perforce, therefore, we had to produce detailed summaries of all thirty-four interviews, each consisting of about one page of close typescript. Readers could then compare the five transcriptions with their corresponding summaries to see the kinds of judgements we were making in producing these abbreviated accounts, and in this way we tried to be consistent with our preferred 'open' research methodology.

In keeping with our professed methodology, we presented our findings as a 'commentary' on the 'rich' materials presented in the report. Although most transcriptions were not available, we felt that the summaries were detailed enough to enable readers to form some sort of judgement about each teacher's perceptions, even allowing for 'distortions' generated by us in producing and shaping up the summaries, although we tried hard to maintain the descriptive mode. What follows is one example of these individual teacher summaries.

Summary of GIST Interview B.4

This male woodwork teacher has been in the school three years and was teaching there prior to the appearance of the GIST project. He mainly teaches in the lower school.

When it did come to the school he was very apprehensive about it because he believes that boys and girls have separate roles in life. He felt that the project was unnecessary. On the other hand he can see that 'educationally speaking' boys and girls in the first two years of secondary school are broadly similar in ability to do craft subjects. Girls, however, have a better attitude to their work and are keener and more disciplined, so they probably achieve more.

This teacher runs a woodwork club of 11 and 12 year olds and half the membership is made up of girls. In his view, the girls are more interested than the boys. It appears that as the girls get older they are directed away from woodwork and metalwork by peer group leaders. This teacher seems strongly wedded to his theory and feels the school could influence the situation by manipulating the groups and by providing more continuity. It is in the third year that the interest of the girls falls away. In this school there is a split of sites between lower and upper schools, the third year being located in the upper school, some distance away.

In the lower school there has been a policy for some years now that all the children come into contact with all the craft subjects. This involves boys doing domestic science and needlework as well as the girls doing woodwork and metalwork. He understands that GIST is trying to encourage girls to go into science, craft and technological subjects and to make them aware that there are career openings for girls in these areas.

Earliest contacts with the project took the form of a meeting between four craft teachers and two members of the team. It was followed up with visits from lady woodworkers, garage mechanics and jewellery makers and men working in the domestic science area. The craft teachers were also given booklets of facts and figures about girls' and boys' achievements in science, but this teacher could not remember much about them now. The information from GIST constituted one small part of the information he received related to his work as a teacher in the school. He has mnay other things to think about in school life. He is always pressed for time.

This teacher was not observed in class and was not aware that the GIST team did that. Nor was he aware of any questionnaires or attitude testing.

He does not feel that the presence of GIST has made any difference to his classroom practices or his views. He is just interested in getting good work from the children. However, he does encourage some of the better girls to carry on with their craft work more than he used to.

One criticism he has is that he feels that the GIST team are too remote from the everyday hubbub of school life. He feels that projects could be better directed at helping teachers with overall discipline and attitudes and with getting pupils to have a more positive attitude towards society.

Bringing in women who do 'traditional male' jobs is probably the best feature in his view because it gets through to the children. All the paper work does not have much effect at all, he has too many other more important things to think about.

In addition to an introduction, summaries and transcriptions, we also summarized the main points made in the interviews in two cross-cutting ways: in terms of a profile of each of the four schools broken down according to the interview schedule and in terms of the perceptions of the three groups – science, CDT, other – in each school.

We also gave a very brief pen sketch of each school as we perceived it through the interviews, an example of which follows:

> In this large school, the greatest impact of GIST is in the science areas, with some effect on CDT. The very layout of the school tends to reduce the possibilities of frequent contact with other departments which might stimulate more interest and knowledge about GIST. Within CDT, and especially science, staff are knowledgeable about GIST even if not directly involved. Their supportive attitude is reflected, at least as we interpreted it, in the humour most attached to its work, e.g. 'PIST' (Persons into Science and Technology), being 'GISTED'. There is positive support from senior staff. This attitude is developed in an overall environment which seems orderly, controlled but reasonably relaxed. Overall, the GIST initiative seems to have been well received in this school. However, we found it very difficult to identify and locate concrete instances of changes to specific classroom practices.

Having produced synopses for all four schools, we than took the next step of summarizing staff perceptions across all four schools. We found that in all four schools there was a high degree of consensus and clarity about GIST aims. In essence, they were to improve opportunities for girls in the science and CDT areas. To do so involves changing attitudes, breaking down sexual stereotypes and hence teacher practices. Few teachers perceived themselves as crucial targets of the GIST initiative. The project was largely viewed as interventionist in the lives of pupils, rather than the lives of teachers. This point may illuminate why some teachers were surprised that the GIST team had not been more concerned to explain to *pupils* the nature of the initiative.

Most staff claimed some involvement in the GIST project and overall the level of involvement was high. Most frequently cited – and easily recalled – were the VISTA visting speakers, the Polytechnic Conference and the administration of tests and question-naires. Observation of classroom teaching was also mentioned in all but one school (school C).

Most of the staff felt that GIST had not changed their attitude though awareness might have been sharpened. There were two extreme individual views: for one person GIST had brought illumination, but another claimed GIST had made indifferent persons more negative.

On balance staff seem almost grudgingly to concede that there have been even marginal changes in their actual classroom practices. Statements are vague, e.g. more aware since being observed, but positive references are to materials, presentation in option booklets, choice of projects.

In all four schools, positive references were made to at least one member of the GIST team, and in three schools to the whole team, in terms of hard work, enthusiasm, sincerity or professionalism. In terms of activities, the VISTA visits were the most frequently mentioned. There was more diversity among the four schools in identifying the 'worst feature' of GIST. In all four schools there were staff who referred to the pressure on their time and the need to appreciate the fact that there are other demands on it. There were critical comments of the conference in schools C and D and again in these two schools an overtly feminist approach was perceived.

In terms of their individual theories, nearly all staff felt there is a genuine problem of underachievement, though it is usually seen as a general problem for boys as well as girls.

As for the causes of underachievement, there was general agreement about the importance of external factors, especially the strength of tradition, mainly in terms of parental attitudes, in shaping the differential opportunities of boys and girls relating to courses in general and science and CDT in particular. The causes were mainly seen to be external. The quality of teaching and the teacher practices were also brought out, but not so strongly and was hardly touched on in school C.

Staff felt that school *can* make a difference, and reactions were mainly positive. Several respondents replied somewhat indignantly that the very *raison d'être* of school is to make change. Most felt, however, that changes can only be slow, over a generation. In short any changes made in the attitudes of current pupils will be rewarded by the changes in their children in due course. Most staff are agreed that it is important to keep trying to make these changes.

Within the same department and with one or two individual exceptions, there were not strong positive views about the GIST project. Conversely, in only one school was there a body of strong negative views (school C). Staff in these directly associated areas were generally aware of GIST.

In the rest of the school, however, there was some variation in the four schools as perceived by the staff in science and CDT. In one school (D) there was general awareness, and some awareness in another school (B). In the other two schools, however, respondents could not detect much impact at all outside the areas of science and CDT.

In all four schools, scientists are committed to the idea of creating fairer opportunities for girls. They are all knowledgeable about the GIST project. Their enthusiasm for it varies from an outright antagonism which seems to derive from personality factors among the female scientists in one school, to reserved expressions of support in the other three schools. Basically, staff feel that they were reasonably aware of the problems. This point was especially emphasized by female scientists who felt they have experienced and overcome the problem.

Again, among teachers of CDT, staff are broadly supportive of the aims of improving opportunities for girls, though there are a couple of 'reserved positions'. There is a feeling that GIST is trying to help, but is not succeeding to any extent. Again, most staff feel that GIST is preaching to the converted, i.e. among those staff not in 'reserved positions'.

We should note, however, that staff see the area as undergoing radical change (i.e. from metalwork and woodwork to CDT). For some, this transformation colours their perceptions of GIST, whilst others do not see any link between GIST and CDT developments.

The four Heads of School are all supportive of the broad aims of improving opportunities for all children and welcome the GIST project as providing some help in the endeavour although they all feel their school had moved some way towards meeting these needs without GIST. They make reservations about some aspects of the approach such as zealotry, the possible neglect of boys, and happenings at the Polytechnic Conference. In short, they feel that their school had developed some way towards meeting these needs before the advent of GIST. In effect, GIST was a positive though more or less marginal influence.

Among other respondents not directly related to GIST there is some variation ranging from one person who had never heard of GIST to another who was extremely supportive.

So far, so good, but could we say anything more about the GIST project as perceived by the teachers in these thirty-four interviews? What sort of a message was here for the GIST project? How was it going? Was it going well or badly? How should all this descriptive data and quasi-descriptive commentary be interpreted?

FURTHER INTERPRETATION

In our commentary, we tried to tackle these questions and embarked on what we explicitly termed a more 'speculative' vein.

We were impressed by the fact that all the respondents nominated by the GIST team were quite knowledgeable about the project and were able to sustain talk easily about it for a thirty or forty minute period in relation to a range of specific questions. Of course, we were aware that they (like us!) were not simply displaying their knowledge of and involvement with GIST, but were also at one and the same time inevitably displaying other aspects of their school identities. For example, heads were being heads, heads of year groups were being heads of year groups and physics teachers were being physics teachers. That is to say, each respondent was not only talking about GIST, but talking about it in relation to his or her position in the school. Further, that person was inevitably going on to say something about that position, what it is to do that job and how GIST helps (or does not help). Thus heads saw GIST as injecting enthusiasm, fire, new blood in a situation of staff shortages, while teachers on the ground were much more pointed in looking for direct help in practical teaching and were particularly appreciative of stimulating materials or visitors. In short, the conception of their position in the school shaped up perceptions of what features of the project were valuable. Thus, teachers valued the introduction of new teaching materials as against the administration of questionnaires, aids for the practical management of the classroom as against theoretical questions about the nature of girls' underachievement in craft, technology and science.

Although we were imrpessed by the teachers' involvement as shown by the interviews, we did wonder what changes the GIST team would agree were legitimate indicators of success. What would teachers have to be saying – or perhaps more pertinently saying they were doing – for success to be achieved?

What sorts of changes in practices were they looking for? Are the claims about 'greater awareness', 'greater sensitivity' enough, or do the changes have to be hardened into institutionalized practices in the school? Whatever the answer to these questions, in our view as independent evaluators there are clear if variable signs of GIST having made some impact in all four schools we visited. That these signs have emerged from a methodology which could only allow teachers to construct accounts of where they were, and where they are now, may be taken as some indication of the impact of GIST. For most of the teachers, despite their multifarious concerns and pressing other interests, could display in some detail their involvement with GIST. That such involvement was not, for the minority, always positive, cannot decry the fact of this involvement. In all schools, consciousness of GIST concerns with equal opportunities for girls was high for staff in science and CDT, and in all schools there was considerable agreement that GIST had heightened this awareness.

Certainly, at the outset of our evaluation exercise, the GIST team gave us a glimpse of their perceptions of relative success. They were able to categorize the four schools as 'one good, two medium, and one poor', but of course they did not reveal to us, the evaluators, which schools fell into which categories, or the criteria informing their judgement. We have already raised the question as to what success in a school could look like. From our materials it is clear that the very concept of school tends to differ in its nature, dimension, and central concerns, depending on the organizational position, involvements and relevancies of the staff speaking to that concept. Perhaps we should note a not unimportant aside here as well: some schools in the GIST project were undergoing massive staff changes relating to LEA reorganization, and school B in our sample is one of these schools.

In their own final report (Kelly, *et al.*, 1984), the GIST team might be read as being somewhat pessimistic about the outcome:

> The results of the GIST project might be something of a disappointment to anyone who thought that schools alone could solve the problem of girls' under-achievement in science and technology. But of course schools cannot act alone; they are enmeshed in the wider social structure. Parents, primary schools, peers and employers all influence children's attitudes and their choices. Teachers are reluctant to change their routines, and men as a group have no wish to relinquish their power. Against these odds it is perhaps more surprising that GIST had any impact at all than that its impact was limited.

Our own view, however, is that it was no inconsiderable achievement for a small team of four to have made such an impact on sixty plus staff in eight schools. Could much more have reasonably been expected?

We think not, given the type of interventionist model of action research adopted by the team. Even though independent evaluation was not a feature at the outset, the model was of the kind which would normally have built it in. For it was not the sort of model which basically emphasized 'action' at the expense of 'research'. Instead it tried to combine an interventionist strategy with a scientific model. This awkward combination of targets, recognized by the GIST team, gave rise to some confusion and complaints from teachers.

One teacher complained that teachers themselves were not involved in initially shaping up and developing the research. Another teacher felt that the pupils' views should have been more directly involved if the aim was to change such views. The GIST team was concerned to study what goes on in schools, yet also to change what goes on. The problem resulting from the more traditional research aspects of the project was a tendency to externalize the team in relation to the school staff, i.e. making for an 'us' and 'them' situation, albeit not as extreme as that associated with most research *on* education. The externalization was compounded by the basic view of the GIST team that to change pupils' opportunities, teachers' attitudes must change. As our interviews showed many staff did *not* appreciate that interventionism was directed at *them*. On one of the few occasions when this message came across, at a specially convened conference at Manchester Polytechnic, some staff were very alienated by one of the speakers. Again, although most staff did express positive views about improving opportunities for girls, they did not attribute this attitude to the influence of the GIST team.

Of course, any attempt to change attitudes necessarily implies criticism: here it is criticism of the most fundamental kind, of teachers' professional competence. What else can it amount to if the very *raison d'être* of the project is that staff do not treat girls fairly? Thus it was extremely difficult for the GIST team to 'come clean'. Nevertheless, despite their in camera approach they seemed able to gain strong support from those staff and schools where they were personally greatly involved in bringing in speakers and materials. But the sheer scale of the programme and the need to produce sound scientific results, as shown by attitude and changes in option choice, meant this approach could not be pursued comprehensively.

To change attitudes is hard: to change attitudes to basic fundamentals like sexual identity, job opportunities, and the ways of teaching stemming from these attitudes, is even harder. Perhaps any disappointment the GIST team feel as an outcome of our investigation of teacher perceptions of their project is a product not only of the scale of the research, but also of the scale of their social as well as educational ambitions.

18

The Alternative Curriculum Strategies Project

MIKE COCKETT

INTRODUCTION

Manchester's Alternative Curriculum Strategies project had its origins in a city-wide curriculum review undertaken in 1981 in preparation for secondary school reorganization. At that time it was recognized that the present examination-dominated curriculum for 14–16 year olds was itself the cause of many difficulties for both pupils and teachers in schools. Alternative Curriculum Strategies were to be found that would offer all pupils a chance of success and not just those whose abilities happen to fit the present examination framework.

The principles underlying these proposed alternative strategies can be summarized as follows:

– Pupils will respond better to a curriculum that is practical, experiential and which is clearly related to the 'real' world in which they live.
– Learning strategies should be developed that promote co-operative rather than competitive learning.
– The schools should be more open to their communities and the resources of the communities should be used in developing the alternative curriculum.
– Pupils should be included in the decision making process in relation to their own learning and this should be the heart of new more co-operative relationships between teachers and pupils.
– New forms of assessment and accreditation should be developed which offer all pupils a chance of success.

It has been up to the individual schools to invent and implement the practical programmes that give body to the principles described above. Because the project has evolved in this way it is not possible to describe *the* alternative curriculum strategies. Each school has developed its own way of working and there are quite radical differences between them. This can be illustrated by describing the roles that two of the project leaders fulfil within their respective schools. In one school, the decision was taken to select a small 'full time' target group and to allow other pupils to opt for a part established and part alternative curriculum. The project co-ordinator for a variety of reasons took an extreme entrepreneurial role in relation to the curriculum. He used the resources of community education, individuals within the community, colleges of further education, polytechnic students, the Rural Preservation Association and any other individuals or organization that could respond to the need and desires of both 'full time' and 'part time' pupils. A mode of operation developed that was very responsive to pupils' expressed wishes and which could cope with increasing numbers of pupils as they became disenchanted with some of their subject options and wished to find alternatives.

In contrast to this is the role of the co-ordinator in another school. In this school a decision was made that the alternative curriculum should be available to all pupils and that the selection of a target group of 'lower attainers' was philosophically undesirable. The co-ordinator's role in this school has been in some ways more restricted. He has had the task of organizing a series of 'alternative' activities for all pupils in the fourth and fifth year. The sheer weight of numbers meant that there had to be a greater emphasis on secure routines and less on responding to individual needs. The entrepreneurial role still existed but was directed much more at setting up activities and new courses which then become part of the routine of the school year. Much energy is spent on making sure transport arrangements work effectively, on making sure that pupils arrive on time, on managing the change-over from one activity to another and on other management rather than curriculum functions.

The roles that the co-ordinators have developed are, in part, related to their personalities. The point is that there is no one way of working, but rather a range of strategies aiming to make the most of local circumstances and to put into practice locally developed ideas.

STAFF DEVELOPMENT

Any major initiative is accompanied by a call for accompanying staff development. The implication has been that there are those 'experts' in the field who can pass on their understanding and expertise and who would be the providers of courses. This was clearly not a useful model for ACS staff development. If the individual schools varied in their interpretations of the alternative curriculum, then their staff development needs also varied. In addition, if the project really was to break new ground, then the staff themselves would soon be more 'expert' than any outsider. In practice, some common needs were identified and in other cases, proposals made by one or two schools were accepted by other schools as meeting their needs as well.

A decision was made to follow through the basic principles of ACS work into staff development and therefore the activities were designed to be practical, experiential, co-operative, etc. So, for example, in the very early stages there was a common need to explore the notions of a practical curriculum and negotiated learning. A weekend course was organized in which staff took part in practical activities involving varying degrees of negotiation and through those activities began to shape methods of work that would suit them and their circumstances.

On other occasions, specific skills were felt to be lacking, such as the ability to make TV programmes using simple video equipment. In these cases it has been possible to provide simple skill training by 'experts', but the curriculum uses of the skills are still up to the interest and inventiveness of the individual teacher.

Other staff development work arose naturally out of the co-operative effort of teachers in each school. In one case this has been relatively formalized in team meetings at which teachers bring up problems and the team proposes possible solutions.

Once again, just as the curriculum itself is responsive to the needs of pupils, so the staff development programme needs to be responsive to the needs of teachers. This is not simply a matter of putting on the courses teachers ask for but also of being responsive to needs that may only be indirectly evident. A lot depends here on the perceptions of the school co-ordinators and the project leader.

TEACHERS IN TEAMS

A recurring theme throughout the course planning, implementation and staff development has been the organization of teachers in teams. A project of this sort is bound to establish some sort of collective identity. There are negative effects of such an identification but on the positive side is the sense of belonging to a team with common goals. The extra staffing has allowed time for team meetings in most schools and this collective planning now seems to be a pre-requisite to successful implementation. Teachers have a forum for trying out ideas; they can receive practical help; they can be given guidance and advice and, perhaps above all, they can share responsibility both for the occasional failures as well as the successes. Of course not every team is an automatic success and the natural tensions can in some circumstances become destructive. This has arisen, for example, where there has been a clear bid for supremacy by one member of a team or where a member is seen not to be making a full contribution. On the whole, however, the ACS teams are remarkable for their collective enthusiasm, for their inventiveness and for their insight into the practical problems of teaching.

It must be remembered that in the background there has been the actual and the threatened industrial action by teachers, and these same people have been collectively characterized as being unskilled and unprofessional. Morale in general has been low in schools and yet, given the time, the finance and the encouragement of the administration, the ACS teachers and the schools generally have responded with enthusiasm and commitment. They have attended regular after school meetings and courses; they have attended two and in some cases three full week-end courses; they have coped with a constant stream of visitors and evaluators; they have produced reports on their work which are both frank and full of insight and with all this they have provided a curriculum that is giving new hope and direction to many disaffected and previously disregarded young people.

19

The Alternative Curriculum Strategies Project at Arden

ROD HILL

At the outset of the course the ACS team at Arden were faced with three major problems. First, the sheer logistics of setting up a new course from scratch. The LEA had deliberately given each institution free rein to determine the nature of its course depending upon the ideas and skills available in each school. This grass roots approach caused a great deal of heart searching and several 'false starts', but eventually proved a blessing in that it provided freedom to respond to the needs and preferences of the pupils. It also allowed flexibility to enable the team to change course in midstream. ACS is generously funded, but spending money quickly and wisely is not easy. Purchasing resources valuable to pupils within the course, which also become shared resources across the school and college, requires foresight and an ability to predict successful learning styles. The purchasing of equipment, the construction of a relevant curriculum and the employment of staff demand a breadth of experience which the ACS team had to acquire as it went along. Whilst support was always available, the team still had to develop at an early stage the necessary administrative competence and the confidence to 'chance their arm', trust their judgement, and learn through monitoring their experience as teachers.

No less a problem was 'involving parents'. Mrs Hodgson's contribution indicates clearly how much work was necessary to win the support of parents and reassure them that what was on offer provided a real second chance at a late stage in their children's school career. From the outset, Mrs Hodgson and Mr Rollins worked on the principle that schools need better communications with pupils' homes and the ACS project in particular demanded high parental commitment. Their work reflected a need for and the successful engendering of a greater sense of partnership with parents.

The second major problem faced by the ACS team proved to be immediate and long-standing. After identifying their target group as those who had underachieved in the mainstream they had to overcome the pupils' sense of previous failure. Their low self-esteem led to cynicism, which was burdensome and crippling. Mr Rollins' contribution clearly records the sense of frustration and resignation which many pupils were quick to express. It was in effect a 'trip wire' to which they continually fell foul. The ACS team has had to work very hard to establish the principle that we are all entitled to our risks and that making mistakes does not mean that you are a failure. Success is the greatest motivator of all for pupils and (as the ACS team was later to discover) for teachers as well. But success is relative and mistakes are also part of the learning process.

The ACS team had to establish its own credibility and sincerity with the group. This entailed two main approaches: constructing an agreed curriculum with the pupils which reflected their needs and preferences; and delivering it through active learning styles. It also entailed building up relationships with pupils and helping them to develop relationships with each other.

The third major problem facing the ACS team was overcoming the preconceptions many staff had of ACS pupils. This, combined with wariness of pupils' wishes to negotiate areas of work (as well as pupils' growing ability to articulate their wishes) led to uncertainty on the part of some staff. As Mr Rollins indicates, a number of teachers, some of whom had only passing contact with ACS pupils, questioned the efficacy of certain approaches with these pupils. To them, their previous failure was evidence that they were at variance with the aims of the school. It soon became clear to those involved in the project that ACS was as much to do with the development of teachers as of pupils. Clearing the ground to offer a better approach to these pupils was only a start. Staff development through a series of inservice training activities was to be essential if the project was to justify its funding and its philosophy. From January 1984 regular meetings were organized at two levels. The Assistant Principal, the Site Co-ordinator and the Assistant Co-ordinator met every week for an hour. Secondly, regular monthly meetings were held after school for all staff teaching on the course. Mrs Hodgson points very clearly to these developments as essential to making the project work. These sessions were periods of 'quality time' where people have an opportunity to reflect and project. A chance to avoid the fire-fighting approach which plagues everyone working on a day-to-day basis. In these meetings staff discussed one another's classroom difficulties, the problems experienced by individual pupils, and the teaching styles that appeared to be successful.

The less formal skills needed when teachers cannot rely on the accepted 'protocol' of the classroom are unfamiliar to most members of staff. If you are encouraging pupils to express themselves through their reactions to the curriculum and seeking to develop confidence in their own opinions, then teachers will need to know how to cope with situations which by and large will be new to them, situations which in the mainstream curriculum may well be seen as threatening. The behavioural problems of pupils also require specific skill in handling difficult situations. How do staff cope with pupils' bad language? How do staff chivvy pupils along when they have failed to achieve the anticipated early success? How do they help pupils set targets and agree approaches to work? What is the art of 'rough cajolery'? How do you build relationships with pupils? When do you take a stand with a pupil and when do you back off and deal with it later?

This introduction has referred to the three basic problems which faced the ACS team in September 1983. The articles which follow provide a clearer picture of the difficulty of giving shape and meaning to what had been initially presented as no more than a well-resourced idea. They did, however, face a further problem; one of sustenance. How did members of the ACS team retain their enthusiasm and sense of commitment in the face of rejection and continued bad behaviour from pupils and criticism from some staff? In the early stages they were continually plagued with a feeling of being out on a limb with nothing tangible as yet to show for their efforts. The solutions lie in the ACS team drawing on each other for mutual support and also in taking positive steps to develop particular skills and attitudes among all staff who taught on the course.

20

Parents, Teachers and the Alternative Curriculum at Arden

LORNA HODGSON

On being appointed as Co-ordinator of the Alternative Curriculum Strategies project for underachieving pupils there were a number of pressing issues on which action had to be taken. What sort of action was another matter, but that the action should be informed, and that it should be monitored as a learning experience for us, seemed essential. What follows is a summary of some of the more sucessful moves that were made in two areas: relationships with parents, and, more briefly, helping other teachers.

INVOLVING PARENTS

I felt that it was important to make sure that all pupils who came on the course had been underachieving. To this end I asked subject teachers to recommend pupils who were underachieving in their subject area: pupils who were not working to their potential. In the event, fifty-six pupils were named as underachieving in at least three subject areas out of a total year group of 189. It seemed important to me, however, that there should be some cross-check on this process. Pupils' first year test scores were compared with their third year exam results to seek a disparity which would confirm underachievement. This was, in fact, confirmed for most of the original fifty-six identified.

The new course was explained to pupils and parents were informed by letter, and a signed acknowledgement requested. However, here again I felt this was not enough and a full explanation of what we hoped to do would be much better given in a personal interview. There might be much more to gain from this as well. In particular, it might lead to parents becoming involved with the course, and the personal interview might also provide us with useful insights. About fourteen parents came into school and I made appointments to see most of the remainder in their own homes, a time consuming exercise received positively by the parents. Many parents said they wished school could have offered them an Alternative Curriculum course and agreed to back up the school in its endeavour on their children's behalf. Many of the parents interviewed found their children to be bored with school, uninterested, lazy, feigning sickness, truanting and generally anti-school in many ways. The pupils themselves considered school to be a 'waste of time', 'boring', 'not related to the outside world', 'subjects of no use, except maths and English'. The interviews with parents were confirming in part what we thought we knew anyway, but it seemed important that this emerged as a third cross-check on the selection process. Both parents and pupils began to show an interest when informed of their involvement in developing their own curriculum, and working with teachers.

There appeared to be more boy underachievers among the fifty-six identified; in reality there were just as many girls. Having taught for many years in secondary schools, it had been my experience that boys tended to be noticed as underachieving by their disruptive behaviour or truancy whereas girls tended to be 'absent in mind' although present in body, and often remained quiet in classes although dismally under-achieving. I felt therefore that it was important to aim for a balance in the numbers of boys and girls in the group for two particular reasons. First, from a purely educational standpoint the course should be properly co-educational as a microcosm of society. Secondly, as ACS is a pilot scheme with intentions of developing into something much larger, then it can only be validated by having boys and girls together in balanced numbers. Once again the interviews with parents seemed to provide some evidence to support my initial appraisal. Girls' parents on the whole seemed to particularly appreciate the special interest shown in their daughters and had been worried by their lack of involvement and interest during their time in secondary school, although some had been previously progressing well and enjoying junior school. I was very heartened by the interest shown by the parents and invited them to come into school at any time to see, or indeed participate in, the course once it had started.

For many years I had felt that getting parents involved more in school activities and decision making could help to change some pupils' attitude towards school, but many of these parents showed no interest in a Parent/Teachers' Association and were very wary of school. Many were afraid of becoming involved, and indeed afraid of teachers. When they saw that I was 'just human', as one mother said when I visited her home, many lost some of their fears and asked to be kept in touch with developments. Comments such as these seemed to reinforce my view that the interviewing strategy was one to retain for the future.

At the end of this exercise I was able to take on twenty-two pupils:

eleven girls and eleven boys. As twenty pupils was the recommended number, it seemed reasonable to take on the extra two who wished to be on the course, especially with the teacher–pupil ratio of 1:11.

With the beginning of the course, a number of approaches were adopted to maintain the involvement of parents. Before the new term started, the pupils, three members of staff, and one father and one mother helped to set up the base room. During the first few weeks five parents came in to view the course at first hand during the day, becoming involved, asking questions and showing an interest in the new ideas. Newsletters were sent to parents to keep them informed and I found that parents responded well. They telephoned school when they had any problems with their child, or even when some problem at home was affecting their child. Indeed at one stage I felt that my co-tutor and I were running a counselling course for parents (the Women's Aid Centre was recommended for one distraught mother and the Law Society for another).

Throughout the first year, a close liaison developed between me, my co-tutor and parents. During most weeks we had communication with one or another of the parents, sometimes to solve joint problems and sometimes for parents to take groups into their homes and teach skills. One mother ran a six-week course of two hours for three pupils, making giant teddy bears and another came into the home economics class and cooked with the pupils. Gradually we have broken down barriers and now in the second year of ACS many parents of fourth and fifth year pupils on the course do come into school much more readily to discuss matters and to give a helping hand with practical work under the teachers' instruction. The chief advantages of close involvement with parents are very clear. Parents are able to make suggestions about particular areas of interest for their child. Parents see what their children are actually doing. We talk to parents to avoid problems. We can monitor closely any absences. We can keep close 'tabs' on pupil problems.

Parents' evenings have been well supported and only parents who were working shifts for example, or had small children, did not attend, but did come into school at other times convenient to them. Pupils were involved with teachers in running the parents' evening and pupils designed invitations, cooked various pastries and made tea. Many parents were able to chat among themselves and learn about how the course was affecting other children. More than one parent commented upon the friendly atmosphere and their pleasure at being able to meet other parents and teachers in this supportive way.

Parents have helped tutors by becoming more involved with the process of education than previously. The tutor can then see more than one side to a particular problem. This can help with the way that problems are dealt with in school, and the reasons for some problems arising. When things go badly wrong it has helped a great deal to be able to involve the parents in the disciplinary process so that the pupils know they are being monitored both at school and at home. Parental involvement has played a major part for me and my new extended team of tutors this year, and many good relationships are developing between these tutors and parents.

WORKING WITH TEACHERS IN THE CLASSROOM

ACS in my view needs a team of people who believe that teaching children is more important than teaching subjects. To this end it is important that a team of people are chosen and brought together on the basis of their interest in children. These people can include senior teaching staff, other teachers, technicians, parents, people in the community, employers, careers staff, FE lecturers, members of the support services and police, outdoor pursuits centre staff, and so on. Part of my role as co-ordinator is to help teachers to develop the new teaching approach skills which operate on the alternative curriculum. Whilst these skills tend to develop quite quickly with tutors who have a large timetable involvement with ACS, the main difficulty lies with teachers who are not *au fait* with our approach, and who teach only one or two hours a week on ACS. It seemed essential for me and my supporting team to make ourselves available wherever possible to help to team-teach in awkward situations. Many of these teachers naturally found difficulties in negotiating the curriculum with pupils, in understanding how tight a structure is needed once negotiation is completed and in building up good relationships with pupils who appeared to them brash and ungrateful despite all the extra monies and resources afforded to them.

Just to adopt an availability strategy did not seem enough however. It was necessary for us to work alongside these members of staff, but *not* do the work for them. Ideally in the first place, teachers were invited to sit in on tutorial sessions with us and see the methods used and the general demeanour and behaviour of the pupils. From this they could get the flavour of an alternative approach which they could then adapt to their own personality and interests.

In the first instance in my position as Co-ordinator I had some difficulty starting these support visits because teachers were uncomfort-able being watched and monitored. ACS had only just started and many staff rightly felt that I lacked some expertise and experience myself. However, they found over the first few months that both I and my co-tutor were willing to learn by our mistakes. This seemed to give some staff more courage to try out new approaches, sometimes with considerable success. This atmosphere of shared staff development, rather than core staff developing the rest, seemed an appropriate one. Many pupils noted in the first months that teachers were treating them differently and began to respond accordingly, at least some of the time. As pupils started to gain confidence, they naturally 'went over the top' at times and had to be pulled back again and again. Tutors and teachers need an infinite amount of patience and resilience when dealing with this new teaching situation – it is certainly not for the faint-hearted. As relationships among teachers, and between pupils and teachers, began to be established certain underlying useful, necessary techniques emerged. The joint approach to staff self-appraisal began to generate strategies which seemed to pay off as, through monitoring our experience, we learnt lessons about overall course structuring and day-to-day relationships with pupils. Courses needed to be of short duration, perhaps two or three weeks, and teachers and pupils needed to contract into these courses so that the pupils learned about commitment. We needed to be able to respond to pupil needs immediately, or the impetus given by pupil interest and motivation was lost. We needed to listen to the pupils' ideas and act upon them when they had a relevance and/or originality. We needed to have a varied and interesting curriculum involving as much practical work as possible. Learning needed to be experiential as pupils very rarely responded to simulated activities and tended not to see these as being worthwhile in their terms. It was quite difficult developing short courses at the pupils' level whilst still appearing to them to be adult and relevant. We found that skills used by some teachers in their subject areas were often applicable to other situations so that staff began to learn from each other once we had started to do more team teaching.

As staff we have been trusted to get on with the job and have done so to the best of our ability. We do make mistakes, but recognizing this through monitoring our experiences is half the battle, and we try not to repeat them. We have used the same method of trusting pupils and allowing them the same space to make their mistakes and this works more often than not. As one part of monitoring our experiences of ACS we were keen to record pupils' impressions of the course as it developed. A formal interviewing programme was also under way, conducted by local evaluators from Manchester Polytechnic. What was interesting was the extent to which feedback from both sources was very similar although constructed under different conditions. Certainly in the very early days the emphasis was on providing a motivating curriculum and I will close by presenting some extracts from pupil comments at that stage. They suggest that there has been some success here, but they also provide perhaps the most important resource of all for staff thinking about future action.

Tina   If I was in school I wouldn't have done the work because there is not much choice even in options. On the course there is more opportunity to do what you would like in lessons. I like doing cookery and doing more of it. I didn't like the work set in ordinary school and I got on badly with teachers. Why can't we save up for a coffee machine? Some of the work units could be cleaned up and varnished.

Kevin   It is better than school because we didn't get a chance to do what we really liked – just copying from books and things, but now we do. The multi-skills workshop is best because we can do our own projects. I still don't like some teachers. Some lads in school say we will get an 'O' level in tea-brewing, but they wanted to come on the course.

Sharon   It is better than school when we just did work from books. Teachers treat us better, treat us like adults not kids messing about. I like my own assignments on beauty care and I will work hard at it. The multi-skills workshop is the best part but I don't like the musical and artistic bits because we don't know what we do.

Terry   In school there was a lot of messing around so you couldn't get on with work. I like residentials, plane-making, English and recreation the best. I like multi-skills because I like making the things I choose. I like it all really. Teachers are better because they don't boss you around and they give you a choice. My mum may come to see the course.

David   It's better than school. We don't get moaned at all the time. I like doing what I want to do. Multi-skills is good because you can go out, where in school they wouldn't let you or trust you. Recreation is good and multi-skills and 'The Birtles'. Teachers are better and don't boss you about so much. Three hours is too much for home economics.

Donna   I like ACS because of Fridays recreation and multi-skills. I like doing what I feel like. Teachers seem to be taking more notice of us. In classrooms we felt treated like little babies, now we have a chance to try to be adults. I didn't like getting the blame for making Glenn scream. The class got accused of stealing a pen but we didn't.

Vanessa   This is better than school because teachers are not telling you what to do all the time. I would probably have 'wagged it' if I had been in school. I like everything. The teachers treat you like adults not babies. Multi–skills and cookery are the best. The Birtles is good because we are with adults who are dead polite. I like visiting the nursery. I feel I do my share in everything. I like being more an individual.

Pat   I feel that I am doing a lot better than if I was in school, because I can do things I want to do such as: poetry, going on visits, without people saying 'you can't do this or can't do that'. I find building a model aircraft too difficult and it needs too much teacher help so I am not interested.

21

Two Bites of the Cherry at Arden

BRIAN ROLLINS

SEPTEMBER 1983

The first weeks were unsure, exciting and very demanding of both time and energy. Gradually over the first few weeks we found time to discuss ideas, styles, pupils, problems, etc., and this was normally done during the lunch-times, after school or in free periods. During this time I felt a combination of frustration, panic, inability, and unsureness because although I had always found it easy to build up good relationships with good and bad pupils alike, I had never worked at such close quarters (ten hours plus per week) with one group of underachieving and, in many cases, disruptive pupils. Much of my time was spent following, supporting, encouraging and gradually adding to Lorna's vast experience and unbelievable enthusiasm. This sometimes meant listening, watching and taking part in activities which I was unsure of, and which sometimes I disagreed with, but at the time I felt that the most important role I could play was a supportive one. I also received an immense amount of support from Lorna as I gradually gained in confidence and started to implement my ideas and thoughts with the group.

The first weeks were full of incidents, shocks, setbacks, conflicts, criticism and much searching for reasons why the pupils behaved in the ways that they did. One of the hardest things to come to terms with was the pupils' treatment of one another, both verbal and physical. They would constantly swear at one another, criticize in the nastiest way possible, and generally 'put each other down'. This meant that as a tutor hardly a minute went by without having to correct somebody's language or behaviour. At the end of the day, usually about 4 p.m. (school finished at 3 p.m.) I would walk the 25 minutes home feeling like a geyser ready to let off steam, and in a state of near mental exhaustion. This would gradually lift, and I would be able to reflect about the incidents of the day.

It was obvious from the start that one of the most important roles I had to play was to raise the pupils' incredibly low self-esteem and this was done both in group meetings, which were not easy to organize and develop, and in one-to-one encouragement. I began to note how often we as teachers put the children down verbally without thinking about it, often in front of their peers. As the weeks went by I became sure that this often unintentional putting down of the pupils, e.g. 'act your age', 'stop behaving like a baby', 'grow up', 'you should be back at junior school', 'there are special schools for pupils like you', 'can't you control yourself', 'you should be in a zoo', etc., etc., has a very negative and counter-productive effect on them. It is far better to refer to the pupils' better behaviour and to then let them compare their bad, or silly behaviour, helping them realize their own mistakes. Gradually the self-esteem of the pupils was raised and evidence could be seen that the pupils were more confident, especially in the company of adults. I am sure that occasionally this raising of the self-esteem was mistaken by some members of staff as cheekiness, cleverness, etc., and could easily cause unnecessary problems. It was as if the pupils actually over-compensated for their original low esteem.

Probably one of my greatest assets as a teacher is patience, and this gave me invaluable help. Much of my time was spent listening to pupils' problems and arguments and then trying to help them to resolve them. I found that if you listen sincerely to pupils you will gain their confidence and they will open up and start to trust you as a person and friend. This has to be a positive step in any teacher–pupil relationship.

Consistency is another skill which I found essential. Most teachers are inconsistent, not out of nature but often stemming from the pressures and demands they are subject to. But to the pupils who see two incidents treated differently, or who are promised something which fails to materialize, inconsistency produces instant conflict. Much time was spent explaining the reason for other people's inconsistency, not in a critical way but in an understanding way.

One of the shocks of the first term which came across from the pupils was how very distrusting the pupils were of teachers generally and some adults. This came across in various ways: interviews, materials from staff discussion and classroom observations.

SEPTEMBER 1984

It is hard to believe now how much easier the first term of the second year of the project has been, with the new group of fourth years. Many of the problems which occurred last year, and were new situations, have now reappeared, but they are so much easier to deal with a second time round.

The vast amount of experience which occurred last year has

obviously helped me to be quicker at reacting in the necessary way, and thus when incidents happen or are about to happen, they can be either dealt with immediately or stopped before they actually happen. In addition to the experience and lessons which we have learnt there are other obvious reasons for a better start to the year. These include the fact that we had much more planning time during the summer term. During this time we had numerous meetings to reflect on the previous year's work, and then to formulate a better curriculum for the pupils. We also spent time discusssing the prospective ACS pupils, the effects they had on each other, and so on with the relevant members of staff, including their tutors, subject teachers and year heads. Much time was spent talking to the staff who were interested in teaching the ACS. They were informed of the methods of work, ideas of how to deal in a positive way with the pupils, and some of the problems which would undoubtedly occur.

The fact that Lorna and I had worked closely over the previous year meant that we had a close team teaching approach and we both tried to encourage all other staff to adopt this approach. Open access to the classrooms by all fellow members of staff was encouraged, not merely to observe but, if at all possible, to get involved, chat with the pupils and so on.

Probably the most important information that we gave staff was our ideas about negotiation. This did not mean a free choice of any topic or project as some staff had interpreted it last year. We encouraged staff to give a limited and carefully structured choice within which there should be some flexibility if the pupils came up with adequate alternatives. We encouraged staff to be as flexible as possible with the subject matter, even if this meant throwing one idea out of the window and starting again. We stressed the importance of building relationships and getting to know the pupils rather than the importance of the subject content. After good relationships have been formed a more structured and relevant subject content can be applied.

I took the group away on a residential trip, very early in the course and although it was only one week (I would have liked it to be four) a very good spirit and comradeship developed. The pupils were able to find new and exciting activities, which they enjoyed. I believe that taking the pupils out of the school environment gives them a fresh start. Much of the negative feedback which they have been used to is no longer there and in outdoor pursuits activities they have a chance to start from the beginning and develop their skills in a mainly non-competitive atmosphere. Each pupil is encouraged to improve his or her skill level, and must become an integral part of the group. This means that if one pupil is particularly talented at one sport he/she will be encouraged to help and motivate the other pupils. I find that most of the pupils respond in a very mature way when they are given responsibility of this kind. Some of the most aggressive and disruptive pupils can be encouraged to help other less able pupils in new situations. During the activities much social and personal education can be effected and this often produces an important insight into the pupils' background, home atmosphere and behaviour patterns. In the evenings, group activities and discussion develop a feeling of belonging and respect. Often hidden talents are exposed. I am sure that all these activities give pupils a chance to raise their self-esteem, and although some pupils do try to show off and dominate the group, it is easy to encourage the others to be proud of themselves for what they have achieved.

Although I am still an optimist, I think that there is a more appropriate realism about how much we can actually change and adapt the pupils' behaviour at the very difficult ages of fourteen and fifteen (last year I naïvely thought that major changes could be made). I now think that we can make positive changes, but that many of these will not appear until later in the pupils' lives.

So far this year there have been fewer conflicts and instances of personal abuse. This is partly due to the composition of the group but also there are far more enthusiastic and experienced teachers on the course who take on the internal school discipline problems and solve them, instead of involving the ACS tutors. Many of the teachers this year have actually come to me to enthuse about a pupil's attitude, improvement, work, etc. This rarely happened last year and is a very pleasant and rewarding surprise. Problems do still occur, but various staff have tried to solve them themselves without first relying on the ACS tutors. Additionally, we have had a very positive Assistant Principal who has supported us and come up with many ideas and suggestions to help the course to be successful. Regular and very rewarding one-hour meetings each week with the Assistant Principal and Lorna and myself have been held. This contact from above has given us previously unfound confidence.

I personally have become more confident and totally committed to the aim of the course and to the ways we have been working. A more correct balance has been achieved between freedom to choose and structured activities.

22

Emerging Strategies at Newall Green

ROY DAVIES

My focus here is on three sorts of 'risks' which seemed to pay off for teachers and pupils at Newall Green. They were 'risks' in the sense that our appraisal and interpretation of the situation required moves into unknown territory: unknown for us at least. A few words on the timetable context come first.

THE TIMETABLE

The ideal timetable envisaged was for project staff to see the target group in half-day or full-day blocks. This was seen as being of great importance to the two tutors (the Coordinator and a co-tutor) who were to spend two and a half days a week with the group. However, every timetable is a compromise and it was agreed that because of the relatively small number of pupils involved in the project it would be wrong to adversely affect the timetable of the rest of the school by giving the target group the highest priority. The resultant timetable (see below) although by no means perfect provided the framework for the first year of the alternative curriculum project.

THE CURRICULUM

Translating into practice the 'desire' to make the learning process more experiental, individual and negotiable was not an easy task. Teachers accustomed to a more 'traditional' approach and pupils unaccustomed to having a say in what they will learn found their new situation at different times, confusing, exciting, difficult, rewarding and impossible. However, successful strategies were identified and developed. The curriculum diet evolved (and still is evolving).

Projects and courses were started with great enthusiasm and discarded within weeks. Successes were built on and failures learnt

MONDAY	TUESDAY	WEDNESDAY	THURSDAY	FRIDAY
Core studies★ Peak District studies★	Art Fashion Ceramics	Science/ Computers Safe Motor Cycling Programme	Art Craft Design and Technology	Core Studies★
Games★ Peak District studies★	Post 16 links Photo- graphy Computers Type- writing and Office Skills Silk Screen Printing Engineering Motor Vehicle Main- tenance	Life and Social Skills★ Instrumental Enrichment Core Studies	Consortium Activity Rural Studies	Recrea- tion★

★Co-ordinator and/or Co-tutor with the group.

from. The following examples of successful strategies illustrate what emerged in our attempt to motivate underachievers and provide them with a more interesting, varied and relevant education.

The Multi-Skills Workbase

A large, open classroom with a raised stage area and adjoining stockrooms was made available to the project. The tutor and co-tutor together with the pupils designed, decorated and fitted the room in their time together. Progress was slow at first but gradually the room was transformed into a workbase which everyone identified with.

The room took on a bright, individual character. Murals, posters and photographs covered the walls. Doors were painted bright red and walls bright blue! A carpeted leisure/discussion area with comfortable seating took up one corner of the room. A recreational area with dartboard, pool table and board games took up another corner. Kitchen units and shelving were bought and assembled. Lockers, tables and chairs were renovated and a workbench and tools installed. Typewriters were repaired and a large stock of paper, pens, coloured felt-tips etc. was built up. Tape-recorders, cameras, computers, a video-recorder and television were all bought and used during the year. A small library stocked with books catering for the whole ability range and a wide variety of interests was established. During the year magazines, books and comics were bought in when a need was expressed. Pupils were also encouraged to write for free materials and did so as their interest in individual projects blossomed.

The group very quickly came to appreciate and value the facilities afforded them. A relaxed but orderly atmosphere was encouraged. Pupils who had previously felt threatened by the school system became more at ease and confident. The crucial part played by the tutors cannot be over-emphasized in the development of the group spirit and of a 'safe' caring environment. Much extra-curricular time was given up to develop projects and foster a community spirit. Pupils came to regard the classroom as a home from home and one of the most effective sanctions was to be banned from the room!

The excellent facilities and favourable staffing ratio (1:12) allowed for a variety of activities to take place in and around the workbase at the same time. During one Friday morning, groups of pupils were involved at one time or another in:

A drama workshop

Painting bookcases made for a local junior school

Decorating the base

Working on individual projects using materials sent off for or bought with ACS funds

Maintaining the school minibus

Planning routes for a cycling expedition as part of the Duke of Edinburgh Award Scheme

A meeting to discuss misbehaviour and the use of sanctions

As the year progressed so the nature of individual sessions changed. The timetable merely served to illustrate the 'shape' of the week. It was the starting point from which we developed an integrated programme where pupils utilized staff as a resource for their own learning.

A growing involvement in the local community, the acquisition of new skills and a growth in the number of group-initiated activities added to the learning experiences available to the group. It also highlighted the need for effective channels of communication between project staff and the importance of short, modular courses.

Group-Initiated Activities

Discussions held during tutorial time led to a variety of group-initiated activities taking place during the year. The leisure interests of the pupils were seized upon to motivate the group and personal qualities such as trustworthiness, responsibility and initiative were demonstrated on many occasions.

Pupils were encouraged to plan, cost, carry out, record and report back on activities such as horse-riding, cycling expeditions and fishing competitions. Staff were on hand to advise and monitor the activities but the actual organization of the activities was undertaken by the pupils.

The importance of the camera as an '*aide-mémoire*' deserves special mention. Photographs provided the stimulus for written expression and evidence of it does serve to illustrate the wide range of activities and learning experience that a school and the Youth and Community service can combine to provide for *all* members of the community. ACS involvement with the centre included:

– Using the centre as a consortium recreation or leisure base.
– Involving ACS pupils in the planning and running of a Mother and Toddler group.
– Making ACS pupils responsible for the design and production and distribution of posters and leaflets for a jumble sale at the centre and helping on the day.
– Local volunteers from the Ashilt Literacy Scheme coming into school to help individual pupils develop their reading skills.
– Unemployed volunteers assisting in the supervision of ACS activities.
– ACS pupils designing and building a ramp to enable disabled members of the community gain easy access to the centre.
– The centre using school facilities in their programme to help local unemployed young people.
– A group of ACS pupils designing and painting murals in a room at the centre set aside for the Mother and Toddler group.
– The school and centre jointly sponsoring a theatrical production at the centre.
– Jewellery and leathercraft courses being held at the centre and jointly funded.

The Wythenshawe Hospital Fund-Raising Project

This project arose from the attempt of Miss Jackie Bolton, a teacher attached to the Newall Green Project, to do something constructive, enjoyable, workable and worthwhile with the ACS pupils whom she saw two mornings a week. Her brief was to set up cross-curricular projects and develop community links. The pupils themselves wanted to do something that would be different, enjoyable, not boring and involve the outside world as well as school.

A community project making soft toys for the childrens' ward at the local hospital was suggested, but the play therapist at the hospital suggested that raising money for the play unit would be a better idea.

It was decided to run a stall at the hospital and sell goods made by the group and jumble collected. The group together with Miss Bolton and a student from Manchester Polytechnic purchased wool, needles and other craft materials. The help of a fashion and clothing teacher was enlisted and sweets, make-up bags and bathroom accessory bags were made. In craft time wooden key-rings, pictures and ornaments were made and in leisure and recreation time, jumble was collected from local householders. The mathematics department helped with the cost analysis and the group's involvement with the computer stimulated some of the boys into following a computer course after the project had finished.

It was agreed that a stall should be set up in the main hall of the hospital and some of the pupils' parents offered to help run a raffle in aid of the children's ward. Cakes and biscuits were made in home economics in the day leading up to arranged dates for the sale.

On both days the stalls practically sold out. After deducting the cost of materials and ingredients a total of £111.83 was raised. This was presented to the play therapist at Wythenshawe Hospital during a special school assembly. The pupils were awarded certificates for their efforts but what was most important was that their efforts had been recognized, valued (to the extent that members of the public were prepared to pay for the fruits of their labour) and appreciated. The pupils' confidence and self-esteem visibly grew and they naturally felt a great deal of pride in their achievement.

As this particular project progressed so more staff became involved. Many cross-curricular links were established, traditional barriers broken down and a more integrated approach developed. The project involves the following subject areas as well as tutorial and leisure and recreation time:

Fashion and Clothing (sewing, knitting and embroidery);

Home Economics (baking);

Mathematics/Computers (estimating and costing);

Woodwork (woodturning and lathework);

English (writing advertising leaflets for distribution around the area);

Art (design of posters for the staff).

`The links that were established with the local community were also important. As well as making many friends in the hospital the school's immediate neighbours in the surrounding district became involved and learned more about their school and its pupils.

THE EMERGENCE OF THE 'DYNAMIC CURRICULUM'

The three examples of successful strategies cited by no means describe the wide range of curriculum development work that took place during the first year of the project. What is hoped is that they give an impression of the more successful strategies that developed as a result of teachers wishing to move away from a content-based curriculum towards a more process-based one. The curriculum evolved as a response to the needs, abilities and interests of the pupils, most of whom had already been labelled failures by the 'system'.

What developed was a 'dynamic curriculum', flexible enough to allow the pursuit of unforeseen outcomes in a project, yet structured enough to provide the assessment techniques and means of accreditation necessary to measure levels of success. Much has been done in the area of assessment, accreditation and profiling; much more still needs to be done if pupils are to receive the reward their labours demand.

Concluding Comments

In the Introduction, we outlined our purposes for putting together the material in this book. There we chose not to provide a tight definition of what we meant by 'action research', preferring to leave readers to come to their own conclusion. We appreciate, however, that the contributions in the book are various, covering a variety of different though overlapping approaches to the practical study of what is going on in classrooms. We are only too aware, however, that the sly synonym 'practical study' for the ubiquitous 'action research', will be seen to beg the question of hard definitions by many action researchers who have taken a stand on what action research is really all about. It should be clear by now that our own approach is to prefer eclecticism rather than a narrowing down and weeding out in terms of some immutable yardstick – although we do have preferences, as we will shortly indicate.

Several of our contributors feel more strongly and make clear what counts as action research and what for them distinguishes action research, in all its varieties, from mainstream educational research. They are unhappy with the character of mainstream educational research and this view unites many of the contributors. This unhappiness stems from the perceived lack of relevance of such research to teachers and schools, but the word 'unhappiness' glosses the variety of ways in which this concern is expressed. Nevertheless, they all contribute to a sense of what is action research in education through a process of eliminating what it is not. In Section A several of the contributors adopt this approach, particularly Anning, Bassey, Cummings and Hustler to some extent, and Rowland, although Rowland is then reluctant to view his work as action research! In the Introduction to Section A, we in fact pointed to the various reservations that the contributors have about mainstream educational research. In keeping with our professed eclecticism we should, however, make it clear that our own position is not to view the action research movement as a substitute for, or necessarily competitive with, mainstream educational research. Certainly there is a clear need for mutual awareness and recognition, leading perhaps to dialogue and collaboration between researchers with different relevancies who might in fact have much to offer one another. On occasion the discovery can be made that they have very similar concerns, or that certain preconceptions about one another's activities were in fact only preconceptions. For example, it has been our experience that educational action researchers can seem at times to go too far out of their way to ignore potentially useful theoretical insights and research strategies, precisely because they are identified with the world of academic or mainstream educational research. There is obviously a tight-rope to be walked if teachers' concerns are to remain where they should be, at the centre of the stage, and if theory, first and foremost, is to be generated and appraised through practice.

As we have noted in the General Introduction, several of the contributors work with available definitions of action research which they have found useful, or have formulated their own. The closest approximation to a definition which we ourselves provide is in fact included in the General Introduction: 'What follows is as close as we would wish to come to a definition of action research where teachers are the practitioners. They subject themselves and their practice to critical scrutiny; they attempt to relate ideas to empirical observations; they attempt to make this process explicit to themselves and others through the written word. Their prime concern is to improve their own practice in a particular situation from the standpoint of their own concern or worry. For them action research seems to be a practical way forward given their concern in that situation. They use and/or design aspects of their action as teachers to find out more about effective teaching and, in our view, they do so rigorously'. Our general strategy has been to provide materials displaying action research in practice and these materials, rather than definitions, in our view, will or will not speak to the reader and be of use.

Nevertheless, we are aware that even 'action research' is developing its own theoretical superstructure, i.e. there is the theory of action research as well as the practice of it. Thus an appropriate task for a conclusion is to guide interested readers to a few possibilities for further reading which connect with the major issues raised in this book. In the recent literature strong attempts are made to argue for and clarify the distinctive nature of 'action research'. Much of this literature is now published in the open market and is therefore much more accessible than in the early days of action research when it was only available locally to the *cognoscenti*. In fact, it now forms a substantial and growing corpus of the theory of action research. Here we will draw attention to those contributions which we find to be most useful in relation to the approach we have adopted in this book, i.e. contributions which open things out rather than close them off.

One very useful and readable little book is *A Teacher's Guide to Classroom Research* (Hopkins, 1985). This book is clearly designed to provide practical guidance for those interested in doing research in their own classrooms. There is, however, some attention paid to why traditional approaches to educational research are not of much use to teachers. At a much more detailed and complex level we would recommend *Issues in Educational Research: Qualitative Methods* (Burgess, 1985b), particularly for the contribution of Dave Ebbutt 'Educational action research: some general concerns and specific quibbles'. Here Ebbutt makes explicit his own thinking about some aspects of educational action research, and then moves to a closer look at action research issues which emerged during the TIQL project. Considerable attention is paid to the paper by John Elliott 'Action-research: a framework for self-evaluation in schools', which has influenced several of our contributors. Dave Ebbutt also discusses *The Action Research Planner* (Kemmis, *et al.*, 1981). *Issues in Educational Research: Qualitative Methods* also contains a contribution from Alison Kelly, one of the co-directors of the GIST project, where she discusses the interventionist model of action research adopted for the project.

The critique of traditional educational research associated with Lawrence Stenhouse is taken further in contributions to *Research as a Basis for Teaching* (Rudduck and Hopkins, 1985) and in a contribution by Lawrence Stenhouse to *Field Methods in the Study of Education* (Burgess, 1985a). This latter book also contains John Elliott's 'Facilitating action research in schools: some dilemmas' where he discussed in detail experiences on the TIQL project. We would also recommend *The Reflective Practitioner* (Schon, 1983), for general discussion of the thinking of professionals about improving their practice. In our view, these sources provide excellent additional materials for those who wish to explore further the differences between action research and traditional educational research. Certainly, we have found them interesting and helpful in clarifying our own thinking, even if we do not always find ourselves in agreement with some of the positions advocated.

As a final word we do think it is appropriate that we, as editors, should point briefly to some preferences about action research which we feel strongly about. To some extent, these preferences stem from the particular academic background of two of us. As sociologists we became committed to approaches concerned with the rigorous description of the bases for order in people's everyday lives. A central question which puzzled us, and still puzzles us, is just how people are able, for the most part, to accomplish their everyday activities in so orderly a fashion. This interest led to a focus on the taken-for-granted knowledge which people use in particular settings as they pursue their practical concerns. More specifically, we found a way into the study of these issues through the analysis of conversation and, in particular, talk in educational settings. Just how the practical business of being a teacher gets done was a central concern, a id we became increasingly convinced that sociologists, and educational reseachers more generally, were not in contact with this issue. Often it seemed as if some researchers did not want to be in contact with such an issue, with the world of teaching not only as teachers routinely perceive it, but also in terms of the daily problems and practical concerns which face teachers. This feeling was in fact renewed for us recently in the context of our limited evaluation of an action research project: the GIST project. With this background, we were led more and more towards involvement with teachers along action research lines, and towards developing contact with action research movements elsewhere.

It is hardly surprising, given the above, that first and foremost we would see educational action research as practitioner and practice centred. It is the teacher's perceived relevancies in the context of the practical job of teaching which must inform, constrain and shape the notion of feasible and worthwhile research for that practitioner in a specific context. For those advocating interventionist action research models and for those who, from the outside, wish to facilitate action research, there must be a concentrated attempt to relate closely to and appreciate these relevancies.

Our second emphasis may appear almost to contradict the first. This is our conviction that collaboration is close to being essential for educational action research. These are, of course, a variety of possible modes of collaboration and a wide range of useful skills which collaborators, who are not classroom practitioners, can bring with them. One strand we see as central: collaboration by the action researcher with some other person who does not share the same set of relevancies, who is in short not doing precisely the same job. This does not necessarily mean finding someone who is located outside the school. For the task of the collaborator is to bring some of the qualities (and at times some of the problems) which a 'stranger' has to offer and Schutz's seminal article, 'The Stranger' (1967) is invaluable. The disjunction of relevancies can serve to make more explicit the action researcher's own practical concerns as well as the more taken-for-granted features of day-to-day practice. This dimension to collaboration clearly requires the 'quality time' which Rod Hill refers to in his contribution. It also requires careful monitoring to ensure that the action research, as it develops, remains practitioner and practice centred.

Finally, we wish to point to what in our experience is the central motivating force for involvement by teachers in action research. It is the same force which Stenhouse (1975), Elliott (1976), Adelman (1981) and many others have recognized, namely the perceived gap between aspiration and performance, the gap between what one would wish to see in one's classroom and school, and what seems to be actually the case. This perception has led and leads some teachers to investigate how through research practices as teachers they can improve the quality of education. Relating to this route forward and providing resources for it, particularly in terms of 'quality time' for teachers, is a practicality which educational authorities are ambivalent about. That ambivalence squanders the major resource in education: teachers themselves.

Bibliography

Adelman, C. (1981), 'On first hearing' in C. Adelman (ed.), *Uttering, Muttering* (Grant McIntyre).

Armstrong, M. (1980), *Closely Observed Children* (Writers and Readers).

Ashton, P. M. E., Henderson, E. S., Herritt, J. E., and Mortimer, D. J. (1983), *Teacher Education in the Classroom* (Croom Helm).

Ball, S. J. (1980), 'Initial encounters in the classroom and the process of establishment', in P. Woods (ed.), *Pupil Strategies* (Croom Helm).

Becker, H. (1970), *Sociological Work in Method and Substance* (Aldine Press).

Bennett, N. (1976), *Teaching Styles and Pupil Progress*, (Open Books).

Bennett, S. M., Desforges, C., Cockburn, A. D., and Wilkinson, E. (1984), *The Quality of Pupil Learning Experiences* (Lawrence Earlbaum Associates).

Blalock, H. M. (1971), 'Aggregation and measurement error', *Social Forces*, vol.50, pp.151–6.

Blumer, H. (1969), *Symbolic Interactionism: Perspective and Method* (Prentice-Hall).

Bogdan, R., and Taylor, S. (1975), *Introduction to Qualitative Research Methods* (Wiley).

Bolam, R., Smith, G., and Canter, R. (1978), *L.E.A. Advisers and the Mechanisms of Innovation* (NFER).

Bruner, J. S. (1966), *Toward a Theory of Instruction* (Harvard University Press).

Bruyn, S. T. (1966), *The Human Perspective in Sociology* (Prentice Hall).

Bullock Report, (1975), *A Language for Life* (HMSO).

Burgess, R. (ed.) (1985a), *Field Methods in the Study of Education* (Falmer Press).

Burgess, R. (ed.) (1985b), *Issues in Educational Research: Qualitative Methods* (Falmer Press).

Capra, F. (1982), *The Turning Point* (Wildwood House).

Carr, W., and Kemmis, S. (1983), *Becoming Critical: Knowing through Action Research* (Deakin University Press).

City of Salford Education Department (1983), *Schools Looking at Themselves*, 1983 (Salford Resources Centre).

City of Salford Education Department, *Profile-82* (Salford Resources Centre).

Cockcroft, W. H. (1982), *Mathematics Counts* (HMSO).

Cockett, M., and Milroy, E. (1983–5), *A.C.S. Newsletter* (Brook House, Manchester M13).

Cohen, L., and Manion, L. (1980), *Research Methods in Education* (Croom Helm).

Cuff, E. C., and Payne, G. C. F. (eds) (2nd edn, 1984), *Perspectives in Sociology* (Allen & Unwin).

Cummings, Carole (1982), 'A first try: starting the day' in G. C. F. Payne and E. C. Cuff (eds), *Doing Teaching*, (Batsford), pp.148–69.

Darwin, C. (1970), *The Origin of Species* (Penguin).

Day, C. (1984), 'External consultancy: supporting school based curriculum development' in *Classroom Action Research Bulletin 6* (Cambridge Institute of Education).

Delamont, S., and Hamilton, D. (1976), 'Classroom research: a critique and a new approach' in M. Stubbs and S. Delamont (eds), *Explorations in Classroom Observation* (Wiley).

DES (1977), *Curriculum 11–16* (HMSO).

DES (1978), *Making Inset Work – Inservice Training for Teachers* (HMSO).

DES (1979), *Matters for Discussion: Mathematics 5–11* (HMSO).

Downing, J. (1970) 'Relevance versus ritual in reading', *Reading* (Basil Blackwell for UKRA), vol.4, no.2, pp.4–12.

Downing, J., Ayers, D., and Schaffer, B. (1983), *The Linguistic Awareness in Reading Readiness Test* (Windsor: NFER/Nelson).

Ebbutt, D. (1982), 'Teachers as researchers: how four teachers co-ordinate the process of research in their respective schools', Working Paper no.10, Schools Council TIQL Project.

Ebbutt, D. (1983), 'Teacher as researcher', unpublished conference paper (Manchester Polytechnic).

Ebbutt, D. (1985), 'Educational action research: some general concerns and specific quibbles' in R. Burgess, (ed.), *Issues in Educational Research: Qualitative Methods* (Falmer Press).

Elliott, J. (1976), *Developing Hypotheses about Classrooms from Teacher Practical Constructs* (Cambridge Institute of Education).

Elliott, J. (1978), 'Classroom research: science or commonsense' in R. McAleese and D. Hamilton (eds), *Understanding Classroom Life* (NFER).

Elliott, J. (1981), 'Action-research: a framework for self-evaluation in schools' Working Paper no.1 (Schools Council TIQL Project).

Elliott, J. (1983), 'School focussed INSET and research into teacher education', *Cambridge Journal of Education*, vol. 13, no.2, pp. 19–31.

Elliott, J. (1985), 'Facilitating action research in schools: some dilemmas' in R. Burgess, (ed.), *Field Methods in the Study of Education*, (Falmer Press).

Elliott, J., and Adelman, C. (1975), 'Teachers accounts and the objectivity of classroom research', *London Educational Review*, vol.4.

Elliott, J., and Adelman, C. (1976), *Innovation at the Classroom Level: A Case Study of the Ford Teaching Project, C.E. 203* (Open University Press).

Elliott, J., and Hurlin, T. (undated), 'Self-monitoring questioning strategies' Ford Teaching Project Chart 2, Nimco (Centre for Applied Research in Education).

Elliott, J., and Whitehead, D. (1980), 'The theory and practice of educational action research', *CARN Bulletin 4* (Cambridge Institute of Education).

Ferreiro, E., and Teberosky, A. (1983), *Literacy Before Schooling* (Heinemann Educational Books).

Francis, H. (1982), *Learning to Read* (Allen & Unwin).

Galton, M., Simon, B., and Croll, P. (1980), *Inside the Primary Classroom* (Routledge & Kegan Paul).

Glaser, B. G., and Strauss, A. L. (1967), *The Discovery of Grounded Theory* (Weidenfeld & Nicolson).

Goodman, Y. (1980), 'The roots of literacy' in M. P. Douglas (ed.) *Reading: A Humanising Experience* (Claremont Graduate School).

Hall, N. (1983a), 'The status of "reading" in reading schemes', *Education 3–13*, (11) pp.27–33.

Hall, N. (1983b), 'The visible language experience of language-experience teachers', *Journal of Language Education* (6), pp.23–7.

Hammersley, M., and Atkinson, P. (1983), *Ethnography: Principles and Practice* (Tavistock).

Hannam, C. *et al.* (1976), *The First Year of Teaching* (Penguin).

Harste, J., Burke, C., and Woodward, V. (1982), 'Children's language and world: initial encounters with print' in J. Langer and M. T. Smith-Burke (eds), *Reader Meets Author: Bridging the Gap* (Newark Delaware: International Reading Association).

Heath, S. B. (1983), *Ways with Work* (CUP).

Henderson, E. C., and Perry, G. (1981), *Change and Development in Schools: Case Studies in the Management of School-Focussed In-service Education* (McGraw Hill).

HMSO (1978), *H.M.I. Matters for Discussion 6: Mixed Ability Work in Comprehensive Schools* (DES).

HMSO (1979), *Aspects of Secondary Education* (DES).

HMSO (1983a), *9–13 Middle Schools* (DES).

HMSO (1983b), *Curriculum 11–16: Towards a Statement of Entitlement* (DES).

HMSO (1984), *Slow Learning and Less Successful Pupils in Secondary Schools* (DES).

Holly, P. (1984), 'Beyond the cult of the individual: putting the partnership into in-service collaboration' in J. Nias (ed.), *Teaching Enquiry-Based Courses* (Cambridge Institute of Education).

Hopkins, D. (1985), *A Teacher's Guide to Classroom Research* (Open University Press).

Hustler, D. E., and Ashman, J. (1985), 'Personal and social education for all: apart or together' in E. C. Cuff and G. C. F. Payne (eds), *Crisis in the Curriculum* (Croom Helm).

Kelly, A. (1985), 'Action research: some definitions and descriptions' in R. Burgess (ed.), *Issues in Educational Research: Qualitative Methods* (Falmer Press).

Kelly, A., Whyte, J., and Smail, B. (1984), *Girls into Science and Technology: Final Report* (Department of Sociology, University of Manchester).

Kemmis, S. *et al.* (1981), *The Action Research Planner* (Deakin University, Australia).

Lacey, C. (1977), *The Socialization of Teachers* (Methuen).

McCutcheon, G. (1981), 'The impact of the insider' in J. Nixon (ed.), *A Teachers' Guide to Action Research* (Grant McIntyre).

Macdonald, B. (1976), 'Evaluation and the control of education' in D. Tawney (ed.), *Curriculum Evaluation Today* (Macmillan).

Merton, R., and Kendall, P. L. (1946), 'The focused interview', *American Journal of Sociology* (51), pp.541–7.

Nias, J. (1983a), *Teaching Research-Based Courses: Possibilities and Problems* (Conference Report, Cambridge Institute of Education).

Nias, J. (1983b), *The Definition and Maintenance of Self in Primary Teaching* (Cambridge Institute of Education).

Nias, J. (1984a), *Teaching Enquiry-Based Courses* (Conference Report, Cambridge Institute of Education).

Nias, J. (1984b), *A More Distant Drummer: Teacher Developments as Development of Self* (Cambridge Institute of Education).

Nixon, J. (1981), *A Teacher's Guide to Action Research* (Grant McIntyre).

Odum, H. W., and Jocher, K. (1929), *An Introduction to Social Research* (Holt).

Open University and Schools Council (1980), *Curriculum in Action* (Open University Press).

Payne, G. C. F., and Cuff, E. C. (eds) (1982), *Doing Teaching: The Practical Management of Classrooms* (Batsford).

Payne, G. C. F., and Cuff, E. C. (eds) (1983), *Talk and More Talk: Studies in Classroom Interaction* (Manchester Polytechnic).

Payne, G. C. F., Huster, D. E., and Cuff, E. C. (1983), *GIST or PIST: Teacher Perceptions of the Project 'Girls into Science and Technology'* (Manchester Polytechnic).

Peyre, J. (1981), *The Development of a Taste for Reading* (Groos).

Riseborough, G. (1983), *Pupils, Teachers, Careers and Schooling* (Manchester Polytechnic).

Rowland, S. (1984), *The Enquiring Classroom* (Falmer Press).

Rudduck, J. (1982), *Teachers in Partnership: Four Studies of In-service Collaboration* (Longman/Schools Council).

Rudduck, J., and Hopkins, D. (1985), *Research as a Basis for Teaching* (Heinemann).

Salaman, G., (1979), *Work Organisation: Persistence and Control* (Longman).

Schon, D. (1983), *The Reflective Practitioner* (Basic Books).

Schools Council (1981), *The Practical Curriculum* (Methuen).

Schutz, A. (1964), 'The Stranger' in B. R. Cosin (ed.), *School and Society* (Routledge & Kegan Paul/Open University), pp.32–8.

Sharp, R., and Green A. (1975), *Education and Social Control* (Routledge & Kegan Paul).

Shipman, M. (1974), *Inside a Curriculum Project* (Methuen).

Shipman, M. (2nd edn 1981), *The Limitations of Social Research* (Longman).

Simons, H. (1982), 'Suggestions for a school self-evaluation based on democratic principles' in R. McCormick (ed.) *Calling Education to Account* (Heinemann/Open University).

Smail, B. (1982), 'Changing the image of women scientists', *Women and Training News*, 9.

Smail, B., Whyte, J., and Kelly, A. (1982), 'Girls into science and technology: the first two years', *Schools Science Review*, 63.

Stenhouse, L. (1975), *An Introduction to Curriculum Research and Development* (Heinemann).

Stenhouse, L. (1985), 'A note on case study and educational practice' in R. Burgess (ed.), *Field Methods in the Study of Education* (Falmer Press).

Stubbs, M., and Delamont, S. (1976), *Explorations in Classroom Observation* (Wiley).

Taylor, J. K., and Dale, I. R. (1971), *A Survey of Teachers in their First Year,*

(University of Bristol).

Teale, W. (1982), 'Towards a theory of how children learn to read and write naturally', *Language Arts* (59), pp.55–70.

Times Educational Supplement (1984), 'The low attainers' 27 January, pp.8–9.

Tripp, D. (1980), 'Reflections on the nature of educational research', *CARN Bulletin 4*, pp.5–15 (Cambridge Institute of Education).

Whyte, J. (1983), 'Courses for teachers on sex differences and sex stereotyping' *Journal of Education for Teaching* 9(3).

Whyte, J. (1984), 'Observing sex stereotypes and interactions in the school lab and workshop', *Educational Review*, vol.36, no.1.

Whyte, J., and Smail, B. (1982), 'GIST as action research' in *EOC Research Bulletin* (Spring).

Willis, P. (1977), *Learning to Labour* (Saxon House).

Wood, R. (1984), 'When three into one won't go' in *Times Educational Supplement*, 16 March.

Woods, P. (1979), *The Divided School* (Routledge & Kegan Paul).

Woods, P. (1980), *Pupil Strategies* (Croom Helm).

Woods, P. (1983), *Sociology and the School: an Interactionist Viewpoint* (Routledge & Kegan Paul).

Index

academic respectability 9
acceptability 9, 10, 115
accountability 2, 78
accreditation 183, 206
action research
    passim
    and traditional research 7, 12, 31, 70,
        126, 181
    large-scale projects 143–246
    recent developments 3–5, 208–9
    small case studies 73–142
    theoretical issues 1–3, 7–17, 19–72,
        207–11
active learning styles 188
Adelman, C. 4, 14, 105, 212, 213
adversary, role of in research 70f.; *see also*
    'critical friend'
age-status (in infant classrooms) 41
Alternative Curriculum Strategies,
    Manchester LEA (ACS) 5, 146,
    183–206
Anning, Angela 11, 12, 14, 15, 56–66, 207
anti-theoretical bias 133
appraisal (of teachers) 2, 42, 47, 78, 142,
    194
Armstrong, M. 32, 212
Ashman, Ian 146, 214
Ashton, Pat 58, 63, 212
Atkinson, P. 14, 107, 108, 214
award-bearing courses 78, 123–32
Ayers, D. 103, 213

Ball, S. J. 117, 212
Bassey, M. 7, 8, 9, 14, 15, 16, 18–24, 207
Becker, H. 112, 120, 212
Bennett, N. 12, 21, 57, 63, 66–72, 212
Bennett, S. M. 123, 212
Blalock, H. M. 107, 212
Blumer, H. 108, 212
Bogdan, R. 108, 212
Bolam, R. 57, 212
Bolton, Jackie 204, 205
Bowes, D. 145, 156, 157, 160–5
brevity, need for 8, 9
Bruner, J. S. 30, 212
Bruyn, S. T. 107, 212
Burgess, R. 209, 212, 213, 215
Burke, C. 96, 214

Cambridge Institute of Education 4, 78
Canter, R. 57, 212
Capra, F. 27, 212
Carr, W. 5, 212
Cassidy, A. 76, 77, 133–42
Centre for Applied Research in Education,
    University of East Anglia 4
child-centredness 79
children, their involvement in learning 8,
    24, 25–35, 51f., 123f.
Classroom Action Research Network,
    University of Cambridge (CARN) 3,
    16
classroom experiences *see* children
Classroom Research Inservice Education
    Scheme (CRISES) 34, 87–94
Cockburn, Anne 12, 66–72, 212
Cockcroft Report 125, 129, 212
Cockett, M. 146, 183–6, 212
Cohen, L. 5, 16, 212
collaboration 2, 9, 14, 15, 36–47, 50, 67,
    70f., 74, 77, 78, 126, 129, 144, 210
critical community 126
'critical friend' 70f., 74
Croll, P. 21, 213
Cuff, E. C. 14, 37, 138, 145, 172–82, 212,
    214, 215
Cummings, Carol 9, 10, 12, 14, 36–47,
    105, 207, 212
curriculum
    aims and objectives 51
    change 34, 58
    development 13, 57, 80
    packages 80
Curriculum in Action 12, 52, 55, 56f.
cyclical nature of action research 77, 125

Dale, I. 105, 215
Darwin, C. 71, 72, 213
data 10, 14, 18–21, 43, 61, 66, 68, 76, 108,
    116, 124, 127, 129, 138f., 179
Davies, R. 146, 201–6
Day, C. 65, 213
Deakin University, Australia 5, 65
Delamont, S. 107, 213, 215
Department of Education and Science
    (DES) 2, 10, 58, 213
Desforges, C. 12, 13, 15, 67–72, 212

diary, use of for research 80f., 108f.
Didsbury School of Education,
    Manchester 38, 137, 200
domination of teacher 44, 136, 139
Douglas, M. P. 213
Downing, J. 95, 103, 213

Ebbutt, D. 4, 74, 77, 209, 210, 213
educational objectives 26, 68
Elliott, J. 3, 4, 14, 15, 58, 66, 74, 75, 76,
    77, 82, 97, 105, 144, 209, 210, 213
environmental character 121
environmental print 98
Equal Opportunities Commission (EOC)
    143
escapism (in the staffroom) 115
ethos
    in school 76, 86, 110
    of classroom 60, 61, 86
evaluation, self-evaluation 48, 51, 52, 60,
    66, 76, 78, 105, 126, 142, 172f.
examinations 62
exclusiveness 56
expectations, teacher 64, 86
experience and knowledge *see* children
expository and explanatory texts 130
externalization 181

feedback 62, 140, 199
Ferreiro, E. 96, 213
fidgeting 22, 23, 24
Flixton Infant School 38
Ford Teaching Project 4, 14, 58, 105, 144
Francis, H. 96, 213
friendship groups 84

Galton, M. 21, 58, 213
generalizations 21, 31, 42, 50, 66, 122, 126,
    131, 133
Girls into Science and Technology Project
    (GIST) 142–5, 148–82, 210
Glaser, B. 75, 107, 109, 213
'good primary practice' 79
Green, A. 57, 215
Groarke, J. 16, 73, 74, 79–86

Habermas 14
Hall, N. 95–104, 214
Hamilton, D. 107, 213
Hammersley, M. 14, 107, 108, 214
Hannam, C. 105, 214
Hargreaves, Margaret 74, 79–86
Harste, J. 96, 214
hearing-impaired pupils 95f.
Heath, S. B. 96, 214
Henderson, E. C. 65, 214
Henderson, E. S. 214
Her Majesty's Inspectors *see* HMI

Herritt, J. E. 212
Hill, R. 14, 146, 147, 187–9, 210
HMI 48f., 67, 69, 125, 134, 214
Hodgson, Lorna 146, 187, 190, 196
holistic approach to learning 27
Holly, P. 4, 214
Hopkins, D. 208, 209, 214
Humanities Curriculum Project 4
Hurlin, T. 144, 208, 209, 213
Hustler, D. 9, 10, 14, 36–47, 145, 146,
    172–82, 207, 214, 215

ideology of teachers 44
independent learning 62
industrial action 141, 186
inservice education 4, 45, 53, 56, 58, 62,
    63, 67, 76, 78, 80, 81, 136, 150, 156,
    188
'intellectual space' 9, 29
interactionist research model 107
interpretative
    framework for judgement 12, 14, 69, 74
    paradigm 76, 107
    teaching methods 28f., 87f.
intersubjective understanding 31
intervention 67, 70, 73, 77, 97f., 135f.
    150f., 172f., 210
interviews 68–9, 75, 109, 173, 175f.
IT-INSET 58

jargon 11, 13, 57, 66
job description 12, 72
Jocher, K. 107, 215
Joseph, Sir Keith 145

Kelly, Alison 143, 181, 209, 214, 215
Kelly grid 63
Kemmis, S. 5, 65, 66, 78, 126, 128, 209,
    212, 214
Kendall, P. 109, 214
knowledge
    experiential *see* children
    taken-for-granted 46, 47, 87, 93, 128,
    209
Lancaster Research Project 57
Law Society 192
learning theory 68
Leicester
    Insights into Learning Project 9, 25,
    32–5
    University 63
Linguistic Awareness in Reading Readiness
    Test 103
literacy phenomena 97
Lower Attaining Pupils Project (LAP) 5,
    146

Macdonald, B. 16, 214

McCutcheon, G. 57, 214
Manchester LEA 5, 146
Manchester Polytechnic 2, 10, 38, 77, 123, 133, 143, 194, 205
Manchester University 143
Manion, L. 5, 16, 212
Manpower Services Commission (MSC) 2, 153
Master degree course (M.Ed.) 77, 123–32
matching and mismatching 66–72, 86
mathematics 49, 64f., 81f., 123–32, 134
Merton, R. 109, 214
Milroy, E. 146, 212
mixed ability teaching 10, 48, 49, 79, 80, 84
monitoring effectiveness 65f., 80f.
Mortimer, D. J. 212
motivation
    for pupils 51, 83, 86, 129, 160
    for research 72

Nias, Jennifer 78, 118, 119, 122, 214, 215
Nind, J. 9, 73, 74, 87–94
Nixon, J. 3, 37, 214

objectivity 9, 14, 108, 135, 138, 144
observation 19, 30, 39f., 61, 67f., 73, 74, 80f., 99, 157–8, 166f.
Odum, H. 107, 215
open classroom 80
Open University 55, 56, 58, 215
Ovens, P. 74, 79–86

parametric analysis 162
Parent–Teacher Association 191; *see also* community
participant observation 107, 124
Payne, G. C. F. 14, 37, 38, 172, 212, 214, 215
pedagogic
    research 21, 77, 124, 126
    theory 57, 66, 133
Perry, G. 18, 64, 96, 214
Peyre, J. 96, 215
phenomenology 14, 87
Piaget, J. 24, 123, 124
Pickles, H. 10, 11, 12, 14, 15, 48–55
positive discrimination 165
print-related activities 101
probationary teachers' problems 105
professional
    development 76, 78, 142, 155
    knowledge 36–47; *see also* taken-for-granted knowledge
    status 42, 72
project leaders, role of 184
project work 82
pupil resistance 138

qualitative data *see also* data 14, 41f., 76, 108f., 145
Quality of Pupils' Learning Experience (QPLE) 67f.
'quality time' 15, 81, 146, 188, 210, 211
question and answer session 139
questioning attitude 72, 153
questionnaires 30, 136, 141, 157, 172
queueing 8, 22

radical changes 12, 58, 142
reading schemes 95
record keeping 57
'red book three' 51
reification (of theory into practice) 124
relationships with parents *see* community
Research Consultative Group (RCG) 33, 34
research leaders 142
residential trips 199
'rich data' 138, 173, 175
Riseborough, G. 118, 215
roleplay 50
Rollins, B. 146, 187, 188, 197–200
rotating timetable 83
Rowland, S. 8, 10, 13–15, 24–35, 74, 93, 207, 215
Rudduck, Jean 4, 78, 209, 215

Salaman, G. 121, 215
Salford LEA 11, 12, 48f., 212
Schaffer, B. 103, 213
Schon, D. 209, 215
Schools Council 4, 12, 42, 74, 79, 82, 133, 136, 215
The Practical Curriculum 49; *see also* Curriculum in Action
Schutz, A. 106, 111, 116, 121–2, 210
science in school 49, 62, 148–82
secondment 32
senior management in school 15, 76, 77
Sharp, R. 57, 215
Shipman, M. 14, 143, 215
Simon, B. 21, 213
Simons, H. 16, 215
singularities *see also* generalizations 21
situational and substantive self 120
Slater, S. 145, 156–9
Smail, Barbara 143, 144, 214, 215, 216
small group work 59–60, 62, 80–4, 135, 137, 153
social and personal education 200
Social Science Research Council (SSRC) 2, 143
staff
    development 76, 184f., 188, 194
    roles 53, 54
standards 110

status of teachers *see* professional status
Stenhouse, L. 3, 4, 16, 58, 59, 66, 105,
  108, 209, 210, 215
storytelling 8, 23
Strauss, A. 75, 107, 109, 213
streaming and setting (in junior schools) 81
Street, Lilian 16, 77, 78, 123–32
Stubbs, M. 212, 215
subgroups within school staff 116
symbolic interaction 75, 107, 108

talk in classroom 10, 44f., 83f., 88f., 135f.,
  194f.
tape-recordings 10, 19, 39f., 64, 74, 82f.,
  88f., 130, 131, 136f., 173f., 202
task for literacy 96
Tawney, D. 214
Taylor, J. 105, 215
Taylor, S. 108, 212
Teacher Pupil Interaction and the Quality
  of Learning, Schools Council *see*
  TIQL
teacher
  resistance 77, 140
  expectations 64
Teale, W. 96, 215
teams, teachers in 185f.
Teborsoky, A. 96, 215
Technical and Vocational Educational
  Initiative *see* TVEI
Thompson, J. 145, 148–55
Times Educational Supplement 117, 146, 216
TIQL 4, 10, 74, 77, 79, 82, 133, 209

traditional research *see* action research
Trafford LEA 38
transcriptions *see* tape-recording
transfer of learning 62
Tranter, Diane 14, 75, 76, 105–22
Trent Polytechnic 19
triangulation 4, 14, 58, 109
Tripp, D. 14, 216
TVEI 153, 154

unanticipated outcomes 78, 129, 137, 206

video in classrooms 12, 45, 63f., 202
VISTA programme 150, 151

Ward, G. 145, 166–71
Whitehead, D. 213
Whyte, Judith Byrne 143, 144, 145, 166f.,
  214, 215, 216
Wilkinson, E. 212
Willis, P. 107, 216
Women's Aid Centre 192
Wood, R. 216
Woods, P. 14, 115, 212, 216
Woodward, V. 96, 214
workcards 50
Wythenshawe Hospital, Manchester 204,
  205
written work in class 30

York Street school 21f.
Youth Training Scheme (YTS) 153